www.tredition.de

Egon Harings

Germany and two World Wars

From the German Reich to the end of the Nazi regime

www.tredition.de

© 2018 Egon Harings

Verlag und Druck: tredition GmbH, Hamburg

ISBN
Paperback: 978-3-7469-5499-8
Hardcover: 978-3-7469-5500-1
e-Book: 978-3-7469-5501-8

Prologue

This book addresses two world wars, two wars of horror and terror.

On 28 June 1914 were the two shots that killed the Austrian Archduke Franz Ferdinand and his wife. The double murder, which was committed by the young Bosnian assassin Gavrilo Princip, had been prepared by nationalist Serbian conspirators from the secret society "Black Hand" and should compel the Serbian Prime Minister to extreme steps.

Europe held its breath. Vienna didn't want to start a war without German backing. Emperor Franz Joseph received the required backing from Berlin. Wilhelm II even urged Austria to a settlement with Serbia. On 5 June 1914 he even made out a blank check to Vienna. However, Vienna was slow with the settlement. But on 23 July 1914 Vienna delivered an ultimatum to Belgrade. The note with the ultimatum contained a demand that would undermine the sovereignty of Serbia, if it had been met. Belgrade rejected the note after it had underinsured Russian help. On 25 July Serbia ordered the mobilization. Austria followed with a partial mobilization and declared war on Serbia on 28 July. On 30 July Russia ordered the general mobilization and Austria responded one day later. On 1 August France announced the mobilization and Germany followed. England put its navy on the alert. Then, on 16 August, Japan ranked in the front of the German opponents and demanded the Chinese area around Jiaozhou Bay, which was in German hands. The First World War had broken out, the first war of material battles and mass extermination. Then, 1918, the world looked different. Tens of millions of people had lost their lives, lost in a senseless war. New states emerged, which were reason for future conflicts.

Many monarchies no longer existed after the war. It was November 9, 1918, when Philipp Scheidemann proclaimed the Republic in Germany. It began a new era of German history, starting with the Weimar Republic.

The Weimar Republic existed only fifteen years. With it also perished the "Second German Reich". There were the turbulent years in which the one sought to build and to consolidate the new state, while others tried to destroy it again. The terms of the Versailles Treaty had to be met. This led to the battle in the Ruhr area (Ruhr-Pott), which was occupied by Allied troops. The Versailles Treaty was also the cause of the horror inflation and the high unemployment. In addition to this, there was still the general economic crisis. For the Nazis these were reasons enough to blame others for the misery.

In 1933 Hitler comes to power. Hindenburg, the German Reich President, had dropped out for personal reasons Chancellor Heinrich Brüning and General von Schleicher presented Franz von Papen as Chancellor. Franz von Papen repealed the SA ban that was a tribute to the NSDAP. But for this step the Nazi Party did not thank. Von Papen did also not reach a significant improvement of the miserable situation in Germany. Hindenburg was looking for a way out of this situation and believed to have found this way with the appointment of Hitler as Chancellor. Thus, on 30 January 1933, Hitler has seized power. He ousted von Papen and formed a cabinet of "national collection." Paralyzed in an almost hopeless struggle against the enemies of the

Republic and at odds with each other, the democratic parties resigned, leaving Hitler to power.

In 1934 President von Hindenburg died and Hitler also assumed the role of President. There were also no parties in the meantime, with one exception, the NSDAP, which determined everything. – With the "Law for the Reconstruction of the Reich" were wiped out the countries' sovereignty. The full power over the press, radio, film, and public opinion was backed by Hitler's chief propagandist Goebbels, who also forced into line the whole German culture by laws, threats and persecutions. It followed the burning of books and boycott of Jewish businesses. But the worst was yet to come, the arbitrary persecutions, arrests and killings of dissidents and the establishment of concentration camps by the SA. But the holocaust was to surpass all this.

Austria became a part of the German Empire (Reich) again. The country of the Sudeten was annexed and Hitler demanded more. The world is facing a war. The Nazi rulers are getting ready, they want it, they want to lead the nation in the cruel war that the world had never experienced before, a war that was to be more cruel than the First World War.

We write 1 September 1939 and a new cruel wartime has begun. The war started with the attack on Poland. A British-French ultimatum with the request to cease hostilities remained unanswered. Thereupon the UK and France declared war on Germany on 3 September.

Poland was defeated in a five-week campaign. Eastern Poland was occupied by Soviet troops. A German-Soviet border and friendship treaty sealed the partition of Poland. Eastern Poland received the Soviet Union, Gdansk (Danzig) and parts of western and northern Poland received Germany. The remainder of the country was declared a "German General Government" (administrative zone), where established a brutal occupation regime.

In order to forestall an Allied landing operation, Germany attacked Denmark and Norway on 9 April, 1940. Denmark was occupied without fight; Norway ceased the fighting in July. Then, on 10 May, the western campaign began. Belgium, the Netherlands and Luxembourg were overrun. Little later, German troops occupied Paris.

The Second World War was planned by Germany as a race-ideological war of extermination with the aim of acquiring habitat in the east and was also implemented accordingly. But Germany lost this insane war. The disaster began with the lost battle for Stalingrad. Instead of winning habitat, after the war Germany was forced to cede large areas in the east. There were areas that were colonized by Germans for centuries.

In the last months of the cruel war also the great escape of the Germans began, the escape of horror, as it was the sinking of the "Wilhelm Gustloff". – "Wilhelm Gustloff" was the name of the German refugee steamship, which took off from Gdynia (Gotenhafen) on 30 January 1945. On board of the steamship were 10,000 refugees, mainly women and children, who hoped to escape the hell by this ship, the hell that broke over East Prussia. Taken by Soviet torpedoes, the ship sank. Not even 1,000 refugees were saved; the others were torn with the ship in the depth or died on the troubled sea, because they were not saved, could not be saved because there were not enough ships, which departed in search of shipwrecked. It was the greatest disaster in the history of seafaring. But, who knows the "Wilhelm Gustloff" and the sinking of this ship? About the sinking of the Titanic was much written. But the world knows nothing about the sinking of the "Wilhelm Gustloff, although this sinking was much worse than the sinking of the Titanic. – This book chronicles the sinking of the "Wilhelm Gustloff".

The war of horror

The First World War

We write the year **1914**

The Austrian successor to the throne, Archduke Franz Ferdinand (a nephew of the Austrian emperor), and his wife, Duchess Sophie of Hohenberg, visited the new province Bosnia. But on 28 June they were not met with a friendly reception in Sarajevo, the capital of Bosnia. In this town mainly lived Serbians, who were not pro-Austrian. So it was bound to happen what many people feared. A Serbian student, Gavrilo Princip, murdered the Austrian married couple short time after they were sitting in their car again. Gavrilo Princip was 19 years old. After his arrest he declared that he had acted in revenge for the suppression of the Serbian nation. The result of the investigation was: the Bosnian nationalism was in narrow contact with the Serbian Prime Minister Nikola Pašić, who aimed at a Great Serbian Empire.

The picture on the next page

The reason to a terrible war,

the First World War

The Austrian Archduke Franz Ferdinand and his wife Sophie on the way to their car. Shortly afterwards they are assassinated.

On the next page

A Berlin newspaper informed

that the Austrian successor

to the throne and his wife

were murdered

Der österreichische Thronfolger und seine Gattin ermordet.

Gavrilo Princip had now murdered the man, who just supported the peaceful balance of power amongst all nations of the Austrian-Hungarian Empire, so he also supported a peaceful life with the South Slavs. Gavrilo Princip had the radical secret organization of Serbia, "Black Hand", behind himself. This terrorist group was managed by the head of the press department of the Serbian General Staff, Colonel Dragutin Dimitrijević; but that became known first many years later. Now the government in Vienna had to make a decision. Was the murder of Franz Ferdinand and his wife only an act of one individual or was it the Serbian attack against the Austrian-Hungarian superpower?

The political circles of Europe officially abhorred the assassination and expected a swift retaliation. But they did not accept a degradation of Serbia to a satellite state of Austria-Hungary, what the Austrian government intended. In Austria, the opinion prevailed that Serbia would be responsible for the assassination and only a campaign against Serbia would again establish the peace on the Balkan Peninsula.

The head of the Austrian General Staff, Franz Conrad von Hötzendorf, demanded the immediate war against Serbia, but Foreign Minister Leopold Count Berchtold and the Hungarian Prime Minister, Stefan Count Tisza, hesitated. They recommended first to consult the German government. The Hungarian magnates (= members of the high nobility) then demanded to wait till the time after harvest, because the fields would be adversely affected by the marching up of troops. Now they wanted to wait for the departure of the French president, Raymond Poincarė, who was at the moment in St. Petersburg/Russia. After that an ultimatum should be delivered to the Serbians.

The hawks of Austria-Hungary will get the upper hand according to the opinion of the German ambassador on 30 June; he informed the government in Berlin as follows: "Hier höre ich … vielfach den Wunsch, es müsse einmal gründlich mit den Serben abgerechnet werden. Ich benutze jeden solchen Anlaß, um ruhig, aber sehr nachdrücklich und ernst vor übereilten Schritten zu warnen" (Here I hear … in many cases the wish, it must be thoroughly settled up with the Serbians: I take every occasion to warn calmly, but emphatically and seriously, against overhasty steps.) Emperor Wilhelm II was annoyed about that and the hesitation of the Austrians. Often he anxiously, but sabre-rattling outwardly, brought a war psychosis about. On 4 July he made the following note: "Jetzt oder nie" (Now or never) it must be settled up with the Serbians. The crisis of July of this year began to ride.

Wilhelm II had put his foot down, but it produced no effect: all his orders required the countersigning of the chancellor according to the German constitution; since the "Daily-Telegraph affair" was especially paid attention to it. Now the chancellor, Theobald von Bethmann Hollweg, had to decide on war or peace. The war was inevitable in von Bethmann Hollweg's opinion. His alternative wish: to weaken Russia's power for ever and to break up the triple entente (alliance) between Russia, France and England.

In the time between 3 and 6 July Alexander Count Hoyos, the head of the Austrian-Hungarian cabinet and so also of the foreign minister Berchtold, explored in Berlin the German attitude and opinion about the general situation in Europe. The permanent sub-secretary Zimmermann – he substituted for the permanent secretary Gottlieb von Jagow, who was on holiday – warned against the war against Serbia, because it would involve the whole of Europe in the Austrian-Serbian conflict.

On 5 July, at noon, Emperor Wilhelm II received the Austrian-Hungarian ambassador, Ladislaus Count of Szögyény-Marich, at the "Neues Palais" (New Palace) in Potsdam. The ambassador asked the emperor the question, whether the government in Berlin would approve an attack against Serbia. Emperor Wilhelm II assured without hesitation that Austria might count on the "vollen Unterstützung Deutschlands" (full support of Germany).

At the same day Wilhelm II received von Bethmann Hollweg. The German chancellor made the following note: "Diese Ansichten des Kaisers deckten sich mit meinen Anschauungen" (This opinion of the emperor tallied with my view of the affair) – On 6 July Szögyény could informed the government in Vienna as follows: "Wir können … mit Sicherheit darauf rechnen, daß auch der Reichskanzler, ebenso wie sein kaiserlicher Herr, ein sofortiges Einschreiten unsererseits gegen Serbien als radikalste und beste

Lösung unserer Schwierigkeiten am Balkan ansieht" (It is safe to say, … , that also the German chancellor, as his sovereign, the German emperor, consider an immediate action against Serbia as the most radical and best solution of our trouble on the Balkan Peninsula).

On 5 July, about five o'clock in the afternoon, Wilhelm II conferred with the military leadership. He put the question to the German war minister, General Erich von Falkenhayn, whether the German army would be prepared in case of a war. Falkenhayn said a short "yes" without any reservation. At the same time von Bethmann Hollweg informed the German ambassador to Vienna as follows: "Kaiser Franz Joseph könne sich aber darauf verlassen, daß S.M. im Einklang mit seinen Bündnispflichten und seiner alten Freundschaft treu an der Seite Österreich-Ungarns stehen würde" (Emperor Franz Joseph may rely on His Majesty – Wilhelm II -, that His Majesty remains loyal to Austria-Hungary, what he also does as ally and old friend of Austria).

Wilhelm II started off on his traditional northland journey, regardless of the crisis. Before he went aboard of his ship, he still announced, if Russia mobilizes he'll immediately declare war on Russia.

On 7 July, Count Hoyos reported on his talks in Berlin to his government in Vienna. Now the Austrian cabinet decided to come to a "tunlichst rasche Entscheidung des Streitfalles mit Serbien im kriegerischen oder friedlichen Sinne" (swift decision of the conflict with Serbia in the sense of war or peace). On 8 July the German ambassador to Vienna, Tschirschky, urged the Austrian-Hungarian foreign minister, Leopold Count Berchtold, to take action against Serbia immediately. But Count Berchtold was dependent in his decisions on the Hungarian minister president (Prime Minister) Tisza, who refused to take instructions from Tschirschky.

The military leadership of the German Empire worked out operational detail plans in the meantime. The real cause of the war, Austria-Hungary's wish for a victory over Serbia, was overlapped more and more by military considerations of Germany. So the General Staff drew up the draft for the ultimatum to Belgium; that even happened before the answer of Serbia to the Austrian ultimatum of 23 July. This draft referred the General Staff to the "Auswärtige Amt" (Foreign Ministry of Germany) on 26 July then.

The draft of the Austrian ultimatum – Serbia received this ultimatum on 23 July – was already completed on 19 July. Now on 23 July, Serbia should answer within 48 hours. The demands of Austria-Hungary were so formulated that Serbia must reject. But the answer of Serbia was a great surprise; Serbia accepted all points of the ultimatum with the exception of one point: it refused an Austrian delegation the investigation of the background of the assassination in Serbia.

In London the anxiety increased in the meantime. On 27 July, the English permanent secretary, Sir Edward Grey, proposed the governments in London, Berlin, Paris and Rome may intervene between the government in Vienna/Austria and St. Petersburg/Russia, but not between Vienna and the government in Belgrade/Serbia. – The German government in Berlin refused the proposal of a conference in London: It would be impossible to Germany, to drag an ally off to a European tribunal because of a conflict with Serbia. At the same time Berchtold asked the emperor Franz Joseph I for the declaration of war on Serbia with the information that there would be already combats close to Temes-Kubin, what was not true.

On 28 July, Austria declared war on Serbia. Sir Edward Grey once more tried to avoid the worst; 29 July he intervened in Berlin and also tried to work on Austria-Hungary to stop the Austrian advance towards Belgrade; Austria-Hungary should also entrust other superpowers, the mediation of its disagreements with Russia. It was in vain. Also Tsar Nicholas II was in the meantime not willing to finish the conflict peacefully. On 30 July followed the general mobilization of the Russian army and one day later the German army mobilized too.

Now it came in rapid succession: on 1 August mobilized France; also on 1 August Germany declared war on Russia; then on 2 August Germany directed the demand to Belgium to let German troops marching through. On 3 August Germany declared war on France. Romania and Turkey remained neutral at the beginning of the war.

Then, also on 3 August, the German troops marched into Belgium, what produced the declaration of war of England on the German Empire on 4 August.

"Serbien muß sterben" (Serbia must die), "Jeder Stoß ein Franzos" (Each thrust a Frenchman), "Jeder Schuss ein Russ" (Each shot a Russian), "Hier werden noch Kriegserklärungen angenommen" (Here we still take declaration of war) – these were epigrams, which decorated the railroad cars, which the German soldiers took to the fronts in the west and east. These epigrams reflected also the spirits of wide sections of the German population; it was not only the spirits of conservative-minded or national-minded people, but also the spirits of social democrats.

Many people, not only in Germany, welcomed the war enthusiastically and came closer together to "defend their threatened native country". Nobody could foresee that there were following material battles and barrages, attacks with poisonous gas and flame throwers, submarine war and attacks of tanks, hunger and revolution. Many people still remembered the beginning of the war in 1870: "Bis Weihnachten sind wir wieder zu Hause" (Till Christmas we are at home again), that were the words of farewell of the German soldiers in those days.

Now the German troops should act according to the so-called "Schlieffenplan" (Plan of General Chief of Staff Count von Schlieffen, 1833 – 1913), i.e., to seek the decision in the west. Mighty German armed forces should, from Belgium coming, by their right wing push the French troops beyond Paris against the Swiss frontier and the Vosges Mountains by a comprising movement. Then, in a gigantic battle, the French troops should suffer a crushing defeat by the German troops there. Then the mass of the German army should only march against Russia, because the Russian deployment was considered to be slow and clumsy, so that it would be possible to put the Russian army off by slight armed forces till the final defeat of France would be clear.

Germany had declared war on Russia and France without to wait for the initiative of them, so that it looked like the real peace breaker. Germany had also broken the neutrality of Belgium by the disregard of effective treaties. Now von Bethmann Hollweg, who had arranged that all, declared in front of the members of the "Reichstag" (Imperial Parliament): "Das Unrecht, das wir damit tun, werden wir wieder gutzumachen versuchen, sobald unser militärisches Ziel erreicht ist" (The wrong that we do by it, we try to put right again as soon as we have reached our military mark). These were foolish words. Also he should not have spoken the foolish words to the English ambassador: "Der Neutralitätsvertrag mit Belgien ist nur ein Fetzen Papier" (The treaty of neutrality with Belgium is only a scrap of paper). England was challenged anyhow by the breach of the neutrality and threatened in its interests. In 1912 England had already assured France that it would come to its aid in case of a German attack. From 4 August on also England was at war with Germany and from 6 August on Austria-Hungary with Russia. Other declarations of war were following in the next weeks. Italy and Romania didn't feel obliged to keep the alliance with Germany and Austria, because they were of the opinion that Austria had broken the peace by the attack on Serbia. So the two blocs, the so-called "Mittelmächte/Central Powers" (Germany and Austria) and the powers of the "Entente" (France, England and Russia), were facing each other. The "Entente" formed so a common front together with Serbia and Montenegro against the "Mittelmächte", a front that was in the offing since a long time before the outbreak of war. The "Mittelmächte" were less successful in diplomatically struggling for other allies than their adversaries. Whilst Germany and Austria-Hungary could only win Turkey and Bulgaria over, the adversaries could win the most of the states of the world over to their side in the course of the war, amongst them were Japan, the former German allies Italy and Romania and above all the USA and all colonies of England and France and also the British Dominions (Canada, Australia, New Zealand, India and so on).

During the first days of the war the German troops were successful in the west. The Belgian and then the French army was thrown back, amongst both armies were also British contingents. The German troops got into North France like a storm and soon they crossed the Marne (river). In August they were already before Paris. The "Schlieffenplan" seemed to lead to a success.

On 11 August, France declared war on Austria-Hungary; since today was Germany also at war with Montenegro. The German warships, the cruisers "Goeben" and "Breslau", broke through the naval blockade of the enemy on this day. Some days later they reached the large Turkish city Istanbul, where both ships were sold to Turkey. From October both ships formed the core of the Turkish navy against the Russian "Black Sea Navy".

On 12 August, England declared war on Austria-Hungary. Also on this day the present "suffrage bishop" of Posen, Likowski; was appointed Archbishop of Posen and Gniezno. Now he used his first pastoral position to admonish the "Poles of the Prussian provinces to devote themselves to emperor and empire".

On 14 August, Japan demanded from Germany by an ultimatum to withdraw its ships from East Asia and from the Jiaozhou Bay in China, which was taken on lease by Germany, till 23 August.

On 19 August, the battle of Gumbinnen began in East Prussia. Von Puttwitz, who was commander-in-chief of the German troops in Prussia, feared the encirclement by Russian troops; therefore he broke off the battle. The German troops now withdrew and Russian troops occupied a big part of the German province East Prussia.

Whilst it wasn't going well in the east, contrary to all expectations, the German troops had more success in the west. On 20 August they had already occupied Brussels, the capital of Belgium. In the East Germany was still waiting for such a success, which wasn't standing in view. On 22 August was conferred therefore the supreme command of the German troops in East Prussia, the "Eight Army", on General Paul von Hindenburg, who was already pensioner. Also on 22 August the French offensive was stopped in the southwest of Germany, in Elsass (Alsace).

On 23 August, it happened what was to be expected: Japan declared war on Germany. Now began the war in Asia too.

There were also combats in Africa. Here the adversary of Germany made a quick success. On 26 August the German troops capitulated in Togo. British and French troops occupied this country. Later the German colony "Togo" was divided amongst England and France. Also on 26 August began the battle of Tannenberg/East Prussia under the supreme command of General von Hindenburg. The Russian "Narew Army" was encircled and had to surrender on 30 August; 93,000 Russian soldiers were taken prisoners. Von Hindenburg was promoted "Generaloberst" (Colonel General/Supreme General) the day before. On 26 August also the first Russian-Austrian battle began by Lemberg in Galicia (today Lviv in the Ukraine). There the Russian troops were successful and could occupied this Austrian town on 3 September. Then on 8 September began the second battle close to Lemberg (Lviv), which came to an end by the Austrian defeat on 12 September. But the Austrian troops could prevent the invasion of Hungary by Russian troops.

On 28 August the first naval battle took place. The British navy penetrated into the North Sea and sank three German cruisers off the island of Heligoland. – On 29 August troops from New Zealand occupied the German island "Samoa". There the German soldiers had surrendered without fight.

On 2 September mobilized Turkey whilst the German chancellor, Theobald von Bethmann Hollweg, gave his first press conference to American correspondents in Berlin. At this conference he warned against the aftermath to the "Kulturgemeinschaft der weißen Rasse" (Civilization of the white race), if Great Britain includes Asians and negros/blacks in the combat against the German Empire and made an appeal to the "sense of justice of the American nation" too.

Germans to the front; it should be a happy journey

By the "Pact of London" Great Britain (England), France and Russia bound themselves on 5 September to make no separate peace with the German Empire or Austria-Hungary.

On 6 September began the battle of the Masurian Lakes/East Prussia. "Generaloberst von Hindenburg " encircled the Russian "Niemen Army" and defeated it on 15 September. By it East Prussia was finally liberated from the Russians.

On 9 September, it was a Wednesday, chancellor von Bethmann Wollweg sent during the height of the battle on the Marne (river in France, before Paris) a "war platform" (Septemberprogramm) from the German headquarter in Coblence to Berlin with the claim of the German Empire to the middle of Europe. On 9 September also Helmuth von Moltke, head general of staff of the German army, made a momentous mistake. From his headquarter in Luxembourg he gave the order to the German troops in France to withdraw towards Aisne line. That happened, because he was unaware of the real front line. So the advance of the German troops became a positional war by this withdrawal now. On 14 September, Moltke was relieved of his duties because of his wrong views of the situation. His successor became "lieutenant general" Erich von Falkenhayn. – During the withdrawal of the German troops in France the "Eight German Army" under the supreme command of "colonel general" von Hindenburg defeated the Second Russian army (Army of Wilna/Vilnius) on 15 September and pushed the remainder of the Russian soldiers back to Russia. During these combats the Germans captured 30,000 Russians. Whilst the Russian army was defeated by the Germans Russian troops could encircle the Austrian fortress Przemsyl on 16 September and besieged it till 11 October.

On 18 September began Japan with the siege of Tsingtau (Qing-dao/China), the capital of the German colony Kiautschou (Jiaozhou). One day later British troops landed in the "Lüderitz-bucht" (Lüderitz/ German-Southwest Africa), whilst German troops besieged the French town Reims and the battle on the Marne (river) was still lasting. On 22 September also began hard combats by Verdun/France and the German submarine "U 9" sank three British cruisers off the coast of Holland. This success of the German navy made clear the importance of the new "submarine weapon".

On 23 September, German soldiers conquered the French town Varennes.

On 28 September began the great offensive of the German and Austrian troops against Russia. On 4 October they reached the "Weichsel" (the Vistula/river in Poland), where the advance was stopped for the time being whilst in Serbia the Austrian troops continued to push ahead. On 5 October fled the Serbian gov-ernment from Belgrade to Skopje (today capital of the Republic Macedonia).

On 7 October, the American president Wilson replied to a letter from Emperor Wilhelm II dated 7 September (Wilhelm II had asked the American president to oppose the use of so-called "dumdum projectiles" and oppose the guerrilla activity of the civilians in the occupied regions). He did it with the note that "he will remain himself really neutral".

On 9 October, the Belgian defenders of the seaport Antwerp surrendered after a siege of 12 days and the members of the Belgian government fled into the North-French seaport Le Ha-vre.

On 10 October, German troops began with the offensive against the French ports at the seaside of the Channel. But they didn't have success, they met with stiff resistance. Short time later both sides had many casualties in the "Battle of Ypern" and the front line came to a standstill. – On 11 October was a German submarine successful again; it sank the Russian cruiser "Pallada" off the Baltic coast.

In Belgium the German troops continued conquering, the towns Gent and Lille were conquered on 12 October, Brugge/Bruges on 14 October and Ostend on 15 October. The British cruiser "Hawk" was also sunk by a German submarine on 15 October.

On 27 October, Russian troops tried a new offensive against German and Austrian troops in Poland. They had partial success, because the German and Austrian troops had to withdraw for the time being.

On 28 October, the assassin Gavrilo Princip was finally sentenced in Sarajevo/Bosnia. He was sentenced to an imprisonment of twenty years. The death penalty could not be imposed on him, because he was not older than twenty years at the moment of the assassination. But five accessories were sentenced to death and ten others to imprisonment of many years. The organizer of the assassination, the head of the Serbian secret service (Colonel Dragutin Dimitrijević), was however not extradited by his government. On 28 October the Turkish navy also attacked the Russian "Black-Sea Navy" by its former German cruisers "Goeben" and "Breslau" without declaration of war; but there was no declaration of war after this occurrence, not yet.

On 1 November, the German government published the first time a prisoner-of-war list, according to this list were in German captivity: 190,000 French soldiers – 190,000 Russian soldiers – 35,000 Belgian soldiers and 16,000 English soldiers. Also on 1 November, von Hindenburg was officially appointed commander-in-chief of all German troops in the east and German war ships under the command of Count Spee sank two British cruisers off the coast of Chile, as a result the British government declared the whole of the North Sea as war region.

Also in the German colonies the English and French continued fighting against Germany. On 5 November defeated the German general Lettow-Vorbeck a British-Indian expedition corps in "German East Africa". During this day also followed the declaration of war on Turkey by Great Britain and France. Russia had already declared war on Turkey on 2 November. Now British troops immediately occupied the Turkish island Cyprus.

On 6 November happened that in Germany, what already happened to Germans and Austrians in England: all British civilians, who were living within the German Empire and were between 17 and 55 years old, were arrested and considered prisoner of war, but women, children and old people were at liberty to leave Germany.

On 7 November the war came to an end for Germany in China. Tsingtau (Qingdao) fell into Japan's hands. The German soldiers had to capitulate since they had shot off their last ammunition.

On 9 November, the German cruiser "Emden" was sunk by the Australian cruiser "Sydney". The cruiser "Emden" was a successful ship of the German navy till this day, it had sunk 1 Russian cruiser, 1 French destroyer and 23 British trading vessels. 56 German marines of the cruiser "Emden" did not experience the naval battle of their ship; they had landed on the Coco Island to occupy it. Now they succeeded in capturing the "three-mast-schooner" Ayesta; after this success they fought their way through to Germany; that happened via Arabia and Turkey. In May of the following year they were at home again.

On 15 November, Russia began with the offensive against the Prussian provinces Posen and Silesia. But it was an offensive without great success.

On 5 December, Italy declared its neutrality and on 6 December came the French government back to Paris after the stabilization of the front line. Till this day Bordeaux was the seat of the government.

On 8 December, a naval battle took place off the Falkland Islands. Vice-admiral Count Spee went down with his flagship "Scharnhorst" during this battle; he was just 53 years old. By this battle Germany lost the cruisers "Gneisenau", "Leipzig" and "Nürnberg".

On 17 December, the Russian offensive in the Prussian provinces Posen and Silesia finally broke down. Now it followed a positional war in the east too. One day later England (Great Britain) annexed Egypt; the reason was the securing of the passage through the Suez Canal for its own ships. Egypt was still a part of the Turkish Empire till the day of annexation by England.

On 24 December, Emperor Wilhelm II declared during his Christmas address: "Wir sind überfallen, wir wehren uns. Das gebe Gott, daß aus diesem Friedensfest mit unserem Gott für uns und unser Land aus dem schweren Kampf reicher Sieg erstehe. Wir stehen auf feindlichem Boden. Dem Feind die Spitze unseres Schwertes und das Herz unserem Gott zugewandt. Wir sprechen es aus, wie einst der Große Kurfürst (Friedrich Wilhelm of Prussia, 1640 – 1688) getan hat: In Staub mit allen Feinden Deutschlands! Amen". (We was attacked, we defend us. God may give that by this festival of peace with him, our God, rises rich victory for us and our land from the hard fight. We are standing on hostile ground. We turn the point of our sword to the enemy and the heart to our God. We express, like once the Great "Kurfürst" – Friedrich Wilhelm of Prussia – it had done: into the dust with all enemies of Germany! Amen)

Now the German government instructed all diplomatic representation abroad to crack down on the dissemination of French assertion of the German guilt of the outbreak of war.

Cardinal Dèsirè Mercier, bishop of Brussels, called upon the Belgians on 29 December to offer resistance against the German occupying power.

On 31 December, the results of the war were so far not good-looking for the enemy of Germany: 310,000 Russians – 220,000 French – 37,000 Belgians and 19,000 English in German captivity, but also 137,000 German soldiers in Russian captivity. Only the British navy could achieve better successes than the navy of the German Empire, the English also confiscated 445 German trade vessels, other 505 German ships were grounded in neutral states. The Germans could only confiscate 124 British ships. – That was a first balance without the dead persons, caused by the combats of this terrible war.

We write the year **1915**

On 1 January, Philipp Scheidemann, who was member of the "Reichstag" (German parliament) and there also at the head of the parliamentary party of the SPD, made the following call to labourers and soldiers: "Haltet aus! Von Euch hängt es ab, was aus unserem Land und aus der Arbeiterschaft wird" (Hold out! It's for you to decide, what will happen with our country and the working class).

On 8 January, the fights began by Soissons and La Bassée, both are towns in the north of France close to the frontier of Belgium; but these fights did not get the positional war moving. Two days later 16 German aeroplanes bombed the English town Dover and the French town Dunkirk and on 19 and 20 January, three German airships (Zeppelins) Yarmouth and Kings Lynn in England. The German press described this line of action as a step towards destruction of the British trade and the British supply.

Philipp Scheidemann; he was a politican and was born July 26, 1865 in Kassel. He died on 29 September 1939 in Copenhagen/Denmark. 1903-1918 and 1920-1933 he was a deuputy in the Reichstag (parliament). 1911-1920 he was in the SPD executive committee. In 1916, during the First World War, he campaigned for a negotiated peace. In 1918 he became Secretary of State in the Cabinet of Prince Max of Baden. During the November Revolution of 1918, he proclaimed the German Republic. Novemer 1918 to February 1919 he was member of the Council of People's Representatives and from Ferbruary to June 1919 "Minister President" (Prime Minister) of Germany. He resigned in protest against the adoption of the Treaty of Versailles. 1920-1923 he was mayor of the City of Kassel/Hessen. In 1933 he emigrated. He wrote the following books: Der Zusammenbruch/The Collapse (1921); Memoiren eines Sozialdemokraten/Memoirs of a Socialist, 2 volumes (1928)

On 13 January, Turkish troops had invaded Azerbaijan and short time later they occupied Tabriz in Persia (Iran).

On 14 January, South-African troops under the command of General Louis Botha conquered the town Swakopmund in German-Southwest (Africa/Namibia). The German troops of "Southwest" were too weak to offer great resistance. In Europe we had another situation, here they were successful. By Soissons they could gain ground so that a large terrain in the north of France was under German control now.

On 24 January, big cruisers of England and Germany for the first time met off the island of Heligoland. During the following battle was sunk the old German cruiser "Blücher", other ships, like the English cruiser "Lion" and the German cruiser "Seydlitz", were heavily damaged. Also two German torpedo boats perished during this naval battle. Now, after the battle, the German government declared the island Helgoland "Festung der Marine" (Fortress of the Navy); the civilians of Helgoland (2,300 persons) had to leave this island, they found their new home for the time being in Hamburg and Altona (today a municipal district of Hamburg). During this month was still set up a distribution place for foodstuffs, which had to share out the grain stocks. Because the grain stocks were not enough, the so-called "war bread" was made longer by an admixture of potato flour from now. Tinned meat and sausage helped for better rations at the front. New companies of the tinning industry were founded in the Braunschweig/Brunswick area mainly. At the end of January were introduced stamps to bread and flour. The daily ration of an adult, which could be bought by a "flour stamp", was 225g flour now.

On 8 February, the decisive battle began in the east. During this "Winterschlacht in Masuren" (Winter battle in Masuria/a part of East Prussia) was fought all along the line Johannesburg-Darkehmen-Tilsit. The "Eight German Army" under the command of Paul von Hindenburg could completely encircle the "Tenth Russian Army" in the Augustow Suwalki area. On 21 February came the battle to an end and the Germans could capture 100,000 Russian soldiers.

On 10 February, the USA protested against the German "naval war declaration". Each attack on American ships would be considered an attack on the American neutrality.

On 16 February also began the winter battle in the west. In the French province Champagne the French army attempted a breakthrough, but this attempt was beaten back by German troops till 30 March. During the last weeks France and Germany had developed the first "battle aeroplanes" with two motors, the "Rumpler" (Germany) and the "Candron" (France). The "allmetal aeroplane", which was developed by the company Junkers some months later, was not yet able to break the superiority of the French and British air force at the front.

On 22 February, the leaders of the German navy declared the unrestricted submarine war. Each trade and war ship was immediately attacked within the war areas.

On 4 March, Russia named its demands in case of victory: The Turkish region around Istanbul, the Bosporus and the Strait of Dardanelles shall become a part of Russia. France and England accepted these demands. Five days later the Russian troops were again defeated, the German troops achieved a great success by Grodno. Another day later the English troops tried to break through in the west, by Neuve-Chapelle. But the English failed in their attempt on 14 March whilst the English/British navy was successful, British ships could sink the German cruiser "Dresden" in the southeast of the Pacific Ocean.

On 22 March, a German zeppelin (air ship) attacked Paris in the night. The German succeeded in making out their marks in spite of the darkness by signal flares, which were fastened to little balloons and hovering over the French capital. The bombs damaged the railway at Gare St.-Lazare and Gare du Nord and also some industrial plants. The next attack by zeppelins followed in May, but now the mark was the English capital London. On 22 March were also successful the Russian troops, that for a long time again. They conquered Przemyśl. By this success they were near to the Silesian frontier and the Hungarian lowlands. Now Germany had to withdraw troops from the west front and to form up a new army, the "Eleventh Army", to avoid a continuation of the Russian advance.

On 5 April, the French army in vain tried to make an offensive on Maas (river) and Moselle (river).

On 6 April Italy demanded, because of its neutrality, from Austria the cession of the southern part of Tyrol (South Tyrol, there were living only German speaking people. Today a part of Italy with two official languages: Italian and German). But Austria rejected this Italian demand; after that Italy prepared for the war against Austria-Hungary.

On 22 April, the German troops began with a second battle by Ypern, this time with the first gas attack. The poisonous chloric gas had a crushing effect. All French soldiers were killed within a front line of 6 km in length. Nobody of the highest leaders of the German army did not believe in this effect before, therefore also no German troops were available for a breakthrough there, even though they had the best possibility now.

On 25 April, British and French ships landed at the seaside of the Strait of Dardanelles (Turkey), where the soldiers of both countries tried to form a new front line now. But they were unsuccessful. As a result of that the "First Lord of the English Admiralty", Sir Churchill, had to give up his job. Only one day later France and England made a security pact with Italy. They promised Italy in case of entering the war against Austria the Austrian-Hungarian countries Dalmatia, Istria, South Tyrol and the town Trieste. Italy now left the "Dreibund" (Triple Alliance/alliance between Germany, Austria-Hungary and Italy) on 3 May.

On 30 April, German aeroplanes bombed the English towns Harwich, Ipswich and Wilton. Also on 30 April, the dynasty Hohenzollern commemorated its five-hundred-year ruling anniversary in the Mark Brandenburg. On 30 April 1415, the "Burggraf" (castle count) of Nürnberg/Nuremberg, Friedrich VI, had received the "Markgrafschaft Brandenburg" (Margravate Brandenburg) by Emperor Sigismund (See German History, Volume 2)

From May 1 to 3 the new "Eleventh Army" of Germany succeeded in breaking through the Russian west front in West Galicia, close to Tarnow and Gorlice. Now the complete front began to falter and the Russians had to withdraw.

On 7 May, the German submarine "U 20" torpedoed the British passenger ship "Lusitania" off the Irish coast, by "Cape Old Head of Kinsale". By the explosion of ammunition on board this ship sank rapidly, so that only 761 out of 1951 passengers could be saved. Amongst the dead persons were 128 Americans. The sinking of the "Lusitania" caused a political crisis between the USA and Germany, in spite of a joint guilt of Great Britain.

On 17 May, the British combat troops had a power of 600,000 men. But also this power did not help to break through the German front between Lille and Arras (French towns close to the Belgian frontier). Then, on 23 May, the English troops, together with the French army, had to stop their attempt to break through the German lines.

On 20 May, the Italian parliament decided to declare war on Austria-Hungary, what also happened on 23 May then.

On 25 May, the German submarine "U 21" sank the British liner "Triumph" and on 27 May the liner "Majestic" in the Strait of Dardanelles (Turkey). Some days later German women the first time protested against the war and for peace. There were more than 15,000 women who moved with their banners towards the "Reichstagsgebäude" (building of the German parliament) in Berlin.

On 6 June, German troops crossed the Russian river Dniester the first time. The same day Emperor Wilhelm II stopped the submarine war against all passenger ships. – The German government feared an end of the American neutrality. Therefore the American president Wilson was by the German government also informed about the stop of the submarine war against passenger ships; but he was only informed alone, apart from that the stop was kept strictly secret.

On 11 June, Serbian troops occupied the capital of Albania, Tirana (Albania was a neutral state!)

On 1 July, the big German-Austrian summer offensive began from the Baltic Sea to the rivers Bug and San in Russia.

On 5 July, the Austrian army succeeded in stopping the Italian offensive by Gradisca and Görz/Gorizia. Only four days later the German troops in the German colony "Southwest Africa" surrendered near Otawi.

On 18 July, the second Italian offensive began on Isonzo (river in the northeast of Italy) with the aim, to break through from the province Venetia towards Istria. But this offensive was again stopped on 27 July. The Austrian troops were too strong to make a success from this offensive.

On 30 July, the Russian troops in Poland were forced to withdraw along a wide front line. The industrial plants were dismantled before to avoid that they fall into the hands of Germans and Austrians; another reason for the dismantling was: Russia was missing of enough plants for the industrial production.

On 3 August, Tsar Nicholas II refused an offer of peace of the Germans, whilst a German submarine captured the American ship "Pass of Bahamas" off the English coast, after that the "Pass of Bahamas" was escorted to the German seaport Cuxhaven. During these days the conquests of the German and Austrian troops in the east were also continued; on 4 August fell the town Ivangorod on the Vistula (Weichsel), on 5 August the Polish capital Warsaw; after that the Russian troops withdrew in a breadth of 2,000 km, from Dniester (river) up to Kurland (since 1918 a part of Latvia. Kurland was a former part of the Holy Roman Empire of German Nation, then in 1561 it came under Polish sovereignty, but as autonomous part and in 1795 it became a Russian province). Russia had 3,000,000 soldiers lost after one year of war; they were killed or were taken prisoner. Now a Polish deputy of the Austrian "Reichsrat" (Upper House of the parliament) pleaded for a kingdom Poland within the Austrian Empire.

On 16 August, the English ship "Baralong", which was camouflaged as unarmed (submarine trap), sank the German submarine "U 27", whilst the triumphant advance of the German army went on in the east; on 17 August, in Lithuania fell the town Kowno (Kaunas), then Bialystok and Grodno. Also on 17 August, a German submarine sank the British passenger ship "Arabic", amongst the dead persons were two Americans; that led to diplomatic quarrels with the USA again.

On 21 August, also Italy now declared war on Turkey. Four days later Poland was divided into two occupying zones: the German "Generalgouvernement Warschau" (General Administration District Warsaw) and the Austrian "Militärgouvernement Kielce" (Military Administration District Kielce). Because Austria and Germany didn't yield to the Polish request for an own state Jósef Pilsudski founded the underground movement "Polish Military Organization". He could here fall back on the veteran troops, who he had led at Austria's side against Russia. Now these units were trained for the combat against Germany and Austria, which had occupied all of Poland in the meantime.

On 6 September, Germany, Austria-Hungary, Turkey and Bulgaria made a military alliance. After a victory Bulgaria should receive the country Macedonia.

On 22 September, a new offensive of the British and French troops began in the Champagne and Artois (West France). On 5 October landed troops of both countries in Salonika (Greece). By it they broke the neutrality of Greece. King Constantine of

Greece insisted on the neutrality of his country whilst the Greek Prime Minister Eleutherios Venizelos supported the action of France and England; therefore he had to resign his post now.

On 6 October, Germany and Austria started an offensive against Serbia and on 9 October, Belgrade, the capital of Serbia, was conquered. The head of the united German-Austrian troops was "Generalmajor (Major General) von Seeckt". One day later Bulgaria declared war on Serbia, as a result France and England now declared war on Bulgaria. Now Romania and Greece declared their neutrality in the Bulgarian-Serbian conflict in turn. – In Germany the foodstuffs were rationed now as ever, only four days in the week meat and sausage were sold.

On 5 November, Bulgarian troops conquered the Serbian railway junction Niš, by it the direct railway line Berlin-Vienna-Istanbul was under the control of Germany, Austria and Bulgaria. Some days later a submarine of the Austrian navy sank the Italian passenger ship   "Ancona".

On 11 November, a meeting of the German chancellor, von Bethmann Hollweg and the Austrian foreign minister, Burián, took place in Berlin. At this meeting von Bethmann Hollweg suggested a union between Germany, Austria-Hungary, Kurland, Lithuania and Poland, the socalled Middle Europe Bloc.

On 14 November, the Czech professor Tomáš Masaryk, who also was deputy of the Austrian parliament, established an "action committee" for the foundation of an independent Czechoslovak state. That happened in Paris (France). There he was supported by the French Prime Minister Briand, who permitted him to form a government in exile. – At the end of November the remainder of the Serbian army fled to Albania.

On 12 December, the design engineer Junkers presented his first all metal aeroplane of the world and few days later the French and British troops withdrew from the Strait of Dardanelles. Now they took position in Salonika (Greece).

We write the year **1916**

The positional war went on in the west, but both sides could not achieve successes.

On 17 January, Russia started its offensive against Turkey. Armenia, which was a Turkish province in those days, was occupied by Russian troops till the end of July. The Russian troops also succeeded in Persia (Iran), but there they were defeated by Turkish troops in June and August.

On 18 February, the war in the German colony "Kamerun" (Cameroon) came to an end. The biggest part of the German troops had already left this colony on 9 February. Now the German soldiers were in the internment camp of the Spanish colony "Rio Muni". The last German units now surrendered after the capture of Yaoundé, the capital of Cameroon. Some days later the German army commando tried a decisive battle at the west front, because France and England were supported by massive assistance deliveries from the USA for a long time. Mark of the German attack was the French fortress Verdun. Then, on 25 February, German troops conquered the little fortress Douaumont before Verdun. But that was also the only success of the German troops before Verdun, where all hell had now broken out. It began a "slaughtering battle" for both sides, which was lasting till July.

On 27 February, it followed a sharp protest of the German government against the confiscation of a German liner in Portugal.

But the protest was unsuccessful, so that Germany declared war on Portugal.

On 29 February, Germany again took up the intensified submarine war (= also the war against trade ships) at the insistence of the "Chief General of Staff, Falkenhayn", what led to tensions amongst the German leadership. As a result of that Tirpitz's request of dismissal was accepted by Wilhelm II on 17 March. The dilemma was the aim of an unrestricted German submarine war against England, but which should avoid the war joining of the USA too.

In March a German submarine had sunk the French steamer "Sussex". Therefore the USA threatened to break off the diplomatic relations if Germany continues the intensified submarine war. Now the German admiralty ordered to continue the submarine war according to the international prize regulations only (Prisenordnung = warning-search-salvage of passenger). By it Germany complied with the American demand, but the submarine weapon lost its effect.

On 29 April, the English troops surrendered in the Turkish province Mesopotamia (today Iraq). General Townshend and 10,000 English soldiers became prisoners of war of the Turks.

There was a trial of strength between the English and German navy off the Skagerrak (Strait between Sweden and Denmark). During the naval battle the Germans showed that their young navy was England's equal. England's losses were big, but Germany couldn't break the English sea blockade in spite of that. The German ships returned to their ports and the marines had the feeling that they had achieved a great success. It was only a tactical success of the German navy but no decisive battle on sea.

In June the Russian troops were successful against the Austrians. General Alexej Brussilov took a military action against the Austrian troops in the southern sector between Prut and Styrknij. There they could defeat the Austrian army. The Austrians had many casualties and more than 200,000 Austrian soldiers were taken prisoner. A few days later the Russians continued to push back the Austrian-Hungarian troops in Volhynia (Russian province, today a part of Ukraine). The result was that the whole of the southeast front began to falter. At the end of June Turkey launched an offensive against the Russians in Persia (Iran) to keep off another military burden of the Austrian troops in Volhynia. The Russians were thus compelled to withdraw their troops from Volhynia.

In July the combats were still lasting in the German colony "Deutsch Ostafrika" (today Tanzania). But the Germans got out of a decisive battle of the English army over and over again. At the end of July Austria could no longer hold the position at the front in Volhynia and Galicia. Austria needed the military support of Germany. Now von Bethmann Hollweg, the German chancellor, decided in favour of "Generalfeldmarschall (Field Marshal General) von Hindenburg" in view of the differences of opinion between the leaders of the army – Generalstabchef Falkenhayn wanted to have a military decision by Verdun, but Generalfeldmarschall von Hindenburg first a success in the east. Von Hindenburg became the commander-in-chief of all troops in the east, also the commander-in-chief of the Austrian troops there. – In the south the Italians could achieve some successes. Early in August they conquered the town Görz, whilst the Russians under the command of General Brussilov were able to fight through to Bukovina. But there the Russian offensive broke down in spite of successes in Volhynia and Galicia. During these battles Russia lost 1,000,000 soldiers!

On 17 August, Russia arranged Romania's entry into the war. Romania should receive the Bukovina, Siebenbürgen (Transylvania) and Banat for the war against Germany and Austria-Hungary. Then, on August 27, the declaration of war on Austria-Hungary followed really. Now it threatened a total disbandment of the Austrian army. 600,000 new (Romanian) soldiers against Austria-Hungary, Austria could not handle alone that. Now Germany set up a new army in view of this situation. This army should operate under the command of Erich von Falkenhayn and attack Romania from Siebenbürgen (Transylvania = an Austrian-Hungarian province/country in those days). On 28 August, General von Mackensen, advancing from Bulgaria, invaded Dobruja (Romanian province) with a mixture of German-Bulgarian-Turkish units. On 28 August, Germany also declared war on Romania and Italy. The declaration of war of Bulgaria and Turkey on Romania followed then on 1 September.

The biggest and most terrible material war of the war history came to an end on 9 September. Above all the names of the forts Douaumont and Vaux became symbols of immense blood sacrifices on both sides. When now the battle was finally brought to an end, the "blood pump" had also pumped out the blood of the veins of Germany's army. More than 500,000 French and German soldiers were killed before Verdun. Then were killed 700,000 English and French soldiers and 500,000 German soldiers during the futile counteroffensive of the English and French army on the Somme (river), where all hell had broken forth after the inferno of Verdun. The English had put in action the first time tanks during the battle on the Somme. These tanks had overrun the German lines and killed thousands and thousands of German soldiers. But in spite of that the English were not able to reach their goal. The Germans could capture one of the wonder weapons and had reproduced it then.

In September followed the Russian attempt to break through in the Carpathian Mountains. But Russia was unsuccessful and had to suffer a defeat. Since the Austrian military positions against Italy had also stabilized in autumn and Romania was defeated till December, the military balance between the enemies was restored till the end of this year. But the way to Germany for the necessary raw material of the world was interrupted by the English sea blockade. Only Germany's adversaries had that material at their unrestricted disposal. Also the aftereffect of the blockade became increasingly clear to the civilians. Now it was also proclaimed the "total war", i.e., severe rationalization of the foodstuffs, woman labour in the defence industry and more. At the end of this year the situation changed for the worse, there was a famine in many regions of Germany that caused many sacrifices amongst the civilian population. During the winter time, the so-called "Steckenrübenwinter" (turnip winter), the people had to make do with "Steckrüben" (turnips) as compensation for potatoes and bread. They made some dainties from the turnips, so turnip pudding, turnip cutlets, turnip dumplings and many other sweet things. But the morale of the soldiers in the army and of the civilians worsened, especially since they saw that some profiteers, who made a good profit during the war, were living in luxury.

In December Germany, Austria-Hungary, Turkey and Bulgaria made a peace offer because of the common bad situation; but France and England refused it, because in their opinion it did not contain precise proposals. Also the attempt at mediation of the American president Wilson was unsuccessful. The weakness of the German peace politics was the lack of a consensus of the targets. Agreement peace or victory peace was the question. The opinion of the rulers was "victory peace". Large sections of the population also expected a compensation for the enormous sacrifices that they had made.

The internal peace of the parties was also broken by the question of right politics for the future. In March the parliamentary party of the SPD had already separated with a left group around Karl Liebknecht and Rosa Luxemburg, who now called themselves "Spartakusbund" (Spartacus) and became the core of a new party, the "**U**nabhängige **S**ozialdemokratische **P**artei **D**eutschlands" (**USPD**/Independent Social-democratic Party of Germany).

We write the year **1917**

It was a year without the wished military decision for both sides. Whilst the American president Wilson stood for a "peace without victory", Wilhelm II decided, under pressure of military arguments and against the intention of the chancellor, on a new unrestricted submarine war, i.e., each ship (also neutral ships), which sailed into a certain prohibited zone around Great Britain, is to be attacked and to be torpedoed. The warning against the inevitable entry into the war of the USA was off the table by the arguments: England would surrender and make peace because of the counter-blockade that would still happen before the entry into the war of the USA.

The USA had a liking for France and England anyhow; the declaration of the unrestricted submarine warfare was crucial for the American declaration of war on 6 April. Now followed the first military intervention of the USA in Europe and Germany had a new strong enemy.

American war poster; Hun, here is a German meant

The second big event of this year was the beginning of the Russian revolution in February and short time later the overthrow of Tsar Nicholas II. When now the new Russian government announced to continue the war against Germany, the German government gave the permission that Lenin could go from Switzerland (his country of asylum) through the region of Ruhr (Ruhr-Pot) via Sweden to Russia, to bring about the Russian counterrevolution, which should then bring the war to an end for Russia. Then, in October, Lenin overthrew the new Russian government (October Revolution) and in December he reached an agreement of armistice with Germany.

The front Line during the First World War

The allies of Germany: Turkey, Romania, Bulgaria, Austria-Hungary

British blockade

Scandinavia

Baltic Sea

North Sea

Germany

France

Austria-Hungary

Black Sea

Mediterranean Sea

Africa

Arabia

S' = Switzerland (neutral)

— Front Line 1917

-.-. Front Line 1918

We write the year **1918**

On 3 March, Russia accepted the hard peace terms after difficult negotiations in Brest-Litovsk. Russia had to renounce the following territories: Livonia (today: one part belongs to Latvia, another part to Estonia), Kurland (today a province of Latvia), Estonia,

Lithuania, East Poland, Finland and also for a short time the Ukraine and Belorussia. – Also all members of the family of the Russian tsar were killed by the new rulers of Russia, the communists.

In January the American president Wilson had presented a definitive programme for a peace of reconciliation. Wilson's "Fourteen Points" demanded amongst other things, re-establishment of Belgium and Luxembourg, withdrawal of the German troops from Russia and the right of self-determination of all nations within the Austrian and Turkish Empire. Wilson developed this programme mainly because of a better, peaceful, democratic world after the war. But in Germany reigned sceptical reserve; not all points seemed to be worthy of discussion, only at the end of the war the German rulers again remembered the "Fourteen Points".

The hope, which the leadership of the German army had connected with the submarine war, did not come true. England was not forced on its knees in spite of the losses of ships and American troops could earlier go into action at the west front than it was to be expected. Till July some hundreds of thousands of rested American soldiers were already in France; it is true that Russia had left the war in the meantime, but that didn't immediately bring the expected relief for the German troops in the west. In spite of that all Germany was not prepared to make a compromise peace. It thought rather of putting all its eggs in one basket and reaching the breakthrough in France by a powerful offensive. This offensive should then force the military decision. But Germany had no possibility to compensate the casualties by reserves.

In the time between March and July the German armies once more stormed against the positions of the enemy. They made big territorial gains, the English troops were forced to cross the Somme (river) and the Germans reached the Marne (river) again. Now they threatened the French town Compiégne in the north of Paris, but they failed to reach the breakthrough towards Paris there, too.

On 18 July, Marshal Foch, who was commander-in-chief of all troops of the allies in France and Belgium, began the counteroffensive. He had fresh American troops at his disposal; also he had new matériel, above all an overwhelming number of tanks.

On 8 August, the English tanks broke through the German front line, so that day became the "Black Day of the German Army". Now the Germans had to withdraw to the so-called "Siegfriedstellung" (Siegfried Line/Siegfried = a hero of the Germanic legend). Then from the "Siegfriedstellung" they fell back to a resistance line, which was still on Belgian and French territory at the moment of armistice.

Germany could not take any more, but also Bulgaria, Turkey and Austria-Hungary were not able to continue the war. Then, on 30 September, Bulgaria made a treaty of armistice with its enemies, Turkey followed on 30 October.

On 27 October, the new Austrian emperor, Karl I (Emperor Franz Joseph I died in 1916), informed the German emperor, Wilhelm I, the people of his nation would not be able to continue the war, also they were not willing to do that, therefore he will apply for an armistice.

On 3 November, Austria-Hungary agreed the armistice and the Austrian Empire began to disintegrate.

Ludendorff, one of the highest commanding officers of the German army and equated with "Generalfeldmarschall von Hindenburg" (the head of the General Staff), apparently lost his head in those days. On 29 September, he demanded an immediate armistice after the failure of the west offensive, because he was afraid of a catastrophe to the German army in case of a large-scale attack by the enemy. Therefore he was dismissed at the insistence of the German government on 26 October.

To offer the armistice must be a capitulation of Germany; that knew the government in Berlin and also the headquarters of the German army. Therefore the new German chancellor, Prince Max of Baden (in 1917 von Bethmann Hollweg had resigned his post because of differences of opinion with the German General Staff), consulted von Hindenburg once more on 30 October and received the following information: "As far as one can possibly judge we have no possibility, we need to force the enemy to peace". That was a clear admission of the military leadership of Germany that the war was lost by a defeat. The German government now asked for peace. In the night from 3 to 4 October the government sent a wire to President Wilson with the request for armistice on basis of the "Fourteen Points".

On 3 October, the highest leadership of the German army had approved to forestall an expected demand for democratization of Germany of a government of parliamentary members only. Now were also members of the "Zentrumspartei" (Centre Party) and social democrats in the new cabinet. The undemocratic "Dreiklassen-Wahlrecht" (Three-class-right to vote) of Prussia was immediately abolished.

After the admission of the defeat by the military commanders revolutionary events took place in Germany. In the last days of October the marines of the German navy, who were in the Bay of Kiel, began to mutiny because it was rumoured that they had to leave the naval ports for a last heroic battle on the high seas, so they would save the honours of the navy, which had berthed in their ports for a long time without to go in action.

Early in November the unrest spread to many German cities; it was created labourer's and soldier's boards. On 7 November, the Bavarian king fled from Munich. On 9 November, the "German Republic" was proclaimed in Berlin; on 10 November, Emperor Wilhelm II left Germany and went to the Netherlands, into exile. Also the other German sovereigns resigned now.

The end of the World War; 8 November 1918, armistice negotiations in Compiégne (France)

, Extraausgabe Sonnabend, den 9. November 1918.

Vorwärts

Berliner Volksblatt.

Zentralorgan der sozialdemokratischen Partei Deutschlands.

Der Kaiser hat abgedankt!

Der Reichskanzler hat folgenden Erlaß herausgegeben:

Seine Majestät der Kaiser und König haben sich entschlossen, dem Throne zu entsagen.

Der Reichskanzler bleibt noch so lange im Amte, bis die mit der Abdankung Seiner Majestät, dem Thronverzichte Seiner Kaiserlichen und Königlichen Hoheit des Kronprinzen des Deutschen Reichs und von Preußen und der Einsetzung der Regentschaft verbundenen Fragen geregelt sind. Er beabsichtigt, dem Regenten die Ernennung des Abgeordneten Ebert zum Reichskanzler und die Vorlage eines Gesetzentwurfs wegen der Ausschreibung allgemeiner Wahlen für eine verfassunggebende deutsche Nationalversammlung vorzuschlagen, der es obliegen würde, die künftige Staatsform des deutschen Volk einschließlich der Volksteile, die ihren Eintritt in die Reichsgrenzei wünschen sollten, endgültig festzustellen.

Berlin, den 9. November 1918. **Der Reichskanzler**

Prinz Max von Baden.

Es wird nicht geschossen!

Der Reichskanzler hat angeordnet, daß seitens des Militärs von der Waf kein Gebrauch gemacht werde.

German newspaper "Vorwärts"

Resignation of the German emperor

Birth of the Weimar Republic on November 9, 1918. Scheidemann calls the republic from a balcony of the Reichstag in Berlin.

Under the impression of all these occurrences the German delegation of armistice, at the head of this delegation was Erzberger (a politician of the "Zentrumspartei"), had a meeting with the victor of the war in the forest of Compiégne. That meeting took place on 8 November; the negotiations were carried on by Marshal Foch, the victor of the war. Then, on 11 November, the treaty of armistice was signed. That was the end of the terrible war, the biggest tech battle of nations till that day. The first time aeroplanes, submarines, tanks, machine-guns, motorcars and poison gas were used.

The "First World War" was over, but the peace was not yet reached.

On 1 December, the members of a soldier's conference passed a vote of confidence to the new German government under the leadership of Chancellor Ebert. That happened in Bad Ems (a little town on the Lahn, river in the country Rhineland-Palatinate) Then an "Imperial Conference of the Labourer's and Soldier's Boards" was called for the 16 December in Berlin.

On 3 December, the last German soldiers left all territories on the left side of the Rhine and in Posen, the Prussian province in the east. Also on 3 December, the archbishop of Posen, who was also Primate of Poland, celebrated the freeing from the German power by a divine feast service. On 4 December, Wilhelm Marx and Carl Trimborn, both were members of the "Zentrumspartei", proclaimed the independent "Republic Rhineland" during a mass rally in Cologne.

Whilst on 6 December German "Free Corps" acted as protectors of the members of the new government in Berlin, British troops occupied the towns Cologne and Bonn.

On 8 December, Ebert and Scheidemann warned at a rally in Berlin against the "anarchic demands of socialism of the Spartakisten" (Spartacists, members of the "Spartakusbund" = the socialistic union of Karl Liebknecht and Rosa Luxemburg). But Karl Liebknecht made a call for a "world revolution" only.

On 9 December, French troops occupied the city Mainz and the German university of Straßburg/Strasbourg. The university was liquidated and the professors were dismissed now. Straßburg was a French city again. (Later, it was to be a German city again, but then for a short time only).

On 15 December, the "Nationalliberale Partei" (National-Liberal Party of Germany) changed its name. The new name was now: "Deutsche VolksPartei" (DVP/German People's Party). The political leader of this new party became Gustav Stresemann (later more about him)

On 18 December, the "Bayrische VolksPartei" (BVP/Bavarian People's Party) threatened to separate Bavaria from the German Empire in case of a victory of the "Spartakus Partei" (Party of the socialistic union "Spartacus").

On 19 December, the members of the conference of the labourer's and soldier's boards in Berlin spoke for the creation of a parliamentary system in Germany and agreed to the election for a constituent assembly. The demands of the "Spartacists" were not accepted. A system of boards was rejected. It was aimed at a system of nationalized industries; but only for industries again, which were suitable for nationalization.

On 24 December, the soldiers of a so-called "Volksmarinedivision" (people's naval division) in Berlin revolted in front of the royal palace. It was a left-extreme troop of mercenaries. They took Ebert, Landsberg and the city commander Wels (all of them were members of the SPD/Social-democratic Party of Germany) hostage. Since they had killed 56 soldiers of the German army and 11 marines of the German navy, the German government paid the demanded wages and renounced the reduction of the troop of mercenaries.

On 27 December, the new Polish state took over the administration of the former Prussian province West Prussia and on 30 December Wilhelm Pieck (who was later president of the DDR, German Democratic Republic) chaired the meeting of the "Spartakusbund" in Berlin. During this meeting the delegates voted for the foundation of a communist labourer's party of Germany.

The famous German physicist Max Planck

Max Planck was born on 23 April 1858 in Kiel (capital of Schleswig-Holstein) He died on 4 October 1947 in Göttingen (town in Lower Saxony). In 1885 he became professor in Kiel and 1889 in Berlin. 1930 – 1937 he was president (chairman) of the "Kaiser-Wilhelm-Gesellschaft" (Emperor-Wilhelm-Society), since 1894 member and later "constant secretary" of the "Preußische Akademie der Wissenschaften" (Prussian Academy of Sciences). Planck's main sphere of work was the theoretical thermodynamics. In 1900 he calculated the radiation energy of the black body and could specify the energy density u' in the black body a certain radiation frequency v and a temperature $\check{T}$ (Plancksches Strahlungsgesetz/radiation law of Planck). The model of his calculation required that the wall of the black body consisted of harmoniously swinging oscillators. Now it followed that the oscillators couldn't take on a continuously changing energy, as it taught the classic mechanics and the electrodynamics, but only the discreet values of limits of the multiple of $h v$ Here is h an universal nature-constant, the "Plancksche Wirkungsquantum" (Planck's Constant): an universal nature-constant by the dimension of an effect (energy time), the most important figure of the quantum theory and atomic physics. Max Planck got the Nobel Prize for the quantum theory in 1918. He also made contributions to theory of relativity (Einstein)

Max Planck published many physical brain works, for example: "Einführung in die theoretische Physik/Introduction to Theoretical Physics" (5 volumes, 1916 – 1940), "Vorlesungen über Thermodynamik/Lectures on thermodynamics" (1897); he also published contributions for the nature philosophy, so the brainwork "Wege zu physikalischen Erkenntnis/Way to the physical knowledge" (1943) and a scientific self-biography with the same title.

The "Kaiser-Wilhelm-Gesellschaft" was later renamed in honour of Max Planck, the new name is today: "Max-Planck-Gesellschaft/Max Planck Society" (an institute for promotion of sciences, since 1948 in Göttingen).

Max Planck was a great German physicist and was awarded the Nobel Prize.

The Weimar Republic and
the son of Alois Schicklgruber from Austria

We write the year **1919**

The First World War was over and more than 9,000,000 soldiers were killed in action during the fights; so Germany mourned over 1,800,000 dead soldiers,

Russia over	1,700,000 dead soldiers,
France over	1,400,000 dead soldiers,
Austria-Hungary over	1,200,000 dead soldiers,
Great Britain over	950,000 dead soldiers,
Italy over	460,000 dead soldiers,
Turkey over	330,000 dead soldiers,
The United States over	120,000 dead soldiers.

But also other countries had to complain many victims and the civilians of all these countries had also suffered. Many people died because of malnutrition, died of epidemics like typhoid, cholera or tuberculosis. It was the same number of dead persons as the number of dead soldiers. Villages, cities and fields were devastated, especially in France and Belgium; need, misery and hopelessness paralyzed many people, who escaped alive.

The ancient European system of states, which had determined the history of the continent and the world for centuries, had broken down. The three European super monarchies, Germany, Russia and Austria-Hungary, had ceased to exist. In Russia the civil war between Bolsheviks and their opponents raged. In Germany the republic was proclaimed and Austria-Hungary began to disintegrate. Austria and Hungary separated as independent states. Austria lost large parts of its territory: Bohemia, Moravia (today both together: Czech Republic, there were living more than 9,000,000 inhabitants in those days, 6,000,000 Czechs and 3,000,000 Germans, the so-called "Sudetendeutsche"/Sudeten-Germans), Austrian Silesia, Galicia (today: one part belongs to the Ukraine, another part to Poland), Dalmatia (today a part of Croatia), Oberkrain (Slovenia) and the southern part of Tyrol (Italy; there are still living more than 250,000 German speaking people today) and the seaport Trieste (today an Italian seaport). Austria lost also the countries Bosnia and Herzegovina and some very little territories of its countries Styria and Carinthia. But also Hungary lost large territories: Siebenbürgen/Transylvania (there were living also 700,000 Germans; today a part of Romania), Bukovina (today: one part belongs to the Ukraine, another part to Romania; also there were living many Germans), Slavonia (today a part of Croatia), Croatia, Banat (today: one part belongs to Serbia, another part to Romania; also with a German population), Slovakia (which joined with Czechia to the new state Czechoslovakia) and a little narrow stripe at the frontier of Austria; this narrow stripe received Austria now and got the name Burgenland (Land of the Castles; perhaps because some towns have the ending –burg there, for example Ödinburg, Mattenburg and so on). Only Ödinburg and a little district around this town Austria had to give away to Hungary again, after a referendum under pressure of the Hungarian army, although the Germans (Austrians) of this town were in the majority. The Hungarian name of Ödenburg is today "Sopron". So Austria and Hungary also lost many territories with a big German population. – The official name of the remainder of Austria was now: Deutsch-Österreich (German-Austria; but that for some months only), later then only "Österreich/Austria" without to lay stress on German.

The Germans clung to the promise of the American president Wilson and pinned their hopes on him. But what did he understand under the word justice? Germany was also vicious and aggressive to him, was guilty of the war, therefore justice couldn't mean equal treatment of aggressor and sacrifice in his mind's eye. Also it did justice to the matter in his opinion that Germany, what had brought its adversaries on the brink of the defeat, had to pay for the caused damages as chief culprit of the war.

15 January, Karl Liebknecht and Rosa Luxemburg, both just 47 years old, were murdered by government soldiers in Berlin. That happened without procedure. The dead body of Rosa Luxemburg was only found some weeks later in the "Landwehrkanal" (a canal in Berlin).
18 January, the representatives of 27 victorious states convened in the French Foreign Ministry in Paris. Germany and its Allies, but also Russia, were absent because they were not allowed to come. This conference was in glaring contrast to Wilson's demands for an abolition of the secret diplomacy. All important decisions were made by the super powers behind closed doors. The little powers could only consent at the few plenary sessions.

The draft of the peace treaty was essentially a work of three statesmen, who disagreed on the important questions. Thomas Woodrow Wilson, history professor of the University Princeton, was the idealistic advocate of a world system of free states with equal rights, which should be united in an alliance of nations. In future controversial issues should be settled by means of democratic procedures and with it wars should be prevented. The French Prime Minister Georges Clemenceau (he lived 1841 – 1929), who was nearly 80 years old, was sceptically faced with the vision of Wilson. He had witnessed the French defeat and occupation of France in the year of 1871 and the cession of Alsace and Lorraine and he knew that Germany had more inhabitants than France and was superior in economic force. The security interests of France demanded in his opinion a weakening of Germany by cession of large territories in the west and in the east and the imposition of high reparation. But he was also prepared to make compromises, if Wilson and the British Prime Minister, David Lloyd George (1916 – 1922), refuse excessive demands. The English Prime Minister Lloyd George saw this goal also in the weakening of Germany, but that as competitor in the international trade and in the colonial politics. But he often supported the interests of Germany too, because he knew that a too heavy burden of the defeated adversary would not make a peaceful member of the community of nations from him, but it would bring the risk of new conflicts.

6 February, Friedrich Ebert officially opened the German constituent assembly (Nationalversammlung/National Assembly) in Weimar and on 11 February Ebert was elected 'Reichspräsident' (President of the German Empire). He immediately put Philipp Scheidemann in charge of the formation of the government. – Scheidemann was member of the SPD like Friedrich Ebert and born on 26 July 1865 in Kassel/Hessen. In October 1918 he became permanent secretary in the cabinet of Prince Max of Baden and on 9 November 1918 he had proclaimed the 'German Republic'. He died on 29 November 1939 in Copenhagen/Denmark. – By the grand opening of the constituent assembly was born the so-called **"Republic of Weimar",** but not yet officially what happened later.

Friedrich Ebert; he was born on 4 February 1871 in Heidelberg. He came from a humble back-ground. His father was a tailor. During his time travelling as a journeyman he came to the trade union movement (1889) and the SPD. In 1893 he became editor of the Citizen Newspaper of the SPD in Bremen, in 1900 Labour Secretary and member of the Bremen citizenry (city council). In 1905 he was part of the SPD executive committee in Berlin. From 1912 he was a member of the "Reichstag". Then in 1913 he was at the head of the SPD. On 2 November 1919, he was elected president of Germany by the members of the Weimar National Assembly. Ebert died on 28 February 1925 in Berlin.

Other important events of the year 1919:

16 February
The cease-fire of the Allies was prolonged for an unlimited period. This day the Allies also drew the boundary (temporary frontier) of Germany in the east. Poland should get the province Posen, but West Prussia should still remain a constituent part of Germany.

18 February
In Essen, the large industrial city in the region of Ruhr (Ruhr-Pot), the participants of the conference of the "Arbeiter- und Soldatenräte" (Workers' and Soldiers' Councils) called the general strike. At this conference more than 100,000 labourers and soldiers were present. Here now the following strike broke down under the fire of the German army because communistic activists, who were instructed by the Bolsheviks, tried to instigate political unrest like in Saxony, Thuringia, Braunschweig/Brunswick and Hamburg. Also in Bremen the German army was put in action to bring the "Räteherrschaft" (rule of the councillors of labourer and soldier) to an end, although they had only 27% of the votes of **USPD** (**U**nabhängige **S**ozialdemokratische **P**artei **D**eutschlands/Independent Social-democratic Party of Germany) and **KPD** (Communistic Party of Germany).

25 February
In the whole of Germany a general strike broke out now. This strike was called by the "Spartacists" (members of the Spartacus League/a communistic organization). Also this strike was closed by German troops.

3 March

This day the general strike broke down in the middle of Germany. That happened since General von Maercker had imposed the death penalty on plunder and armed resistance.

This day the KPD again called upon the people to overthrow the German government in Berlin. As result it was called the "Belagerungszustand" (state of siege/political measures against riots). But the troops took nine days to break the last resistance, which was heated up by a call of the USPD for a general strike. The combats claimed 1,200 victims. Also on 3 March, Poland made demands for the re-establishment of the Polish state within the frontier of the year of 1772.

4 March

In Bohemia and Moravia (the Czech part of the new republic Czechoslovakia) the Germans demonstrated in masses against the prohibition to take part in an "Austro-German National Assembly". The riot was put down by the Czech armed forces; 54 Germans were killed.

8 April

The Allies reached an agreement about the seat of the new-founded League of Nations, it was Geneva/Switzerland.

7 May

In Versailles (France) the Allies handed over the peace terms to the German delegation (The Germans already arrived on 29 April in Versailles). Now the German government had a time of 14 days for the discussion of the peace terms. If Germany rejects these terms the Allies had to take up the war actions again.

The peace terms of the Allies were:
Acknowledgement of the sole responsibility for the war; the cession of all colonies, the cession of Elsaß-Lothringen (Alsace and Lorraine), cession of the Memel territory (Memelland = eastern part of East Prussia), cession of West Prussia, cession of Posen, cession of the "Hultschiner Ländchen" (very little territory in the east, it was a part of Upper Silesia), cession of Eupen, Malmedy and St. Vith (towns in the Eifel), cession of Upper Silesia and cession of the northern part of Schleswig; delivery of 75% of the yearly production of iron and zinc, delivery of 28% of the yearly output of hard coal, delivery of 20% of the yearly harvest of potatoes and cereals, reduction of the army to 100,000 soldiers; heavy weapons were prohibited. The amount of the additional reparation was still to clear. – Count Brockdorff-Rantzau, the negotiating head of the German delegation, protested against the sole responsibility for the war. The press of the adversaries of Germany differently reacted to the peace terms: The "Daily Herald" of London: "The peace terms of the entente are shameless and tasteless; they are the prologue to new race hatred and to a new war" (The Daily Herald was to be right in the end!). The French press cheered: "France has got the maximal demands". But the French newspaper "L'Humanité" said: "The French proletariat refuses to sign the peace terms".

12 May
The "National Assembly" of Weimar declared against the acceptance of the peace terms. That unanimously happened during a special session in Weimar.

14 May
Two of the murderers of Karl Liebknecht, the soldier Runge and the colonel-lieutenant Vogel, were sentenced to two years of

custody only. But colonel-lieutenant Vogel was already freed by a commando of officers on 19 May. He went into exile to the Netherlands.

16 June
The Allies refused every German suggestion of change to the peace terms and even tightened up the appointment of blame. The only concession was the permission to hold a referendum in Upper Silesia.

18 June
Also the German "peace delegation" suggested the German government to reject the peace terms.

20 June
Also the German chancellor, Philipp Scheidemann, and the German Foreign Minister, Ulrich Graf (Count) von Brockdorff-Rantzau, refused the signing of the peace terms of the Allies. Philipp Scheidemann also resigned with all members of his cabinet now and Gustav Bauer of the SPD formed the new government, together with the "Zentrumspartei" (Party of the political Centre). This day Germany sank even a part of its naval ships, which were still abroad.

23 June
Today the "National Assembly" in Weimar approved the terms of the peace, but without acknowledgement of the sole responsibility for the war and the extradition of "war criminals". This qualification of Germany rejected the Allies and threatened to take up again the war activity. Thus the "National Assembly" had to approve the terms of peace under pressure of the Allies. On 24 and 28 June the German delegation signed the "dictate

peace" of Versailles under the leadership of the new Foreign Minister, Hermann Müller.

3 July
The "National Assembly" of Weimar (German parliament that had the seat in Weimar/Thuringia during the first months after the "First World War") selected the colours of the revolution of the year of 1848 as colours of the national flag (black-red-gold/yellow) and some days later the Allies called off the sea blockade against the German Empire.

31 July
The majority of the "National Assembly" of Weimar agreed to the new constitution of Germany as "German Republic". With it was officially born the "Republic of Weimar" too.

11 August
Today the German president, Ebert, signed the new constitution of the German Empire and determined this day as national holiday.

12 September
In the brewery "Sterneckerbräu" in Munich for the first time a son of the family Schicklgruber took part in a meeting of the "Deutsche ArbeiterPartei (DAP/German Workers Party). The following question was under discussion: "Wie und mit welchen Mitteln beseitigt man den Kapitalismus? (How and by which means can I eliminate the capitalism?) Main speaker was the leader of the „Kampfbund zur Brechung der Zinsknechtschaft" (Union of fighters for breaking the slavery of interest), Gottfried Feder. But who was the son of the family **Schicklgruber**? His father was **Alois Schicklgruber**, who was born as illegitimate child

in the year of 1837 in "Waldviertel" (Forest-District = Region in Lower Austria). Alois' father was in turn Johann Georg Hiedler or Johann Nepomuk Hüttler. But who really was Alois' father could never be determined. Alois went to Braunau (town in Upper Austria on the river Inn, at the Bavarian frontier). There he got married the third time and changed his surname in 1876 (by this time he had the name of his mother Anna Maria Schicklgruber). He chose the name of his alleged father, Hiedler or Hüttler. Probably by a phonetic misunderstanding of the notary the name was changed to Hitler. **Alois Hitler** died in 1903. He had with his third wife 6 children; the fourth child was **Adolf**, who was now at the meeting of the "Deutsche Arbeiterpartei". Adolf Hitler was born on 20 April 1889 in Braunau. His three siblings, who were born before him, didn't live when he was born. He had to leave the "Realschule" (secondary school/junior high school) in the year of 1905 because of bad grades. So he remained without vocational training. His interests in art (painting, architecture and opera, especially Wagner's operas) led him to Vienna, where his tow applications for admission in the painting school of the academy of arts was refused. "Orphan money" (his mother died 1907), inheritance and the sale of own paintings (mostly drawings) made it possible for him to live relatively free from cares most of the time, although he had said later, that he had to live in material misery and had to scrape through as construction labourer. **Adolf Hitler's** world view formed the offended feelings of a man, who was craving for admiration and had dreams about successes as artist and architect, but who also had a lack of drive like a loner on the brink of the society. **Hitler** was also formed by political and social tensions, which surrounded him, and by reading matter that he read unsystematically. In his world view dominated the "right of the strength" and the hatred of the Jews as threat to the "Germanic lord's race". He also had a love-hate relationship to the opinion and habit of living of the middle-class. But a political line was not yet in the offing. – In 1913 **Adolf Hitler** evaded the Austrian military service by the resettlement to Munich, but there he voluntarily went into the Bavarian army in the year of 1914 and became "Meldegänger" (walker for messages) on the Western Front. In 1915 he became lance corporal and received the military medal "Eisernes Kreuz 1. Klasse" (Iron Cross of First Class) before the end of the war. Now, during the meeting of the members of the "Deutsche Arbeiterpartei" (DAP) in Munich, he became member of this party too. Some months later the DAP changed its name and called itself "**NationalSozialistische Deutsche ArbeiterPartei**" (**NSDAP**/National Socialist German Party of Labourers)

2 October

The French "National Assembly" ratified the peace treaty with the German Empire. – Many European nations had adopted the 8-hour-day in the meantime; now also followed the new "Kingdom of the Serbians, Croatians and Slovenians", which existed since December 1, 1918.   This kingdom in 1929 changed its name to Yugoslavia (South Slavia).

10 October

20,000 metalworkers of the Saarland were on strike. Their demand was: withdrawal of the black soldiers of the French occupying forces, because the inhabitants of Saarland felt threatened by these soldiers.

24 October

In Berlin it was signed the German-Polish agreement about the military evacuation of the territories, which Germany already had to give to Poland.

28 October
In Belgium, the German children of Eupen, Malmedy and St. Vith were forbidden to go into a public school. The whole of that former German territory in the Eifel should become a constituent part of the French-speaking province of Belgium (Wallonia).

12 November
Sir Reginald Tower took over the administration of Danzig on behalf of the "League of Nations". Then, some weeks later (10 January 1920), the official name of this former German city was changed. Now it was an independent "Free City" and was named "Freistadt Danzig" (Free City of Danzig/Gdansk).

18 November
Von Hindenburg made an accuser against the peace politics and striking labourers of himself at the parliamentary fact-finding committee: "Die deutsche Armee ist von hinten erdolcht worden." (The German army was stabbed to death from the back). So was born the "Dolchstoßlegende" (Dagger Thrust Legend), which became the political catchphrase of the Rights during the following years.

25 November
The German Empire and Poland made an agreement about the evacuation of West Prussia.

10 December
In Munich **Adolf Hitler** made one of his first speeches for the **DAP** (Deutsche ArbeiterPartei)

21 December
The Netherlands granted the former emperor, Wilhelm II, full right of asylum and refused to follow an application of extradition, if the Allies demand that.

This year, the year 1919, the Rhineland was also occupied by Allied troops. British troops had occupied the northern part and French troops the southern part. Because no one knew the exact area ratios, the boundary between two occupied zones was drawn on a map. That happened by drawing a stroke in a semicircle. The result: now there was a small open space between two strokes. This space, a small area near Kaub on Rhine, had the shape of a bottleneck (Flaschenhals). That "Flaschenhals" was an error that the Allies only noted when they had occupied the Rhineland already. But they could not correct their error, they had previously agreed on the establishment of the boundary. The population of the small area cheered; there were about 8,000 people who were free now. They could determine about their country, they belonged to no other country. So they declared their area an independent state and called it "Free State Bottleneck" (Freistaat Flaschenhals). Trains drove through Bottleneck, but they were not allowed to stop there. The population was forbidden to take economic links with the neighbours, thus smuggling flourished and Bottleneck had vineyards and so wine to offer, which was smuggled out now. The people of Bottleneck printed their own money; they created their own economy and were happy. In 1923 it was over, however, with the dream of an independent state for ever. French troops occupied Bottleneck and dissolved it.

Castle Pfalzgrafenstein in the middle oft he Rhine near Kaub

The story of the coffee filter paper

The inventor was a housewife; her name was Melitta Bentz.

Melitta Bentz had a brilliant idea **in 1908**, to percolate coffee by using paper.

In 1919, first round filter made of porcelain.

In 1925, the typical red-green brand packaging appears on the market.

In 1932, first quick filter conical.

In 1936, patenting of the currently known filter bags.

In 1941, banning the production of coffee filter paper.

In 1945, seizure of the manufacturer's plant by Allied troops.

In 1960, first quick filter made of plastic.

In 1989, first natural brown filter paper made of unbleached cellulose.

coffee filter paper

We write the year **1920**

Germany had lost large territories in the east, so the province Posen, almost the whole of West Prussia and a part of Pomerania and East Prussia was separated from the German Empire by the so-called "Polish Corridor" towards Baltic Sea. This solution was to be especially disastrous in the future and was to give a pretext to **Hitler** to attack Poland later. In Upper Silesia a referendum about the possibility of an annexation by Poland should still follow; the same referendum should then follow in the southern part of East Prussia and in the eastern part of West Prussia too. But the little territory Hultschin (Hultschiner Ländchen) with 48,000 German inhabitants should get Czechoslovakia without referendum.

There was already unrest in the beginning of this year. On 13 January it was dispersed a big demonstration against a "law of plant's councillors" (Betriebsrätegesetz) of the "USPD" and "KPD" in front of the "Reichstag" (German parliamentary building). That happened by machine-gun fire of the German army. 42 demonstrators were killed.

On 3 February, the Allies handed over their extradition list to the German Empire; this list comprised 900 names. The names of Hindenburg, Ludendorff, Tirpitz and Bethmann Hollweg were also put on the list. But the president of the German peace delegation in Paris refused to take this list. He announced his resignation and on 10 February the German crown prince made the Allies an offer of having him at the disposal instead of the 900 persons whose names were put on the extradition list. Then, on 5 February, the "Deutsche Reichsrat" (Upper House of the German parliament) and the "Preußische Landesversammlung" (Prussian Country Assembly) protested against the extradition or the attempt of the Allies to reach an extradition respectively.

Germany and Austria after World War I

Memelland 0.15 million German residents

Germany's territorial losses and losses of Austria with German population:

West Prussia 2.5 million inhabitants (Poland)

Upper Silesia 1 million inhabitants (Poland)

Sudetenland: 3.1 million German residents (Czechoslovakia)

Burgenland 0.1 million inhabitants (Hungarian part of today's)

South Styria and a small part of Carinthia 0.1 million inhabitants (Yugoslavia)

Remained after a referendum in Germany and Austria

═══ territorial losses
══ occupied zone

"After the First World War"

Baltic Sea

North Sea

Northern Schleswig 0.16 million inh. (Denmark)

Germany

The country "Bottleneck"

Eupen and Malmedy 0.05 mi. inh. (Belgium)

Alsace and Lorraine 1.9 million German residents (France)

Lake Constance

Austria

South Tyrol 0.25 million German residents (Italy)

On 8 February, the last German troops left the "Freistadt Danzig" and on 10 February the last German troops also left the former German territory Memel (Memelland), which was administered by the Allies now, like Danzig. (In 1923 Memelland became a part of Lithuania)

On 10 February it was also started the referendum in Schleswig. The northern part of Schleswig voted with 74.2% for the union with Denmark, whilst the southern part of Schleswig voted with 80% for Germany on 14 March; so was Schleswig divided amongst Germany and Denmark. Denmark also received with the northern part of Schleswig the German-speaking towns Tondern and Apenrade.

On 24 February, in "Hofbräuhaus" of Munich a mass meeting of the "Deutsche Arbeiterpartei" (DAP) took place. During this meeting the name of the DAP was changed, the new name was now: NationalSozialistische Deutsche ArbeiterPartei (**NSDAP**/National Socialist Worker Party of Germany). In the course of this meeting **Adolf Hitler** also announced the 25-Points-Programme of the new party.

On 1 March, France and Germany made an agreement about the administration of the Rhine ports of Straßburg (now Strasbourg) and Kehl in Baden. The leadership should take over a French harbour director.

The month March also brought the first outbreak of the rivalry of antidemocratic right groups, which more and more undisguised arose. Pent-up aggression amongst the mostly monarchist-influenced officers reached its climax when the reduction of the army, which was agreed upon by the peace treaty, was to be tackled. Now radical "Freikorps" (Free Corps) proved to be nucleus of the rebellion. On 13 March, the "Marinebrigade

Ehrhardt" (Marine brigade Ehrhardt) under the command of General von Lüttwitz together with rebels under the leadership of the private man Wolfgang Kapp had started to make a putsch against the German government. Wolfgang Kapp was general manager of the "Ostpreußische Landwirtschaftskreditbank" (East Prussian Agriculture Credit Bank) and was founder of the „Deutsche VaterlandsPartei" (**DVP**/German Native Country Party, founded in the year of 1917) together with Admiral Tirpitz. Wolfgang Kapp was advocate of all-German ideas and propagated the counterrevolution against the "Republic of Weimar". Now he didn't want that his "Free Corps" is disbanded and also General von Lüttwitz with his marine brigade tried to prevent the German government from doing the same. After the invasion of Wolfgang Kapp and General Lüttwitz with their rebels in Berlin, they delivered an ultimatum to the German government. Now for the German government only remained a cry for help to the army. "Reichswehrmininster" (Minister of Defence) Gustav Noske was fobbed off, at the moment of biggest threat, by the head of the German army, Colonel General von Seeckt, with the following words: "Reichswehr schießt nicht auf Reichswehr" (The Imperial Army does not fire on the Imperial Army). So the German government had not any backing and fled headlong via Dresden to Stuttgart. The (German) imperial army stayed meanwhile in the background and watched the spectacle calmly. The inadequate organization of this putsch (Kapp-Putsch) and the reaction of the labourers were the reason that the assumption of power by the real wirepuller, the national-minded "administrative lawyer" Wolfgang Kapp, remained a political farce of some days only. The resolute general strike of the labourers and the fact that also employees and officials did not put their trust in Kapp's adventure ran the putsch into space. Wolfgang Kapp fled to Sweden after his failed putsch.

The allied diplomats congratulated the German government on the failed putsch. Then, on 20 March, the government returned to Berlin again.

It came onto the side of the democrats an exaggerated satisfaction relating to the strength of the democratic attitude of the people after the "Kapp-Putsch", additionally to the disillusionment about the unmasking performance by the military personnel. But the confidence in the government grew by no means after this victory, on the contrary. The working class was in vain waiting for social measures, which were put in view, for a long time; also its influence in the companies was considerably cut when members of the work councils took the place of "Arbeiterräte" (Workers' Councils) by law. But the government was at the same time lenient towards the reactionary "Free Corps". The persons concerned of the Kapp-Putsch" had even do not expect more than a symbolic punishment. Who would listen, could even learn about the organization of new secret unions by Wolfgang Kapp, but with the old goals that had failed for the time being. That happened although he was wanted for arrest together with his companions. Indignation and disappointment therefore brought the labourers together to form self-help groups in the region of Ruhr, in Saxony and Thuringia. KPD and USPD found open ears to their realization that government and parliament had failed and would only be agents of the "Offizierskaste" (caste of the officers), whose interests were again in absolute contrast to the interests of the working classes. The labourers wanted to take action against the enemies of the empire on their own initiative and with it to protect their legitimate interests. In addition, in the large cities of the Ruhr (Ruhr-Pot) was formed a proper "Red Army" at the instigation of the KPD (Communistic Party of Germany).

Now something happened that no one could understand; the German government sent regular military units together with the notorious "Free Corps" into the regions of unrest. That happened on 2 April after vain attempts at mediation. The "Brigade Ehrhardt" was even allowed to advance against the labourers. During the civil war, which broke out now, the combative parties were spared nothing. When the military personnel had their "Säuberungsaktion" (Purge) finally brought to a successful end, they could realize that the government was saved again by indescribable brutality.

Because the "Reichswehr" (German army) had occupied the cities Dortmund, Essen and Bochum during the unrest in the region on the Ruhr (= demilitarized zone according to the peace treaty), French troops occupied the cities Frankfurt, Darmstadt and Hanau on 6 April. That was a reason for new German-French tensions. The countries Bavaria, Württemberg, Baden, Saxony and Hessen condemned the invasion of these cities by the French troops and spoke against the disbandment of the so-called "Einwohnerwehren" (civil defensive forces) there.

Tensions between Left and Right. Deutsch-Nationale (right political group) insult Reichsbanner members (left political group)

15 March, after the disbandment of some "Free Corps" by the German government on 29 February, now followed the order about the disbandment of the remainder of the "Free Corps". Two days later the French troops also evacuated the cities Frankfurt, Darmstadt and Hanau again.

18 April, Adolf Hitler founded the first local group of the NSDAP; that happened in Rosenheim (little town close to Munich). One

day later Russia and Germany signed an agreement about the exchange of prisoners of war.

24 April, France and Germany made an agreement about taking over of the administration by French authorities in Alsace and Lorraine (Elsass-Lothringen).

6 May, Danish troops occupied the northern part of Schleswig, which now belonged to Denmark according to the referendum.

11 May, in Paris the Allies handed over a new list with names of war criminals to the German peace delegation. But now there were only 45 names.

21 May, by a greetings address of the president of the German Empire, by words of thanks of the chancellor and the president of the German parliament, Fehrenbach, the "National Assembly of Weimar" was closed. The law on the termination of the military jurisdiction could not be passed by the National Assembly because the parties of the Rights had already left the parliament before. The passing of this law ought to be the last measure of the "National Assembly" in Weimar.

6 June, the first election of the "Republic of Weimar" was held. The so-called "coalition of Weimar" suffered big losses now, whilst the right-wing and left-wing parties could reach big gains in votes. The allocation of mandates now:

SPD - Socialists	113 (1919: 165)
USPD - Independent Socialists	81 (1919: 22)
KPD - Communists	2 (1919: 0)
Zentrum/Centre Party together	
with BVP/Bavarian People's Party	89 (1919: 89)
DDP - German Democratic Party	45 (1919: 74)

DVP - German People's Party   62 (1919: 22)

DNVP - German National People's Party   66 (1919: 42)

This day elections in some countries (Landtagswahlen) were also held, so in Bavaria, Württemberg, Oldenburg, Anhalt and Bremen.

17 June, German troops marched into the southern part of Schleswig again; it was that part, which still belonged to Germany. One week later the party leaders of DVP and Zentrum announced that they have reached no formation of the government. Germany must have promptly a new government therefore the former president of the "National Assembly of Weimar", Konstantin Fehrenbach (Zentrum/Party of the Middle – Centre Party), formed a new government from Zentrum, DDP and DVP without participation of SPD.

11 July, a referendum took place in the southern part of East Prussia, the administration district Allenstein. 98% of the inhabitants voted for Germany. By it the district Allenstein remained a part of Germany. Also in one part of West Prussia took place a referendum, namely in the districts of the towns Marienburg and Marienwerder. Here 92% voted for Germany; so also these districts remained a part of Germany with the exception of a little territory on the right side of the Vistula (Weichsel), which received Poland.

13 August, **Adolf Hitler** gave a speech about the subject "Warum sind wir Antisemiten?" (Why we are anti-Semites?). This meeting took place in "Hofbräuhaus" in Munich. There **Adolf Hitler** also named Jews, during his political talk, "die Rassentuberkulose der Völker" (the race tuberculosis of the nations).

17 August, there were repeated demonstrations in Upper Silesia, which still belonged to Germany (till the time after the referendum). In the course of these demonstrations there were clashes between German and Polish ethnic groups. As a result the French army went into action there.

21 August, the German peace delegation protested in Paris against Polish encroachments, which especially happened in the city Kattowitz (today Katowice/Poland). During the unrest in Upper Silesia Poland proclaimed the general strike of the miners, who belonged to the greater part of the ethnic group of the Poles; that happened on 20 August in Kattowitz.

23 August, Polish troops occupied the "still-German" administrative districts Kattowitz, Beuthen and Tarnowitz. As a result the inhabitants of Breslau (capital of Silesia) attacked the Polish and French consulates on 26 August. Now the German Empire assured the government in Paris and Warsaw of the immediate investigation of the occurrence in Breslau and apologized to France and Poland for this. But the French government in Paris made a claim for damages now, Germany should take over the costs that were caused by the destruction of the consulate in Breslau, additionally to it France demanded an act of atonement from German authorities. Also the German army should pay its respect to the French flag. But all this the German government in Berlin rejected.

4 September, the acts of violence of Polish rebels went on in Upper Silesia. Now the German government made a protest to the president of the "peace conference" in Berlin and to the French, Italian, British and Polish government. Germany also made a protest to the Vatican because of the Polish acts of violence.

7 September, the first party conference of the "Großdeutsche Volkspartei" (Great-German People's Party) took place in Salzburg/Austria. This party conference spoke for an Austrian referendum about the affiliation with the German Empire.

20 September, the KPD gave up its epithet "Spartakusbund"; this epithet had reminded until now, the year of its foundation, the year of 1917. Also this day the "League of Nations" decided on the cession of the German towns in the Eifel (Malmedy, Eupen and St. Vith) to Belgium. Now Germany had to give up this territory, although there were 82.5% of the people of German nationality.

10 November, the new constitution came into force in Austria. This constitution revoked the law of 12 November 1918, which designated: "Deutsch-Österreich ist ein Bestandteil des Deutschen Reiches" (German-Austria is a constituent part of the German Empire). Austria now became an independent "Federal Republic", first president of the "Federal Republic of Austria" became Michael Hainisch; the first chancellor of this republic became Michael Mayr.

15 November, the "Freistaat Danzig" was proclaimed (Free City State Danzig); that happened by a solemn ceremony. The first government of this new state (the most inhabitants were Germans) was in charge of the president of the senate, Heinrich Sahm (1920 – 1930).

16 November, Czech rebels were running riot through Prague and attacked the German inhabitants. The reason for this behaviour was anti-Czech demonstrations in Eger (German town in Bohemia/Czechoslovakia; the name today: Cheb in the Czech Republic) Now the German Theatre of Prague was occupied by

the Czechs and performances should only follow in Czech language there.

3 December, the party conference of the DVP (German People's Party) began in Nuremberg. There the first speaker was Gustav Stresemann. He spoke about the general political situation. The DVP was one of the strongest parties of the Republic of Weimar in those days. This party had more than 800,000 members. – Gustav Stresemann was born on 10 May 1878 in Berlin. He was economist, then, in 1902, he became "Syndicus of the Union of the Saxon Industrialists". 1907 – 1912 and 1914 – 1918 he was member of the "Reichstag" (German parliament) for the National-Liberal Party, 1917 – 1918 he was even party leader. In 1918 he was co-founder of the new party **DVP** (Deutsche VolksPartei/German People's Party). 1919 – 1920 Gustav Stresemann was "Member of the National Assembly" in Weimar and then, from 1920, a member of the "new parliament" (Neuer Reichstag) in Berlin. During the First World War he advocated annexation's aims and took part in the overthrow of Bethmann Hollweg. During the war he also demanded internal reforms as prerequisite for a victory. As monarchist he was only faced with the "Republic of Weimar" reservedly. But later, as chancellor of the German Empire, he prepared the consolidation of the new republic.

We write the year **1921**

On 1 January, the German president sent good wishes for the New Year to the Austrian president by telegram. The same did the Austrian president and sent a greetings telegram to the German president. In their telegrams the two presidents emphasized the unity of Austria and Germany.

The representatives of Germany, at the top the German president Ebert, commemorated the fiftieth anniversary of the foundation of the "Second German Empire" on 18 January. The day after the "Reichstagspräsident" (President of the Parliament of the German Empire), Löbe, ceremonially opened the parliamentary session with a commemorative address to the moment of the foundation of the new "German Empire" fifty years ago. The communists called this parliamentary session as an "imperialistic meeting".

On 24 January, during a conference in Paris without Germany, the Allies decided to impose a payment of reparation of 269,000,000,000 Goldmark on the German Empire; this amount Germany should pay within a space of time of 42 years; additionally to it Germany should hand over to the allied creditors 12% of its export of each year (that also for 42 years), that ought to have a value of 1,500,000,000 Goldmark each year. (It was madness, without reality!)

Unsere einzige Rettung ist Deutschland!

1921, the people of the Austrian country Salzburg wished to be Germans!

Jetzt heißt es: Hilf, wer helfen kann.
Doch Niemand will uns hören.
Drum schließt Euch frisch an Deutschland an,
Dort wo wir hingehören!

Salzburger!
Stimmt geschlossen am 29. Mai
für den Anschluß an Deutschland!

On 27 January, **Adolf Hitler** for the first time wrote an editorial in the newspaper "Völkischer Beobachter". The NSDAP (National-Socialistic German Worker Party) had purchased this newspaper publisher on December 17, 1920. On December 25, 1920, this newspaper then appeared as organ of the NSDAP in Munich.

On 3 February, a mass meeting of the NSDAP took place in Circus Krone in Munich. **Hitler** made use of the note of the Allies about the payment of reparation, which was delivered to the German government on 29 January, and made vehement word attacks on the Allies under the subject: "Zukunft oder Untergang" (Future or downfall). 6,000 persons were present at this meeting of the NSDAP, although the NSDAP had not more than 3,000 members.

On 5 February, in Berlin the German chancellor and the ministers of the German countries discussed the note of the Allies. They wanted to meet the condition of the Allies to eliminate the population weirs (Einwohnerwehre) that were formed after the war. Therefore they gave the Bavarian government an ultimatum to disarm immediately its weirs, which were still the sole civilian armies within the German Empire.

On 20 February, elections to the Landtage (Parliaments of the countries) of some German countries were held, so in Prussia, Hamburg and Bremen. In East Prussia and Schleswig-Holstein were held by-elections to the "Reichstag". The result of these elections was a considerable gain of votes to the extreme right- and left-wing parties; so the SPD lost, but USPD and KPD gained mandates and on the right wing DNVP and DVP made considerable gains whilst the DDP lost mandates. - One day later the Allies refused the counterproposals of the Germans regarding the payment of reparation at a conference in London. Since the Germans had refused the payment because of the insane amount, the Allies began to occupy Düsseldorf, Duisburg-Ruhrort, Mülheim and Oberhausen on 8 March. Before they had still given Germany an ultimatum to pay the demanded reparation, but the Germans had under protest left the conference of London because of this ultimatum and the German delegation had then left London on 1 March.

On 20 March, a referendum in Upper Silesia was held. The only question was: "Upper Silesia belongs to Germany or to Poland?" 60% voted for Germany and 40 % wished that this part of the Prussian province Silesia become a part of Poland. The result of this referendum, which was favourable to Germany, the Polish lawyer Wojciech Korfanty, who was also polling commissioner of this referendum, tried to dodge. Korfanty, who was a former Member of Parliament in Prussia (Prussian Landtag) and leader of the Polish Party there and also a member of the "Reichstag", called upon the Poles to rebel against the German rule and to fight for a Polish Upper Silesia (Korfanty Rebellion). So the rebellion began on 23 March. But the Polish rebels met with stiff resistance of the German inhabitants, which found help by the "Self-Protection-Units" under the command of General Höfer. After the deployment of British troops in June the victorious German units and the defeated Polish rebels withdrew into their starting points again. Then, in October, the division of Upper Silesia followed; that was a recommendation of the President of Czechoslovakia, Eduard Benesch. Germany had to give away 3,200 km² with 900,000 inhabitants to Poland. Cities with German majority, like Kattowitz/Katowice (57% Germans) and Königshütte/Chorzów (75% Germans; 1921 – 1934 the name of this city was Królewska Huta) and 75% of the hard coal and 80% of the lead and zinc production of this region received Poland. But the takeover of this region by Poland only took place on 9 July 1922.

On 5 May, the Allies of the Conference of London fixed a deadline of 4 days to accept the new resolutions. This meant to Germany: Disarmament according to the peace treaty, extradition of the German war criminals and the payment of (now only) 132,000,000,000 Goldmark, but 1,000,000,000 Goldmark of this sum was to pay immediately. The conference members threatened with the occupation of the whole of the region Ruhr if Germany refused the demands of the Allies again. But the German government now accepted the conditions of the Allies.

We write the year 1922

This year the political conflict reached its peak, what many people had feared. It was worn out another ruling coalition within a brief time, the cabinet of Wirth (Wirth was chancellor since the previous year). Wirth had to recognize that he could neither count on a respite of payment nor on mediation in the matter of reparation by the American president. After crumbling of this basic pillar of his politics he was so helpless in this desperate situation that he was moved to say the following: "Erst Brot, dann Reparationen" (First bread, then reparations)

The commission of reparation set up a committee of reparation on 19 April. This committee should audit the German ability to pay. Now representatives of the USA, who had refused the request of Germany one year ago to mediate because of the excessive reparations, were members of this committee too. But also this committee reached no satisfactory result for Germany.

In November the non-party economic expert Wilhelm Cuno formed a new government. But also the members of his cabinet were without party membership, they were experts with self-confidence. Chancellor Cuno (also he only was chancellor till 1923) steered for confrontation with the Allies from beginning of the ruling time of his bourgeois minority government. The "Deutsch Nationale Partei" (DNP/German National Party), which supported him, encouraged his government to make tough politics, especially to France. The present so-called "Erfüllungspolitik" (politics of fulfilment) should have an end now. But this new line of strength was an idea in a very unfavourable moment, because Germany had to accept the French Prime Minister Raymond Poincaré as partner. Raymond Poincaré was an irreconcilable and strongly national-orientated Frenchman. Now the new German government in vain hoped for a moderating influence of England. When it was to see that the German Empire tried to protract the payment of reparation, Poincaré was looking for a pretext to emphasize his opinion to Germany. He put out feelers to some European capitals to check a possible reaction to the French step to make really true the threat to obtain "productive securities".

The inflation; one German billion = 1,000 English billion!!!
During the summer time of 1923 the Germans had to pay for 1
US-Dollar 354,000 Deutsch Mark and in Ocotber of the same
year 25 billion Deutsch Mark (Reichsmark)

We write the year 1923

2 January, the commission of reparation sat in conference in Paris again. But on 4 January this conference already failed because of the stiff attitude of France and Belgium. The breaking off of the conference forced up the US-Dollar to an insane height; 1 US-Dollar = 8,800 DM, but the things were still going from bad to worse.

11 January, 90,000 French and Belgian soldiers invaded the region of Ruhr (the so-called Ruhr-Pot). This took effect like a bombshell. All cities of the Ruhr were occupied. Germany showed its indignation by a "feierlichen Protest vor der ganzen Welt" (ceremonious protest to the whole of the world). Helpless rage and an outcry of the greatest part of the inhabitants of the region on the river Ruhr made it easier to the government of Cuno to propagate politics of passive resistance to the invaders. France should dearly pay for the hoped-for mineral resources and outputs. Poincaré soon knew that not the refusal of the payment of the reparation was the aim of the German politics but the humiliation by France.

The inhabitants of the Ruhr passionately took trouble for the humiliation by the invaders. Refusal of labour, acts of sabotage and nightly raids produced conditions of a civil war. The brutal repulse of the French troops aggravated the situation. A few hundred inhabitants of the Ruhr risk their life and many people became martyrs of the national affair of Germany.

The German government under the leadership of Cuno was of the opinion that the passive resistance would bring the occupation to an end within some weeks. But the German chancellor soon had to listen to reason, because it was an error that the invaders would leave the Ruhr. Now Cuno's government was brought down to earth again; the German government was also absolute unable to take action whilst France built up an own administration in the region of Ruhr. Germany had to deliver the hard coal of the Ruhr to France, but France had not to pay that, additionally to it the German state had to support the inhabitants of the Ruhr by enormous sums of money, which caused an increase of the inflation. Now Germany was missing of supplies of hard coal from the Ruhr and the breakdown of trade and industry of an important region (Ruhr-Pot) made the unemployment and the economic situation worse. The crisis-ridden economic situation of Germany had not yet permitted a way to peace production with a view to the future, too. It was simply suicidal to bank on politics of strength of military solutions in view of this situation. But combat troops were still formed and armed secretly, which could lead to an escalation of the situation. Great parts of the German army with its patriotic partisans banked in irresponsible way on national enthusiasm and a deep-seated disappointment of thousands and thousands of former front combatants, who were released from the army without to have gained ever a foothold in civil life. But the situation could not be mastered by sabre rattling. Now democratic politicians had to take over the thankless part of the losers again, although other men (normally) had to take the responsibility for the consequences of German-national self-overestimation.

Whilst the "Ruhr-Pot" (Region of Ruhr) was seething with discontent furthermore, the inflation rose to a new record level on 1 July; 1 US-Dollar = 160,400 Deutsch Mark! 2 July, the pope in a letter to the Papal Nuncio in Berlin condemned the German acts of sabotage in the Region of Ruhr during the passive resistance against the French-Belgian occupation. As a result the German chancellor, Wilhelm Cuno, saw the Papal Nuncio Pacelli on 5 July to talk about the "Ruhr-affair". It is true that also Wilhelm Cuno condemned the acts of sabotage, but he saw in it an expression of a justified excitement of the inhabitants of the region on the Ruhr.

11 July, the German government presented a balance sheet of the occupation of the Ruhr (Ruhr-Pot). It would be used 80,000 French and 7,000 Belgian soldiers in the "Ruhr-Pot", in addition 10,000 French and 1,000 Belgian railwaymen would be used there, who should maintain the supply of hard coal because the German railwaymen would be on strike. -- During the passive resistance were 92 Germans killed and 70,000 inhabitants of the cities on the Ruhr were expelled. 169 schools were closed. In the last five months the occupation troops had only transported the double quantity of hard coal that the Germans had voluntarily supplied within the first two weeks in January. On 23 July there was also in the rest of the German Empire unrest with riot and plunder. As a result assemblies were prohibited in the open air within the country Prussia now.

The progressive rise in price to food stuffs especially contributed to unrest in the whole of Germany too.

2 August, the British government tried to intervene in the Ruhr-affair. But France refused a British intervention. So the disaster continued to take its course.

8 August, the union and management of the German mining industry came to an agreement. The wages should be paid weekly according to the assessed factor of currency depreciation in each week.

10 August, the KPD (Communistic Party of Germany) introduced a motion of no confidence against the government of Wilhelm Cuno. This day also newspapers were prohibited, which made a call for a forcible constitutional amendment; this happened by a so-called "Notverordnung" (decree of emergency) of the "Reichsprsäsident" (President of the German Empire). One day later the "Verfassungstag des Deutschen Reiches" (Constitution Day of the German Empire) was observed. The Prussian State Ministry combined this ceremoniousness with a "Rhein- und Ruhr-Tag" (Rhine – and Ruhr Day). In the "Dresdner Staatsoper" (Dresden State Opera/Saxony) Heinrich Mann made the ceremonial address for the Constitution Day now; in the course of this address he also spoke about the democratic ideals of Weimar.

12 August, all ministers under the leadership of Wilhelm Cuno resigned. The German President, Friedrich Ebert, now put Gustav Stresemann (DVP/German People's Party) in charge of the forming of a new government. Chancellor Gustav Stresemann (he also was Foreign Minister) had enough trouble from the beginning; it was a hard job for him.

Gustav Stresemann, who formed a government with the members of the SPD, Zentrums Partei (Centre Party) and DDP (German Democratic Party), was sworn in as "Reichskanzler" (Chancellor of the German Empire) on 13 August. He was already chancellor of the eighth German government after the World War. Now there were unrest and strikes in Berlin during his swearing-in, which brought the traffic to a standstill totally.

14 August, 43 deputies of the SPD refused the new government under the leadership of Gustav Stresemann, although their party had received 4 ministerial posts. The Reichstag nevertheless

passed a vote of confidence to Gustav Stresemann's cabinet; that happened against the votes of the DNVP (German National People's Party) and KPD. In Bavaria the opposition formed up against the new government under the leadership of Gustav Stresemann two days later and on 22 August, there was a demonstration of distrust against the imperial politics at a meeting of the "Vereinigte Vaterländische Verbände" (United associations of the native country) in Munich. The president of the Bavarian associations saw Stresemann as "blamierter Platzhalter des Genossen Breitscheid" (a placeholder of the comrade Breitscheid, who looks like a fool. - Rudolf Breitscheid was a politician and first member of the SPD, 1917 – 1922 member of the USPD and then member of the SPD again; he was born on 2 November 1874 in Cologne and died on 24 August 1944 in the concentration camp Buchenwald; 1920 – 1933 he was Member of Parliament/Reichstag). Now the president of the Bavarian associations also demanded Stresemann's resignation. As a result Gustav Stresemann visited Munich four days later; it was his first visit as new chancellor of a capital of a German country.

18 September, the largest mass demonstration of "Vaterländische Verbände" took place in Nuremberg (Nürnberg), there they now kept their "German Day". At this meeting of these associations **Adolf Hitler** angrily attacked the German government in front of more than 100,000 people. Then, the day after, the "Deutsche Kampfbund" (German Fight Association) was founded in Nürnberg and some days later **Hitler** became the **"Führer"** (Leader, which was his title in the Third Reich too) of this association. During the meeting of the "Vaterländische Verbände" in Nuremberg/Nürnberg Gustav Stresemann visited Stuttgart, the capital of Württemberg. Here, he made France an offer of understanding in the Ruhr-affair; he offered a "produc-

tive pledge" in case of the withdrawal of the French and Belgian troops.

9 September, a demonstration against the "German Day" took place in Dresden; here 8,000 members of communistic and social-democratic organizations assembled for the "Musterung der Proletarischen Hundertschaften" (review of the Proletarian squadrons); they alleged to have the intent to defend the German Republic against the **"Hitler-Banden"** (Hitler's gangs)

11 September, the unrest spread to Thuringia (Thuringia was a young country; it was founded just some months ago: Before there were many little countries; see the other volumes about German History by Egon Harings). There the social-democratic government of Thuringia was now brought down. That happened in Weimar, the capital of Thuringia in those days. The reason was that the middle-class parties and the KPD had voted against the government, thus the Thuringian government had no longer the majority for important decisions.

Not only the unrest, but also the galloping inflation was alarming in Germany. On 21 September 1 litre of milk costs 5,400,000 DM and postage for one letter 2,000,000 DM.

23 September, it was a very bloody day. There were separatist riots in Cologne, Aachen, Wiesbaden and Trier, whilst right- and left radicals fought against each other in the whole of the German Empire.

26 September, the German government and the "Reichspräsident" proclaimed the end of the passive resistance in the region of the Ruhr. Trade and industry were absolutely ruined. The balance of the resistance on the river Ruhr: 132 dead persons, 11

death sentences were passed, 150,000 inhabitants were forced to leave the Ruhr Region (Ruhr-Pot) according to the order of the occupying troops. With the proclamation of the end of the passive resistance the "state of siege" was now proclaimed to the Ruhr. The executive took over the "Reichswehrminister". – Reichswehrminister = today: Verteidigungsminister/Minister of Defence – DNVP and KPD took advantage of these steps for public protests, but the "Reichswehr" (German army) immediately went into action against these protests. In Bavaria the Minister President (it was von Knilling) had declared the state of emergency because of this unrest and the government commissioner of Upper Bavaria prohibited 14 planned rallies of the NSDAP (Hitler's party)

Two days after the proclamation of the end of the passive resistance in the region of the Ruhr Germany took up the supplies of reparation to France and Belgium again.

The separatist riots in Rhineland went on for the last few days. By clashes between separatists ("Independent Rhineland") and police 5 policemen and 12 civilians were killed in Düsseldorf. Whilst that happened in Düsseldorf the members and followers of the NSDAP marched up in Bayreuth (town in Bavaria); they had their great meeting, the "Germany Day".

3 October, the government under the leadership of Chancellor Stresemann resigned. But the German president, Friedrich Ebert, immediately put Stresemann in charge of the formation of a new government. So Gustav Stresemann began with negotiations of coalition and could present his new (second) government on 6 October. But also this government was a government of a short

time. November 23rd was then the last day of Stresemann's second government period.

10 October, "Reichskanzler" (Chancellor of the German Empire) Gustav Stresemann demanded an "Ermächtigungsgesetz" (law of authorization) for the redevelopment of trade and industry. This day, his party (DVP) let its own minister for economic affairs drop, because he had voted against the prolongation of the working hours from 7 to 8 hours each day for miners and from 8 to 9 hours for labourers. Since also the minister of finance, Hilferding (SPD), was forced to resign from his post, everybody could foresee the end of the government time of Gustav Stresemann. This crises of the government also was to see against the background of the galloping inflation; now: 1 US-Dollar = 242,000,000 DM!!!

On October 10, also the KPD (Communist Party of Germany) joined the government of Saxony; here, Zeigner (SPD) was minister president. Now the communists took over the ministry for economy and finances. At the same moment the fourth supplementary budget for the year 1923 was approved by the German parliament (Reichstag) in Berlin. This supplementary budget was imperative, caused by the passive resistance in the Region of Ruhr. The budget had an amount of 578,000,000,000,000 DM. Only two days later the Germans had to pay for 1 US-Dollar 4,000,000,000 DM.

13 October, the Reichstag in Berlin passed a "law of authorization". Now the government of the German Empire could enact economic laws without consultation with the parliament. During the voting on the "law of authorization" the deputies of the DNVP and KPD left the plenary assembly room. Now the German

government decided on the basis of this law to found the "Rentenbank" (Bond Bank) and to introduce the "Rentenmark" (Bond Mark) as stable currency.

18 October, the extreme right-wing encroachments in Bavaria increased, whilst there was left-wing unrest in Saxony. As the result of the unrest in Saxony Bavaria broke off the diplomatic relations with Saxony, which it still had. Because General von Lossow, the "Wehrkreiskommandeur" (commanding officer of the defence district) in Munich, refused to prohibit the national-socialist newspaper „Völkischer Beobachter" one day later, the „Reichswehrminister" (Minister of Defence of the German Empire) said on 20 October: "Von Lossow is removed from office". This step was the beginning of a serious crisis between Bavaria and the German Empire.

19 October, the value of **1 US-Dollar: 12,000,000,000 DM!!!**

21 October, the separatist riots were expanding in Rhineland. In Aachen a new state was proclaimed, the "Republic Rhineland". But on 2 November this state was already liquidated again, the separatists were driven away.

Now the events accumulated. On October 22, the German government tried to reach the removal of General von Lossow by military and verbal measures in Bavaria and in Dresden the German government tried to stabilize the situation by the entry of imperial troops. The countries Württemberg, Baden and Hessen spoke with regard to the conflict between the German Empire and Bavaria for the unity of the German Empire without reservation.

24 October, the leaders of the Bavarian army, at the head the "Wehrkreiskommandeur" Otto Hermann von Lossow, intended to march towards Berlin; there they wanted to proclaim the "National Dictatorship", if this attempt fail, then they would intend to separate Bavaria from the German Empire. This day the German army also put down a three-day rebellion of the communists in Hamburg and Gustav Stresemann warned France and Belgium one day later not to support the separatists of the Rhineland.

26 October, the Bavarian troops were under the code "Herbstübung 1923" prepared for the action against internal riot.

28 October, the KPD called a general strike in Saxony as the result of the refusal of its demand for resignation of the Saxon government under Minister President Zeigner. One day later the German army went into action in Dresden and Leipzig (the largest cities of Saxony). The "Volksfrontregierung" (People's-Front-Government) of Saxony, a government of members of SPD and KPD, were deposed. Now "Reichskommissar" (Commissioner of the German Empire) Heinze, a member of the DVP (German People's Party), took over the executive power in Saxony.

At the end of October the Germans had to pay for **1 US-Dollar: 130,000,000,000 DM!!!**

2 November, the SPD withdrew their ministers from the German government in Berlin because of the intervention in Saxony. But the remainder of Gustav Stresemann's cabinet was tolerated by the SPD for the present.

3 November, in Warsaw the German government protested against the Polish "Entdeutschungspolitik" (politics against the German population) in the former German provinces, which belonged to Poland now.

5 November, by order of the German president, Friedrich Ebert, imperial troops marched into Thuringia and Saxony to get the communist agitation under control. This entry of the imperial troops caused the resignation of the Thuringian government on 7 November and one week later the dissolution of the parliament in Weimar. During this time the separatist riots spread out in the Palatinate, where the separatists proclaimed the "Republic of the Palatinate" on 12 November.

8 November, the value of **1 US-Dollar: 630,000,000,000 DM!!!**

This day **Adolf Hitler** also called for the "national revolution" and proclaimed the "provisional national government". One day later he marched with his followers demonstratively to the "Feldherrenhalle" (Hall of the Field Marshals) in Munich. There his demonstration came to an end by a massacre; more than 16 persons were killed. **Hitler** had hoped that General von Lossow would follow the putsch, but he didn't it. Now the NSDAP was immediately prohibited in Bavaria. – Also on 9 November General von Seeckt, the head of the military leadership, received the supreme commando over the "Reichswehr" (Army of the German Empire) and by it the executive power in the German Empire (till February 1924). Now it was for the first time possible to hear political news on the radio. So the Germans listened to the radio and could be witnesses of **Hitler's** putsch in Munich directly. – **Adolf Hitler** was arrested two days later!

After the proclamation of the "Republic of the Palatinate" by separatists in Speyer Severing, the Prussian minister of the interior, designed the separatism as an "artificial breeding of the French" on 12 November. One day later the German government in Berlin officially denied the foundation of an autonomous "Republic Rhineland" and the French government agreed to let check the German ability to pay by experts.

15 November, the new currency in Germany, the so-called "Rentenmark" (Bond Mark), was introduced. By it the German inflation came to an end. One day ago the Germans had to pay for **1 US-Dollar = 4,200,000,000,000 DM, now 4.20 Rentenmark (RM) only.**

23 November, the government under Chancellor Gustav Stresemann resigned and General von Seeckt prohibited all organizations of the KPD, NSDAP and the "Deutsch-Völkische Freiheitspartei" (German-National Liberty Party). The French government under Prime Minister Poincarè also campaigned for the German separatists of the Rhineland this day. France's wish was for a long time, an independent "Rhineland".

30 November, a new government was formed in Berlin. Chancellor became Wilhelm Marx (Zentrumspartei/Centre Party)). This new government was composed of a coalition of DVP, Zentrum, DDP and BVP. Also Gustav Stresemann belonged to this government, but now only as Foreign Minister; but the SPD was absent from this government.

4 December, the new German Chancellor, Wilhelm Marx, demanded in his policy statement a law of authorization for the removal of the economic and financial crisis in Germany. This demand became a signal for the governments of some other

German countries to demand a law of authorization to the removal of the own crisis too.

8 December, the "Reichstag" accepted the bill of the "law of authorization for the removal of the misery of the people and the empire" against the votes of DNVP and KPD. This law gave the opportunity to take measures on the economic, social and financial field without preceding parliamentary approval.

10 December, France ordered a slow relaxation of its measures in the region of the Ruhr and began with the withdrawal of its troops; convicts were also dismissed. These were convicts who were in custody because of sabotage and riot against the occupying powers. Now the expulsion of Germans was also stopped.

In Germany another crisis had in the meantime begun, the unemployment; on 15 December 3,500,000 labourers were without job and that was to be not the end.

30 December, a Belgian court-martial sentenced many Germans to life imprisonment in Aachen (the town of Charles the Great) because of sabotage.

Countries of the Republic of Weimar

Anhalt
Baden
Bavaria
Braunschweig/Brunswick
Bremen
Hamburg

Hessen
Lippe (Detmold)
Lübeck
Mecklenburg-Schwerin
Mecklenburg-Strelitz
Oldenburg
Prussia
Saxony
Schaumburg-Lippe
Thuringia
Waldeck (from 1929 a part of Prussia)
Württemberg

Albert Einstein, the famous physicist and Nobel Prize winner

Albert Einstein was born on 14 March 1879 in Ulm (Württemberg). His father, Hermann Einstein, was a Jewish businessman. In 1880 the family resettled. The new place of residence was Munich. There Albert went to the Luitpoldgymnasium (Luitpold High School). Then, in 1894, the parents went to Milan (Italy). Albert followed short time later. In 1896 Albert Einstein enrolled himself in the "Eidgenössische Technische Hochschule" (College of Technology of Switzerland) of Zurich. With a thesis he received his college degree in 1900 there. Now he also became Swiss citizen. 1902, after the death of his father, he became collaborator at the "Eidgenössische Patentamt" (Swiss Patent Office) in Bern (till 1909). 1903 he got married to Mileva Maric. Albert and Mileva had two sons, Hans-Albert (he was born 1904) and Eduard (born 1910).

In 1905 Albert Einstein received his doctorate. This year he also extended Max Planck's quantum theory to the light quantum theory, which was a contentious point for the present. Einstein supposed that also electromagnetic radiation, for example light, must consist of particles, the so-called light quanta or photons. This year he also evolved the "special relativity theory" (since 1915 general theory); by this theory he illustrated the gravitation; he made out the equivalence of mass and energy; which is expressed in the equation $E = mc^2$.

1908 followed the university lecturing qualification at the University of Bern. In 1909 Albert Einstein became professor at the University of Zurich and in 1911 professor at the University of Prague (today Czech Republic). But in 1912 he came back to Zurich, where he was professor at the "Eidgenössische Technische Hochschule (ETH).

In 1913 Albert Einstein went to Berlin, there he was member of the „Preußische Akademie der Wissenschaften" (Prussian Academy of Sciences) and director of the "Kaiser Wilhelm Institute for Physics"

In 1919 the British "expedition of eclipse of the sun" confirmed Einstein's theory of gravitation and relativity and his scientific adversaries unleashed a counter-campaign. This year Albert Einstein got a divorce from his wife Mileva and married his cousin Elsa Einstein, who died 1936.

In 1920 Einstein joined to the Zionist movement. Now he also tried to create a homogeneous field theory, which comprised the gravitation and the electrodynamics, to make a uniform mathematical description of the universe and to keep the thought of the causality, which was jeopardize by the modern quantum physics.

In 1921 Albert Einstein won the Nobel Prize, not for the theory of relativity, but for the interpretation of the photo effect of the year of 1915. Since 1920 Albert Einstein and his theories was exposed to violent anti-Semitic attacks in Germany. Now he also gave as pacifist and Zionist his view on political questions.

In 1933 Einstein was deprived of the right of honorary citizen by the NS-regime and he was a wanted man now; 50,000 Reichsmark (the new currency) as a reward for his arrest. The result was that Einstein emigrated to Princeton (USA).

Einstein moved off of his pacifist attitude and demanded the construction of an atom bomb with his letter to the American president Roosevelt in the year of 1939. He intended to forestall Germany. But later he did not take part in the realization of the atom bomb.

In 1941 Albert Einstein became American citizen. After the Second World War he warned against nuclear weapons, spoke up for a world government and took over the presidency of the "Emergency Committee of Atomic Scientists", which should prevent an atomic war. In the year of 1952 it was offered him the office of the President of Israel, but he rejected. -- Albert Einstein died on 18 April 1955 in Princeton.

The last years of
Weimar Republic

We write the year **1924**

After the ban of the NSDAP came the "Großdeutsche Volksgemeinschaft" (Great German National Community) under the
leadership of Alfred Rosenberg and the "Völkische Block" (Nationalist Bloc) under the leadership of Erich Ludendorff into being.

On January 4, the present minister of finance, Max Heldt (SPD),
was elected new Saxon Minister President. This election was
assessed as a mark for the end of the radical-political actions.
Max Heldt's government was supported by the parties SPD, DDP
and DVP.

On January 7, the American experts of finances and economy,
Charles Dawes and Owen Young, arrived in Paris. There they
took part in the first session of the committee of experts for the
settlement of reparation's affair one week later. Now it developed the general conditions to the German politics quite favour-
ably too, especially after the end of the "Ruhrkampf" (combat in
the region of the Ruhr). England looked for a talk, because a new
start of the German economic policy could mean that the reparation's affair, which was still unsolved, could finally get settled
bindingly now. In view of the enormous English war debts to the
United States met a talk the interests of both states. France saw
itself isolated and relented. A lasting French occupation of the
Ruhr had besides offended against the interests of balance of
England.

There was already a contractual agreement with the new Soviet
Union in Rapallo two years ago. The treaty of Rapallo that was
made in April 1922 stipulated that should be dispensed with
mutual compensation of the costs and damages of war. There

was also the wish to promote on both sides the trade and to enter into diplomatic relations. According to Lenin's motto took the Russians in their outsider's role advantage of the tensions in the capitalistic world to be qualified as a political partner to other nations again. But the distrust of the western world had considerably increased since Germany and the Soviet Union had also agreed upon the cooperation of the "Reichswehr" (German army) and the "Red Army" (Soviet army) Now the German Foreign Minister, Gustav Stresemann, could dispel doubts by a stricter western orientation, but above all to start a long-term orientation of the German foreign politics that the world was missing up to now. A plan that was worked out by the American banker Charles Dawes should reorganize the way of payment of the German reparations. The economic ruin of Germany, above all the peak of inflation (1923) with its decline of purchasing power and flight of capital, also underlined Germany's inability to pay the expected reparations to the victorious powers now. The committee of experts under the leadership of Reginald McKenna noted that only an economic recovery of Germany and the renunciation of acts of violence like the occupation of the Ruhr would make Germany's ability to pay the reparations possible again. Therefore, the plan of Daws was adopted. That happened on 16 August in London. This plan stipulated new conditions of payment and offered helps: Germany should pay 2,500,000,000 Deutsch Mark each year for reparations in the future, beginning in the year of 1929. The German "Reichsbahn" (railway) and the "Reichsbank" (National Bank of the German Empire) were put under international control and a great strain was put on them as securing. Also the revenue of customs and consumption's tax were pawned. The German industry had to find the interest payment for obligations in a sum to the amount of 5,000,000,000 Deutsch Mark. Germany got at the same time a foreign loan of 800,000,000 Deutsch Mark for the redevelopment of its trade and industry.

This settlement helped Germany to get new capital assets and made it trustworthy in financial affairs. Since the occupation of the Ruhr was also finally finished and a rapprochement between Germany and France was started, the "Dawes Plan" proved to be politically and economically fruitful. But the disadvantage was to show itself later, caused by the enormous foreign debts.

On April 1, Adolf Hitler, who had to answer for the attempt of putsch of the year of 1923 in Munich, was sentenced because of high treason to an "imprisonment in fortress" of 5 years. But he was not deported as foreigner (he was born as Austrian, but now stateless!) He even had the chance to get a premature amnesty.

In 1924 — The judgement against Hitler —

Erste Ausgabe — Preis 10 Pfennig

München-Augsburger Abendzeitung

Das Urteil
im Hitlerprozeß

München, den 1. April 1924, 10 Uhr 05 Min.

Unter großer Spannung einer zahlreichen Zuhörerschaft wurde heute vormittag im Saale der Infanterieschule durch Landgerichtsdirektor Neithardt das Urteil im Hitlerprozeß verkündet.

Freigesprochen wurde: General Ludendorff
unter Ueberbürdung der Kosten auf die Staatskasse.

Die übrigen Angeklagten wurden

zu Festungshaft verurteilt
und zwar wie folgt:

Adolf Hitler 5 Jahre Festung

Oberstleutnant Kriebel 5 Jahre

Dr. Weber 5 Jahre

Oberstlandesgerichtsrat Pöhner 5 Jahre

Oberamtmann Dr. Frick 1 Jahr 3 Monate

Hauptmann a. D. Röhm 1 Jahr 3 Monate

Oberleutnant Wagner 1 Jahr 3 Monate

Oberleutnant Brückner 1 Jahr 3 Monate

Oberleutnant Pernet 1 Jahr 3 Monate

Die Hastverschonung gegen Frick, Röhm und Brückner wird aufgehoben. Das Gericht erläßt weiter Beschluß: Den Verurteilten Brückner, Röhm, Pernet, Wagner und Frick wird für den Strafrest mit sofortiger Wirksamkeit Bewährungsfrist bis 1. April 1928 bewilligt.

Den Verurteilten Hitler, Pöhner, Kriebel und Weber wird nach Verbüßung eines weiteren Strafteiles von je 6 Monaten Festungshaft Bewährungsfrist für den Strafrest in Aussicht gestellt.

Die Verurteilung und Freisprechung erfolgte mit vier Stimmen.

Die Begründung des Urteils erscheint in einer zweiten Ausgabe gegen Mittag.

We write the year **1925**

"London kann der Anfang sein" (London can be the beginning), that was Stresemann's hope. He believed to can achieve other successes to Germany by the path that was taken according to the "Dawes Plan." Much to his initiative also came back that on 1 December the treaties of Locarno were signed in London. (On 16 October Germany agreed upon the peace terms with France, Great Britain, Italy, Belgium, Poland and Czechoslovakia in Locarno/Switzerland. This made possible that Germany could become a member of the League of Nations on 8 September 1926) – By Aristide Briand, French Foreign Minister 1925 – 1932, Stresemann could rely on a partner of understanding, who overcame French doubts of security by much patience. The friendly relations of both politicians made open new ways of understanding to the former hostile nations.

By the treaties of Locarno Germany acknowledged for the first time the result of the war; i.e., the frontier with France and Belgium, which was laid down in Versailles. Also Elsaß-Lothringen (Alsace and Lorraine) should remain a part of France. England and Italy took over the guarantee for this agreement. It was also made treaties of arbitration with Poland and Czechoslovakia, which **didn't designate a guarantee of Germany's east frontier.**

Although Germany had been treated as partner with equal rights for the first time since the end of the war, predominated reserve and disapproval in the empire, explained in many cases by missing understanding for Stresemann's goal of agreement with the former enemy.

A great event of this year was the election of Field Marshal General Paul von Hindenburg as new President of the German Empire. It was also a surprise, because he had a monarchist cast of mind. – President Friedrich Ebert died on 28 February in Berlin.

Paul von Beneckendorff und von Hindenburg was born on 20 Ocotber 1847 in Posen (today a city of Poland) and died on 2 August 1934 in Neudeck (his estate in East Prussia) He was first officer and retired from the sercive in 1911 as a General of the Infrantry. In autumn 1914, he was put back into service to take over the defence of East Prussia. He was victorious at Tannenberg and in the area of the Masurian Lakes. In late 1914 he became commander of the German forces in the East, in August

1916, Chief of the General Staff. After the collapse of the monarchy, he led the German troops are ordered to return home, after he organized the protection of the border in the east, and laid down his command in 1919. In 1925 he was elected President of Germany. He was a monarchist, but he accepted the Constitution of the Republic. In 1933 he made a grave mistake; despite concerns he was persuaded to bring Hitler to power. He saw no other option after not was found a majority for a government.

We write the year **1926**

The German Foreign Minister, Gustav Stresemann, complemented the treaty of Locarno by the "Treaty of Berlin" to avoid tensions with the Soviet Union, which was still internationally isolated. This German-Russian treaty of friendship assured the mutual neutrality in case of war. By this treaty Germany had created the basis for a relation of good terms with both important European neighbours too. With the approval of the treaties of Locarno the "Reichstag" had simultaneously spoken for Germany's joining the League of Nations. But the negotiations lasted till September to reach the position of the super powers with equal rights in this world organization: "Ein wahrer Beifallssturm im ganzen Saal, unterbrochen von Bravorufen" (a real thunderous applause throughout the hall, interrupted by bravo cheers), so outlined an eyewitness Stresemann's first appearance at a meeting of the League of Nations on 10 September. His speech the international press celebrated as convincing expression of German intention of peace and understanding. But in the German Empire he was missing the readiness to a great extent, to deal objectively with his politics; but the distance to the aim of his hopes was also too great, because he thought to have the possibility to solve the affair of reparation by his politics in the near future. But that was not possible. He also hoped to can secure peace and by it to reach a "correction of the German east frontier" and the union with "German-Austria" at the same time.

The further foreign development seemed to confirm his critics. The understanding with France suffered a setback when Raymond Poincarè was elected French Prime Minister (1926 – 1929). Raymond Poincarè immediately delayed the departure of the French occupation troops from Rhineland, what led to a tension with Germany. So it did not move much in this matter despite Stresemann's efforts. That changed only in 1928.

We write the year 1927

On 19 January the French Foreign Minister, Aristide Briand, had to justify himself in front of the French chamber because of his talk with Gustav Stresemann in Thoiry; but he denied having made promises to a premature departure of the French troops from the Rhineland. On 5 March was called off the prohibition of speech for Adolf Hitler, who was at large again in the meantime. On 1 February that already happened in Saxony. Then, on March 6, Hitler gave a speech in Vilsbiburg (Bavaria); the subject was: "Zukunft oder Untergang" (future or downfall). And on 9 March he gave the same speech in Munich.

During this year also increased the activities of the NSDAP again. The "Führer" (leader) of the NSDAP, Adolf Hitler, tried to get the financial support by the German industry and in Munich were published anti-Semitic books, for example "Die jüdische Welt-

pest" (The Jewish world plague) and "Kann ein Jude Staatsbür-
ger sein?" (Can a Jew be a citizen?). On August 19, the NSDAP
gave its third "Reichsparteitag" (Nazi Party = national assembly
of the NSDAP) in Nürnberg/Nuremberg. Nürnberg (after Munich
and Weimar) was to be now the city of the "Reichsparteitag" of
the NSDAP for ever.

On 18 September President von Hindenburg inaugurated a war
monument in Tannenberg (East Prussia). During his speech he
repudiated Germany's guilt of the outbreak of the First World
War. As a result the French government and press responded
with indignation. Therefore Gustav Stresemann expressed his
regret in this matter during an interview by the French newspaper "Le Matin" and showed his understanding for the angry reaction of the French press to Hindenburg's speech of Tannenberg. But Gustav Stresemann also said that the cultivation of
war reminiscences is more intensive in France than in Germany.

We write the year 1928

The year had already left its feature on a fading business cycle.
The first German republic went to the third phase with the first
indication of a worldwide economic crisis now; it was a phase of
a creeping internal crisis, which led to the decline of the democratic system of Weimar. The last years were influenced by an
"internal change of conditions", deep-reaching economic shocks
and a depressing material predicament of wide sections of the
population. Trade unions and employees faced each other irrec-
oncilably more and more in view of the catastrophic effect of
the crisis. The trade power position dwindled simultaneously
with enlarging number of unemployed persons. There was for

the moment the possibility to go optimistically into the crisis, because Germany was governed by a parliamentary majority since this year. After many years of abstinence the social democracy had entered into a great coalition with the middle-class parties. But in view of the problems, which were to master, hardly anyone had bet on the durability of the new government under chancellor Müller (SPD).

On 23 September there were extreme right-wing demonstrations under the motto "Das Ende der Locarno-Politik – was nun?" (The end of the politics of Locarno – what next?) That happened although the German government could achieve successes with regard to the departure of the French troops from the Rhineland and a premature annulment of the liability to reparation.

In 1928, the red peril in Germany

We write the year **1929**

On 3 January Heinrich Himmler became leader of the SS
(Reichsführer der SS). The **SS** (**S**chutz**S**taffel/protecting squad-

ron) was founded for protection of the leader of the NSDAP in the year of 1925. Heinrich Himmler expanded this protecting squadron to an internal security organization of the NSDAP (National Socialist German Labourers' Party/party of the Nazis) now. Later he arranged that the SS also held important positions in the police, so that this squadron became the most important instrument to the fight against the political opponents and to the securing of the Nazi regime. – Heinrich Himmler was born on 7 October 1900 in Munich. Since 1923 he was member of the NSDAP and took part in the putsch of Adolf Hitler.

On 9 February was opened in Paris the international conference of experts for the clarification of the German payments of reparation. Participants of this conference were Belgium, France, Great Britain, Italy, Japan and Germany. Owen D. Young, who was director of the New York Federal Reserve Bank (USA), was in the chair at the meetings of the members of this conference, which was closed with the announcement of the so-called "Young Plan" on 7 June. This plan led to a revision of the Dawes Plan and brought a better fixation of the conditions of reparation and more own responsibility to Germany, but also higher economic burdens. The treaty, which was made in Paris, came into force on 1 September and designated amongst other things that **Germany had to pay** to the Allies **2,050,000,000 Deutsch Mark each year** and that **for 37 years**, after this time **then 920,000,000 Deutsch Mark** each year **till 1988**. The control of the "Reichsbank" (German National Bank) and "Reichsbahn" (German National Railway) was abolished and Germany took over own responsibility for all money transactions, but it was threatened with new sanctions according to the "Treaty of Versailles" in case of contravention. The occupation of the "Rhineland" was finally closed now.

September 9, Stresemann's speech in front of the members of the League of Nations

On October 3, Gustav Stresemann, the German Foreign Minister, surprisingly died after a stroke in Berlin. He was just 51 years old. Germany had lost one of its most important persons of those days, therefore the members of the German parliament immediately assembled to funeral obsequies.

On 24 October was the financial world shocked by the stock exchange of New York (USA); all German hopes were shattered. Germany was, like the most important industrial countries, dependent on American money in a fateful way; that was also the reason for a deep depression in all these countries. Now the unemployment in Germany considerably rose too. On 16 December were more than 3,000,000 Germans without job and it was to be worse.

We write the year **1930**

This year, the government failed under chancellor Müller; the reason was an absurd affair. The SPD suggested a fee's rise of the unemployment benefit to cushion the increasing deficit of the unemployment insurance company (Arbeitslosenversicherung). It should be only 1 percent; 0.5% had to pay the employer and 0.5% had to pay the employee.

(**Arbeitslosenversicherung**: this company was founded on 16 July 1927. Unemployed persons, who had gone about a job with "insurance duty" before, were entitled to get money in case of unemployment from the unemployment insurance company. – Everybody, who was employed, had to insure himself against unemployment). In spite of a one-year negotiation and a signalling willingness to compromise, Müller's government could not be saved. Within a coalition, which was paralyzed by a tormenting incapability to act, the SPD feared for its connection to the trade unions and the DNVP showed no inclination to prolong the throes of death of a coalition, into which the party had only gone with aversion.

In view of the national predicament the parties showed an alarming incapability to a responsible cooperation now. It increased the voices, which saw in the incapability of the parties a failure of the democracy. On March 27, the government under chancellor Müller resigned. That meant the beginning of a deplorable end of the first German democracy; now Germany was driven into the hands of the Nationalists in rapid succession.

The splendour of the former "state of authorities" hadn't yet faded. When also the fascination of the "strong man" became effective again by the hope of the powerful state, the national-ethnic propaganda of Germany tore the thin veil of democratic mind of a great part of the people, who were humiliated and made feel economically insecure for years. Labourers, farmers and the people of the middle class radicalized themselves to an alarming extent. The agitators of the Rights incited unscrupulously the masses, which had lost their bearings. "Das System muss weg" (this system must be off) that was the formula for the frontal attack at the Republic of Weimar.

It developed more and more violent arguments from battles of words and parliamentary debates. Now there were facing each other half-military, political combat units with the conservative "Stahlhelm" (Steel Helmet), the communistic "Rotfrontkämpfer-bund" (Red Front Fighter's Legion), the republican "Reichs-banner" (Standard/Banner of the Empire) and the brutal beating troops of the National Socialist "**S**turm **A**bteilungen" (**SA** = Storming Department), which were prohibited for a time. Above all the National Socialists heated up the crisis by having political talks about controversial opinions in the streets. Democrats, Jews and Bolshevists became interchangeable goals of a merciless inflammatory propaganda.

Whilst now was to form a government without SPD by the "Reichstag", in the background prepared national-conservative forces around "Reichswehrgeneral" (General of the Army of the

German Empire) von Schleicher an alternative solution. Heinrich Brüning (Zentrum Party) became chancellor of a minority government, which lived as "half-parliamentary presidential cabinet" on the confidence of the president! The SPD helplessly tolerated this course that eliminated the parliament, because Brüning essentially governed by the article 48 of the constitution in the form of "Notverordnungen" (emergency measures/decrees). He could draw near at hand two goals, which many Germans had longed for quite some time: the end of the payment of reparation and the military equality of Germany.

This year brought still another negative event. The US-credits for Germany were annulled at the end of the year that led to a collapse of the German banks a half year later. The general crises mood, which was aggravated still by the year's spectacular election successes of the NSDAP (a dubious party to the estimation of many people), caused the American financial backers to overreact nervously. Now it threatened to come to an economic collapse, which began already to be in the offing by the decline of the production and the rapidly rising unemployment. The catchword "mass unemployment" didn't illustrate the misery that spread before dole money offices and in some million of households. One year later an unemployed person got less than the subsistence level. The Republic of Weimar wasn't a modern welfare state in spite of all the social improvements.

We write the year **1931**

In the beginning of this year Germany had 65,000,000 inhabitants and 4,400,000 unemployed persons. That was the reason to lower the wages of the miners of the Ruhr(-Pot), they received 6% less pay to cut the costs. This measure should lead to new jobs. Short time later wages of the German and Prussian state employees were also lowered; they received 5% less.

On January 25, a meeting of the German and French Foreign Minister took place in Paris. There the new German Foreign Minister, Curtius, tried to reach a revision of the Young Plan, but Briand, the French Foreign Minister, rejected a revision. So Germany continued to slide into the catastrophe. On 31 January Germany had already 4,900,000 persons without job.

On 10 May was held an election in "Hultschiner Ländchen" (this little country became a part of Czechoslovakia after the First World War, how you know). Now the German parties could obtain 24 out of 30 mandates there, whilst the Czechs obtained the remainder of 6 only.

On 17 May got the NSDAP for the first time the most votes during a regional election. Now this radical party obtained 19 mandates to the regional parliament of Oldenburg, whilst the SPD (the second largest party) only obtained 11 mandates there.

On 12 July were closed all banks and savings banks by an emergency decree of Brüning's government. The reason was Germany's heavy indebtedness. The effect of the payments of reparation played still a great part. On 13 July began a run on the banks and savings banks. The financial catastrophe took shapes for everybody now, therefore were also the stock exchanges of Germany closed. On 17 July were the banks and savings banks already opened again but only for payment of wages, taxes and unemployment benefits. Then, at the end of July, the interests of the banks for debts were considerably risen, because they had to pay themselves more than 4,000,000,000 **RM** (Reichs-Mark = German currency of those days) to foreign creditors.

That was a too clear signal of the financial crisis in Germany, but also in Europe and in the world.

On October 10, the German president, von Hindenburg, met for the first time the leader (Führer) of the NSDAP, Adolf Hitler. Both had their first political discussion together now. After this discussion Hitler went to the conference of the national opposition in Bad Harzburg. Here NSDAP, DNVP, Stahlhelm, Reichslandbund (National Rural League), industrialists, Alldeutscher Verband (Pan-German Association) and some representatives of the former reigning dynasties united into the so-called "Harzburger Front" now. The political aims of the Harzburger Front addressed themselves to the present-day government of the German Empire under chancellor Brüning.

Other two important events of this year were: the NSDAP became largest party in some German countries and the unemployment increased, Germany had already 5,400,000 unemployed persons at the end of this year.

We write the year **1932**

The German president, von Hindenburg, rebelled against the chancellor Heinrich Brüning for personal reasons after his re-election in this year. Now the old game repeated itself. General von Schleicher presented Franz von Papen as new chancellor (1932 – 1933) to the president. Also Franz von Papen was without majority, but he was judged as a flexible and tractable man. The SA, which was prohibited for quite some time, was immediately admitted as organization again by von Papen. It was a bow to the NSDAP; but the NSDAP didn't thank Franz von Papen for this.

Hunger and misery in Berlin – especially the children had to suffer. Of course, the Nazis used this for their propaganda.

In July Franz von Papen could achieve a success at the conference of Lausanne/Switzerland. This conference had been already prepared by Brüning. Now was agreed upon that Germany had to pay once more 3,000,000,000 Gold Mark as last payment for reparation. The German government under chancellor Brüning had first accepted a proposal of the American president Herbert Clark Hoover (1929 – 1932) to suspend the payment for reparation for one year. But Brüning's goal was, to make Germany's inability to pay, also in future, clear to the world. Therefore he pursued a deflating policy that he did also because of the deep-sticking fear of inflation. This policy was a policy of short money, by which Brüning wanted to let Germany financially slim down. But today also everybody knows that he put up with the total breakdown of the Republic of Weimar contrary to the representations, which showed him as last fighter for this republic. – The crisis must get increased so that an "authoritarian state of the stände" (classes: see other volumes about German History by Egon Harings) could take over the republic and the parties would disappear as power factor. The elections of September 1930 could have been a serious warning to this naïve concept. These elections became the great moment of the Nazi-agitators. Above all Josef Goebbels (he was born on 29 October 1897 in Rheydt/Rhineland. He studied "Germanistik" – German studies – and was tempted to be a free author. He became member of the NSDAP in 1925. In 1926 he became "Gauleiter" (Head of Gau/District) of Berlin, then in 1927 he founded the newspaper "Angriff/Attack" and he became deputy of the German Parliament/Reichstag in the year of 1928. Since 1930 he was head of the propaganda department of the NSDAP) and Adolf Hitler wore his "ideology" reinforced to the voters. The voters were frightened to death by street fights, which determined the atmosphere of the electoral battle; also the count of the votes showed an alarming increase of the votes for NSDAP and KPD, which threatened to crush the democratic parties more and more from right and left in the way of the movement of a pair of tongs.

In July was again held an election to the German parliament. Beating troops of the SA caused a stir by street terror till then, nearly 100 persons were killed and more than thousand were injured. The unrest was the reason now that Franz von Papen (he was born 1879 and died 1969) took occasion to bring down the social-democratic Prussian government by help of the

"Reichswehr" (German Army) on July 20. Then he was appointed "Reichskommissar für Preußen" (Commissioner of the German Empire for Prussia) with reference to article 48 of the constitution of the Republic of Weimar. But he acted without fortune and longed for a new "authoritarian state" (which was a naive idea), whilst the National Socialists were celebrated as winners of the election of July. What many democrats had feared that had happened in the meantime, the NSDAP became the largest party of the "Reichstag" (German parliament). Now the NSDAP formed together with KPD (Communistic Party of Germany) and DNVP (German-National People's Party) also an anti-democratic majority, which didn't make possible a parliamentary work. Since it was impossible to Franz von Papen to form a government, he found himself compelled to set a date for a new election. This new election should be held in November now. Election tiredness and empty cashboxes of the parties marked this time of the listless election campaign; the result of this election was the same, no party was capable of governing with a majority, although the NSDAP lost 34 mandates. That was the political end of Chancellor Franz von Papen, but also the end of the Republic of Weimar.

Some famous Germans of those days

Bertold Brecht, author

Bertold Brecht was born on 10 February 1898 in Augsburg. He was descended from a solid middle-class family. After the secondary school time he studied in Munich and got touch with the literary circle there. 1918 – 1922 he wrote the shocking piece "Baal": a scene succession which is about an instinctive boozer. Anti-middle class subjects are also dominating in the second drama "Trommeln in der Nacht" (Drums in the Night/1922) and in the poems of the "Hauspostille" (Manual of Piety /post illa verba)

In 1928 Brecht, now dramaturge in Berlin, he married the actress Helene Weigel. By the "Dreigroschenoper" (Three-Penny Opera/1928) he succeeded in gaining acceptance after expressionist attempts ("Im Dickicht der Städte" – Jungle of Cities/ 1924); now he made a realistic description of the reality (Erst kommt das Fressen, dann kommt die Moral – Gluttony comes first, then morality) and that wrapped up in stirring songs (Und der Haifisch … --- And the shark …, music by K. Weil) In 1929 followed "Aufstieg und Fall der Stadt Mahagonny (Rise and Fall of the City of Mahagonny)

Bertold Brecht turned to the Marxism now: in his literary piece "Die heilige Johanna der Schlachthöfe" (Saint Joan of the Stockyards) was the religion described as instrument of capitalism. In the following years he wrote a whole string of "didactic games", which first supported all social changes.

In 1933 began Brecht's exile crosswise through Europe. His first place to stay was Denmark; there he wrote "Svendborger Gedichte" (Poems of Svendborg)1941 he went to Colifornia (United States) There he found his place to stay for the some years. During his time in exile he wrote his great literary pieces like: "Mutter Courage und ihre Kinder" (Mother Courage and Her Children), "Der gute Mensch von Sezuan" (The Good Person of Szechwan) and "Der kaukasische Kreidekreis" (The Caucasian Chalk Circle)

In 1948 Brecht found a new home in East Berlin (Short time later the capital of DDR/German Democratic Republic = East Germany). There he worked for model performances of his stage games in the theatre "Theater am Schiffbauerdamm" together with Helene Weigel and the "Berliner Ensemble". His lyrics culminated in the miniatures of the "Buckower Elegien" (Elegies of Buckow/1954), for example "Der Radwechsel" (The Wheel Change). His relation to the **SED** (**S**ozialistische **E**inheitspartei **D**eutschlands/Socialist United Party of Germany = the ruling party of the German Democratic Republic) was more reserved. Bertold Brecht died on 14 August 1956 in Berlin. He was a great author, director, theorist and dedicated social critic.

Hermann Hesse, author

Hermann Hesse was born on 2 July 1877 in Calw (town in Swabia/Country Baden-Württemberg). He was the son of a missionary and was reverentially educated and after the attendance at a Latin school sent into the monastery Maulbronn in 1891. But soon he escaped from this monastery and went to Tübingen; there he served his apprenticeship with a bookseller. 1899 – 1903 he lived as bookseller in Basel (Switzerland) and made two travels to Italy. 1904 he published the trend novel "Peter Camenzind". This novel made him famous. It's the story on a young man, who goes back to the nature to find so his own individuality. Hermann Hesse also married in the year of 1904 and lived as free author on the Lake Constance now. After his travel to India in 1911 he moved to Bern/Switzerland with his family.

Now began a marital crisis, which is reflected in his novel "Rosshalde" (1914); his own position as restless wanderer marks the "Knulp" (1915). In 1914 Hermann Hesse vehemently protested against the madness of the war. 1919 he published "Demian", a story on Emil Sinclair, who discovers the wide world of his soul by renouncing his mother's tie: like "Camenzind" had also "Demian" a great effect on the youth of those days.

Hesse moved alone to Montagnola/Ticino (Switzerland) now; it was following a phase of new reflection and new contacts. 1922 was published "Siddharta", which was also an attempt to find the own individuality. 1923 he got a divorce from his wife and became citizen of Switzerland; 1924 he married again.

Hermann Hesse describes symbolically the empire of the ghost in Orient in his novel "Morgenlandfahrt" (The Journey to the East); the empire of the ghost was conjured up again in the novel "Glasperlenspiel" (The Glass Bead Game) then. Hesse was a sharp adversary of the nationalism. 1946 he got the Nobel Prize, 1955 the "Friedenspreis des deutschen Buchhandels" (Peace Prize of the German Book Trade). He died on 9 August 1962 in Montagnola.

Hermann Hesse

Carl Zuckmayer, author

Carl Zuckmayer was born on 27 December 1896 in Nackenheim (Rhine-Hessen, today a part of Rhineland-Palatinate). He died on 18 January 1977 in Visp/Switzerland.

Carl Zuckmayer was married to Alice Zuckmayer-Herdan, who was an authoress. 1939 – 1946 he lived in exile in USA. Since 1958 he was living in Switzerland. He wrote successfully literary works, which were ready for the stage and close to life. All these literary works dealt with the problems of those days: "Der fröhliche Weinberg" (The merry Vineyard – 1925); "Schinderhannes" (1927 – Schinderhannes was a German Robbin Hood during the Napoleonic period in Hunsrück/Dog-Back Mountains); "Katharina Knie" (1929); "Der Hauptmann von Köpenick" (The Captain from Koepenick – 1931); "Ulla Winblad oder Musik und Leben des Carl Michael Bellmann" (Ulla Winblad or Music and Life of Carl Michael Bellman – 1953); "Des Teufels General" (The Devil's General – 1946); "Barbara Blomberg" (1949); "Der Gesang im Feuerofen" (Singing in the Kiln – 1950); "Das kalte Licht" (The cold Light – 1955); "Die Uhr schlägt eins" (The Clock strikes one – 1961); "Das Leben des Horace A.W. Tabor" (The Life of Horace A.W. Tabor – 1964) His lyrics: "Der Baum" (The Tree – 1926) and "Gedichte" (Poems – 1960) His short stories: "Ein Bauer aus dem Taunus" (A Farmer from the Taunus/Mountains – 1927); "Herr über Leben und Tod" (Lord of Life and Death – 1938); "Der Seelenbräu" (Soul's Brew – 1945); "Die Fastnachtbeichte" (Carnival Confession – 1954) ... Carl Zuckmayer also wrote addresses, essays and memoirs.

Käthe Kollwitz, graphic artist and sculptor

Käthe Kollwitz was born on 8 July 1867 in Königsberg/East Prussia. She died on 22 April 1945 in Moritzburg by Dresden.

Käthe Kollwitz was trained to be graphic artist and sculptor in Berlin (1884 – 1886) and Munich (1888 – 1889). Then she worked till 1943 in Berlin. First she made naturalistic graphics with themes from the history of the proletariat (illustration to G. Hauptmann's drama "Die Weber", 1894 – 1898; etching's series about the farmer's war, 1903 – 1908), then followed socially critical poverty illustrations of the industrial districts and worker's area of the big cities, which are marked by generous simplification of form and renunciation of sentimental effects. Her wood engraving works are partly near to the expressionism; all the sculptures and wood engraving works were destroyed during the Second World war, with the exception of a few. – In 1986 was opened a Käthe-Kollwitz Museum in Berlin.

Ernst Barlach, sculptor, graphic artist and poet

Ernst Barlach was born on 2 January 1870 in Wedel/Holstein (North Germany): He died on 24 October 1938 in Rostock/Mecklenburg. He studied 1888 – 1896 in Hamburg, Dresden and Paris. In 1906 he made a trip to Russia, which was decisive for his artistic life. Since 1910 he was living in Güstrow/Mecklenburg then. After literary attempts and early graphic and ceramic works, which were influenced by the "Youth Style", he found his own expressionist creation, to see especially in his ceramic, wooden and metallic plastics (porcelain figures of Russian beggars, 1907; "Drei singende Frauen" (Three Singing Women" – 1911); "Panischer Schrecken" (Panic Fright – 1911); "Der Rächer" (The Avenger – 1914). Barlach's art was influenced by piety and strong sympathy in human misery, which led to an increasing internalization of the expression (Relief "Die Verlassenen/The Deserters" – 1913; "Verhüllte Bettlerin/Veiled Beggar" – 1919; "Die gemarterte Menschheit/The Tormented Mankind"- 1919/20 and more). Plastic main works of the years later are the memorials of Güstrow and Magdeburg 1927 – 1929; "Der Geistkämpfer/The Ghost Fighter" – Kiel 1928; "Die Gemeinschaft der Heiligen/The Community of the Saints" – Lübeck 1930 – 1932. Barlach made also portrait plastics, larger series of wood engravings ("Die Wandlungen Gottes/Transfiguration of God: Third Day" – 1920/21; "Walpurgisnacht" – 1923) and numerous special graphic arts, partly with religious subject matter and in narrow conjunction with the poetical work. During the period of the National Socialism were Barlach's sculptures and graphic works removed from all museums as "entartete Kunst" (degenerate art). Many sculptures of Barlach were destroyed and on himself was imposed a prohibition of exhibition (1937). – Barlach was as poet a main representative of the literary expressionism. His prosaic works: "Seespeck" and "Der gestohlene Mond" (The Stolen Moon, published 1948); his dramas: "Der tote Tag" (The Dead Day – 1912) – "Der arme Vetter" (The Poor Cousin – 1918) – "Die Sündflut" (The Flood – 1924) – "Der blaue Boll" (Squire Blue Boll – 1926) – "Die gute Zeit" (The Good Time – 1929) – Barlach wrote also an autobiography: "Ein selbsterzähltes Leben" (A Self-selected Life – 1928).

Ernst Barlach

The Dritte Reich
and
the beginning of the holocaust

We write the year **1933**

After the "Reichstagswahl" (Reichstag Election/poll for the German parliament) in November 1932 Papen's government didn't have a majority to be able to govern, as we know. Now it followed as last reserve Kurt von Schleicher (1882 – 1934), who had hitherto kept in the background. "Er soll in Gottes Namen sein Glück versuchen" (He should try his luck in God's name) said the German President, von Hindenburg, with a clear indication of resignation. But General von Schleicher had only some grace days as new chancellor, hardly time enough to outline his policy. He still speculated on the possible behaviour of the NSDAP (National Socialist German Labourer's Party/Nazi Party) when Franz von Papen, who was ambitious and had a high opinion of himself, had the first secret connection with Adolf Hitler. In the house of Schröder, a banker of Cologne, Hitler was introduced as political partner to the bosses of the German industry and trade on 4 January. Papen contacted von Hindenburg after that and intrigued against Schleicher. He suggested Hitler, the unloved "lance corporal" from Bohemia, as new chancellor to the German president, what was too much for von Hindenburg. He had always a dislike for Hitler, but von Papen kept on trying to appoint Hitler chancellor. Then, on January 30, the German President von Hindenburg appointed Adolf Hitler, who was surrounded with "loyal" men, chancellor of a cabinet of the "Nationale Erhebung" (National Rise). The chairman of the NSDAP (Adolf Hitler) hadn't seized the power by a revolutionary act, but the power had fallen to him. The democratic parties, which were reluctant to the hopeless fight against the adversaries of the republic, had given up and a senile president (von Hindenburg) had let abuse himself as game figure of reactionary experiments and intrigues. It would be too simple to refer to the weakness of the constitution, because a large part of the people, who had longing for a "healthy system", demanded a state of authorities. The conservative-national politicians like Papen played into Hitler's hands, because their political capability was hardly more far-reaching than the satisfaction of their own vanity. Therefore Papen's bigmouth words some days later had an effect like a bad joke: "Wir haben uns Herrn Hitler engagiert … In zwei Monaten haben wir ihn in die Ecke gedrückt, dass er quietscht" (We have engaged Mr. Hitler … Within two months we have pushed him into the corner that he squeaks). But in fact it didn't take two months, because Hitler passed the "Ermächtigungsgesetz" (Enabling Act) by the "Reichstag" on 24 March. That meant the own deprivation of its power for the parliament. Only the SPD voted against this law; the KPD (Communist Party) was expelled from the parliament in the meantime. But also the SPD was already decimated by persecution and harassment. Now the "SA" in their "Braunhemden" (Brown Shirts) celebrated loudly the late victory at the jam-packed grandstand of the parliament; on 5 March their party, the NSDAP, had not reached the absolute majority at the polls, therefore the shout for joy for this late victory, because the uncontrolled power was fallen without a fight into its hands by the "Enabling Act". The remainder of the democrats took leave with mourning, despair and helpless rage of the first German republic, whilst the Nazis and their sympathizers were in flush of victory.

How was the situation of the last days of the first German republic? When Hitler became chancellor the National Socialist Wilhelm Frick took over the ministry of the interior and Hermann Göring became minister without sphere of activity. Hermann Göring became also temporary minister of the interior of the country Prussia. Then, on April 11, Hermann Göring became

Minister President (Prime Minister) of Prussia. On March 13, Joseph Goebbels, another known Nazi, became already "Minister für Volksaufklärung und Propaganda" (Minister for Public Enlightenment and Propaganda). This ministry was a new government department. In spite of Nazi ministers the weight of the ruling coalition seemed not to have shifted outwardly. Only 4 Nazi ministers faced more ministers of other parties, who seemed to be stronger; so there were the German-national man Alfred Hugenberg as Minister for Economic and Agriculture Affairs, Franz von Papen as Vice-Chancellor and "Reichskommissar" (Reich Commissioner/Commissioner of the Empire) for Prussia, Foreign Minister was von Neurath, Johann Ludwig Count Schwerin von Krosigk was Minister of Finance, Franz Gürtner was Minister of Justice, "Freiherr" (German aristocratic title like baron) von Eltz-Rübenach was Minister of Post and Transport and some other ministers. They should frame the national-socialist partner together with the leader of the "Stahlhelm" (Steel Helmet; that was a union of front-line soldiers and founded in 1918 in Magdeburg. It was the strongest union of the armed forces of Germany and had more than 400,000 members in the year of 1930), Franz Seldte, who was Minister of Labour and Werner von Blomberg, who was "Reichswehrminister" (Minister of the Imperial Army = Minister of Defence) Papen's concept of taming looked promising. Therefor he also announced proudly and outlined the conservative conception with the following words: "Wir haben ihn (Hitler) uns engagiert." He was also self-confident that he will have pushed Hitler into the corner within two months. But he was not alone with this assessment, because not only the conservatives underestimated the dynamics of the partner by their illusion of the national rise (nationale Erhebung), but also the politic left side saw the "drummer" (= Hitler) in the hand of reactionary power circles and thought that Hitler's ruling time would be soon over. Also when the wild terror of the "SA" against the Lefts got more violent, the people consoled themselves by the analogy that the labourer's movement had also ridden out Bismarck's "Sozialistengesetze" (Anti-Socialist Laws) The powers of seduction of historical legends took effect once more, when Goebbels did everything on March 21, the "Tag von Potsdam" (Day of Potsdam), to give new food for the mind to the illusion of the national rise" and the "Versöhnung" (reconciliation) of old Germany with the young movement in front of the "Garrison Church" (Garnisonskirche) of Potsdam and the tomb of Friedrich the Great.

But that the 30 January, when Hitler was elected "Reichskanzler" (Chancellor of the German Empire), was more complex than that let suppose the slogan of the "nationale Konzentration" (national concentration) and that the National Socialism had not only a conservative, traditional characteristic, but was also a revolutionary, dynamic mass movement, that we could already see one day later, but in March it was evident at the latest then.

On February 1, Hitler had already achieved a decisive victory over his conservative partner, when he opposed the coalition agreements enforced elections and thus played the plebiscitary element of its motion off, this time still taking advantage of the state apparatus, against the traditional German-national partner Hugenberg. (Alfred Hugenberg was born on 19 June 1865 in Hannover. He died on 12 March 1951 in Kükenbruch by Rinteln on the river Weser. He became leader of the party DNVP in the year of 1928 and was always an adversary of the Republic of Weimar; therefore he was also looking for a connection with the NSDAP. Till 1945 he was deputy of his party in "Reichstag"/German Parliament). Hugenberg disapproved in principle of election and parliamentary methods, his goal was the strengthening of the authoritarian power of the president. But Papen saw his concept of framing put in jeopardy and Hugenberg yielded at his insistence: on 1 February the "Reichstag" was dissolved. In the time to the election on 5 March the National Socialism unfolded again its double strategy, which had already proved its worth during the fight for the power. Also the Italian dictator Mussolini had practised with success this strategy with his fascist party ten years ago. This strategy looked as follows: legality and violence, propaganda and terror.

The unrestrained use and expansion of the legal power instruments, simultaneous acts of terrorism, which were now protected by the state and revolutionary actions in the streets, were decisive for the gradual conquest of the power. Now the National Socialists held the ministry of the interior in the German Empire and in the largest German country, Prussia, according to the rules of a modern coup d'état, and by it the disposal of the police. Still more, Göring as head of the Prussian police let activate an auxiliary police troop of 50,000 men, amongst them 40,000 SA- and SS-men. The National Socialist party army got by it public powers. On February 17, Göring ordered by his notorious order to fire the officers of this army to put diligently use of the firearm.

All political adversaries were goal of the open terror, above all communists and socialists. Their persecution met with great approval by the conservative government partner and by great parts of the German population. The slogan "Kampf dem Marxismus" (fight against the Marxism), with this slogan Hitler also moved into the electoral battle, but many people did not think that with the state-protected suppression of left-wing parties, the NSDAP had decisive power over institutions and had also a lever for emergency laws, which were also to use against other parties and unions in another stage.

The people ignored temporarily a lot. Even if the measures of the following weeks were partially illegal, so the legality seemed apparently maintained, because no authority, which had the right to protest, brought a protest "in the fight against the Marxism". Basis for that was the right for emergency decrees of the German president according to the Article 48 of the constitution of the Republic of Weimar, simultaneously with the anti-Marxist opinion-making of the Rights. (According to the constitution was the German president the second legislator simultaneously with the people, who could contribute to the laws by plebiscite. So they were direct competitors of the parliament. The German president was additionally vested with the greatest authority; **Article 48**: Der Reichspräsident kann, wenn im Deutschen Reich die öffentliche Sicherheit und Ordnung erheblich gestört oder gefährdet wird, die zur Wiederherstellung der öffentlichen Sicherheit und Ordnung nötigen Maßnahmen treffen, erforderlichenfalls mit Hilfe der bewaffneten Macht einschreiten. Zu diesem Zweck darf er vorübergehend die in den Artikeln ... festgesetzten Grundrechte ganz oder zum Teil außer Kraft setzen/The President may, when public security and order is seriously disturbed or endangered in the German Empire, take measures for the restoration of public security and order, if necessary, intervene with armed forces. For this purpose, he may the Articles in which fundamental rights are determined, temporarily abrogate in whole or in part.) The Article 48 served already in the first days of February of this year to obstruct the activity of other parties, to restrict the freedom of the press and to bring the public servants to heel. The new German government had a lever against the social-democratic and communistic press by the decree "Zum Schutz des deutschen Volkes" (For the Protection of the German People) of the "Reichspräsident" (published on February 4) at its disposal. This lever was reflected in 65 prohibitions till 27 February and other 108 prohibitions till 15 March. It may be possible for a judge to object, but now it was decisive in whose hands were police and internal administration. The disposal of police and justice made the sanction, the lawful approval of revolutionary, violent actions possible. Now, by a "decree of emergency" was also dissolved the Prussian parliament (the parliament of the largest German country) on 6 February. All authority that the Prussian government still had was temporarily assigned to Göring. After this blow the way was free for Göring; the most important offices of the Prussian administration were filled with National Socialists or conservative men. Sharp prohibitions and bureaucratic quarrels obstructed the electoral battle of the left parties now in Prussia.

On 27 February burnt the "Reichstag" (here: the Building of Parliament) in Berlin. This fire still accelerated the actions of persecution, that at least in Prussia. Because not the question, who had set the fire to the "Reichstag" and how was it possible, is important for the history, but the manner how Hitler and Göring made use of this event to conquer the power: Now it presented itself the opportunity to prove the communistic attempt at rebellion and to get the formal basis of large-scaled persecution measures and for the state of emergency by the decree of emergency "Zum Schutz von Volk und Reich" (For the Protection of the People and the Empire) that was already prepared by the German President on February 28. In the night of the fire Göring had still ordered to arrest MPs and leading officials of the KPD; also a ban was pronounced on the press of this party. The same happened with the social-democratic press for the time of 14 days. On the basis of the "Decree of Fire" 7,784 persons were arrested till 15 March, 95% of them were communists.

The "Reichstagsbrandverordnung" (Reichstag Fire Decree) became the gate for arbitrary acts of the German police and National Socialist terror (the terror of the Nazis!). The improvised "regulation of the state emergency" with its vague wording became the real "document of constitution" of the "Third Reich/Empire". All civil basic rights, as freedom of the press and freedom of the person, were generally repealed. Now there was no possibility of appeal for the persons arrested, which they had before according to the past states of emergency. Another way to arbitrary application and extension of the "Reichstagsbrandverordnung" was given by the fact that the Minister of Interior did not issue executive regulation. Now there was also given the possibility, under the cover of legality, to step in the measures of security, and so also in the political proportions of the other countries of the German Empire. In this atmosphere of legalized insecurity of justice and the open terror was held the election for the new "Reichstag" (parliament) on 5 March. But it was only a "half-free" polling, because the both left parties, SPD and KPD, couldn't take part regularly in this election, but in spite of the massive intimidation of their voters the SPD could with 18.3% (November 1932: 20.4%) and the KPD with 12.3% (November 1932: 16.9%) well hold the own part in the cast votes. Also the party "Zentrum" (the party of the middle) could hold the own bastion. In spite of the extreme development of the propaganda, in spite of terror and in spite of a record turnout at the election of more than 88% the coalition of government achieved 51.9% only, the NSDAP (the Nazi Party) alone 43.9% out of this 51.9%. So the NSDAP was not elected by the majority of the voters in this plebiscite. But the coalition of NSDAP and DNVP (German National People's Party) could govern with their parliamentary majority. Hitler aimed in return for it at the bringing the German countries into line by means of the "Reichstagsbrandverordnung" and the new "Heimtückegesetz" (Treachery Act; this law was passed on 21 March); also he intended to eliminate completely the parliament and the other constitutional control bodies by means of the "Ermächtigungsgesetz" (Enabling Act), which was passed now.

The "Ermächtigungsgesetz", which required the approval of the two third of the members of the parliament, had given the possibility to the government to govern for 4 years without participation of the "Reichstag" (German parliament) and "Reichsrat" (Imperial Council = Upper House of the parliament, like the Upper House in Great Britain). But especially the "Enabling Act" had significantly strengthened the position of the Chancellor (Hitler), who now became independent of the "Notverordnungsgesetz" (Emergency Ordinance Act) of the German President, also independent of the consent of Cabinet.

Why could the parties approve of the own deprivation of their power with the exception of the SPD? The parties, which were not participating in the government, were already finished for a long time. The followers of the middle-class parties turned to the NSDAP because of blindness and fear, but also out of opportunism. Also the labour unions and a part of the SPD showed a bent for an opportunist adaptation, because they were worried about their own existence. The free labour unions made a statement of loyalty; the SPD was demoralized by terror and without orientation. These were all advantages for Hitler to enforce the "Enabling Act". His opinion was also that he would be able to prevent the worst by assistance and legalization of the state of emergency and so to save the own organization and existence. But was that the idea to a constitutional state? The Germans had to find soon that there can only be subjection or resistance in a totalitarian state and no collaboration.

Because the KPD could not exercise its mandate – the MPs of the KPD were all arrested or had fled in the meantime – the NSDAP had the absolute majority in the "Reichstag" (parliament) now. Hitler's government was only missing 40 votes to have the two-thirds majority, which was necessary for the passing of the "Ermächtigungsgesetz", therefore he depended on the attitude of the party "Zentrum". But before he had ruled out a possible parliamentary obstruction by a hasty Rules change after that also unexcused absence was considered present.

Also the party "Zentrum" followed the consideration of legality and opportunity and didn't want to put at risk the negotiations for the "Konkordatsabkommen" (Concordat Agreement) between the Vatican and the German Empire. So voted only against the "Ermächtigungsgesetz" (Enabling Act) the SPD under the party leader Otto Wels (he gave a courageous speech to the members of parliament.)

Now it was following the "Gleichschaltung" (bring into line) of the officials (all public servants, so government officials, officers of police and customs and so on) by the "Gesetz zur Wiederherstellung des Berufsbeamtentums" (Law for the Restoration of the Professional Civil Service; passed on April 7). That law gave the absolute power over the non-liked officials to the state now, but it also flattered their traditional awareness of social standing. That this law also the racist thought disseminated in the civil service and "non-Aryan" officials put under the ban on pursuing their career, was only a little blemish for many Germans. (**Aryan:** a derived word from the Indian word Aryavarta = Place of the Aryans. That was also the ancient name of India. The Sanskrit's root of the word "arya" means "valuable, sacred, noble." The Nazis had ethnologically abused this word. They spoke about the Aryan race, Aryan blood, Aryan eyes and hair colour, about a higher standing race as it would be only Germanic nations. It was their crime against the humanity and also one of the causes of the holocaust).

The "Gleichschaltung" (also the German countries were brought in line in the meantime) and the end of the parties, which dissolved in June and July, found a great consent in the German public, because the parliament was in the eyes of the Germans, who were traditionally and authoritarian educated, only a „Schwatzbude" (blabber's place) and the parties were in the opinion of many people unnecessary, egoistic and troublesome for the political decision process. The parties gave up one after another and capitulated to the omnipotence and terror of the NSDAP.

The fire of the "Building of Parliament" (**Reichstag**/gebäude) had already served to hit the SPD hard; so the publication's organs of the SPD were temporarily prohibited and the members of this party were already fair game, also many members were pursued and arrested after the passing of the "Ermächtigungsgesetz". The parties were prohibited or liquidated themselves and arrests on a large scale were started. Also the German-National ally, who had wanted to buy the "drummer" Hitler some months ago, wasn't spared the total pretension of the NSDAP and had to submit himself to the **SA** (**S**turm**A**bteilung/Storm Department = the military police organization of the Nazis) by a so-called "Freundschaftsabkommen" (Agreement of Friendship). The leader of the allied party of the NSDAP, Hugenberg, had to declare his resignation already on 26 June. Some months ago he had taken up his office as ambitious economic dictator.

The "Gleichschaltung" (Coordination/bring into line) of the parties and countries was completed by measures, which were outwardly praised as standardization, but inwardly raised only political structural problems. The law against new formation of parties, which was passed on July 14, made the sole legal party from the NSDAP and sealed the "one-party-state". But although Hitler had combined the power over party and state in his hands, there were conflicts and demarcation disputes by the coexistence of party and state. The German countries had the same problem because they had finally lost their independence by the "Gesetz zur Gleichschaltung der Länder mit dem Reich" of March 31 (Act for Coordination of the Countries with the Reich) Now there were the great variety of wild-proliferating departments instead of independent countries. Also there was not the promised centralization of the Empire. The post of the Minister President (Prime Minister) of each German country was filled by a "Gauleiter" (Leader of the Gau/District; Gau = new name of a German province) and the posts of the ministers by "SA-Gruppenführer" (Group leaders of the SA). Also in Prussia it was caught up on the "seizure of power" of the party (NSDAP) and in the regional executive positions were only employed National Socialists. At the head of the Prussian provinces were immediately employed "Gauleiter" or "SA-Gruppenführer". Despite frequent personal union of the party and state leadership conflicts between the administration and party now remained not out, not least because not all "Gauleiter" had received a government office. Even in non-Prussian countries was not progressed with the personal union of party and government office, the Empire unification because some power-conscious "Gauleiter" at the same time tried to strengthen their own position in the party by the independence of their administrative unit.

The second act for the "Gleichschaltung" of the countries with the Empire was already enacted on April 7. That happened for counteracting the threat of a particular development of power. According to this law were introduced "Reichsstatthalter" (Governors of the Empire), by it was continued to reduce the territorial rights of the German countries. The "Reichsstatthalter" were "Attendants of the Empire" towards the National Socialist Minister Presidents of the countries and also towards tendencies of a far-reaching party revolution. In case of Prussia the institution of the "Reichsstatthalter" meant the next weakening of Franz von Papen, whose present function as "Reichskommissar für Preußen" (Reich Commissioner for Prussia – or better expressed: Commissioner of the German Empire for Prussian affairs) expired by the introduction of the post of "Reichsstatthalter". Now Franz von Papen was pushed out by Göring, who only exercised the function of the "Reichsstatthalter" on behalf of the chancellor (Hitler).

They fell back on the well-tried double strategy of seduction and violence in case of the labour unions, of which power the National Socialists especially feared. In March for the regime it was once more made clear the strong loyalty of the labourers to their organizations. That happened by the election to the works councils. The Nazis therefore avoided the open confrontation and stopped continuing the many wild local actions of the "**Na**tional-**S**ozialistischen **B**etriebszellen-**O**rganisation" (**NSBO**/National Socialist Work Cell Organization) against the institution of the labour unions and their officials. The National Socialists (Nazis) prepared in return for it a central action of "Gleichschaltung" (Coordination). That happened under the leadership of Robert Ley, who was the leader of the organization of the NSDAP and later leader of the "Deutsche Arbeitsfront" (German Labour Front). The following name of the preparation's team to an action of violence threw light on the abuse of words, in which the National Socialists were masters: "Aktionskomitee zum Schutz der deutschen Arbeit" (Action Committee for the Protection of the German Labour)

Now the Nazis declared the 1 May "Feiertag der nationalen Arbeit" (Public Day of the National Labour). The labour unions, which had declared their loyalty to the regime and their limitation to the social sector because of fear of attacks by the SA, lulled themselves into a false sense of hope, that it would be possible now to realize the dream of a united labour union. Therefore they also took part in the gigantic mass meetings, which the Nazis organized all over the empire on May 1. These mass meetings gave Hitler the scope for "singing the Great Song of the German Labourer" and for representing him as "Son of the Nation". But one day later followed the death blow against the labour unions according to Robert Ley's plan. All buildings of the labour unions were occupied by SA and SS under the leadership of the "Party" (NSDAP) and NSBO and the leading unionists were taken into "protective custody". Now minor unionists had to continue the work of the labour unions under supervision of the NSBO (National Socialist Work Cell Organization). Not the NSBO, but the new founded "Deutsche ArbeitsFront" (**DAF**/German Labour Front) took finally over the members of the labour unions and the union's property. By the liquidation of the labour unions was also eliminated the free collective bargaining.

Now the organizing of the farmers followed too. They were united in a monopoly organization, the "Reichsnährstand" (Organization of Nutritional Professions of the German Empire). But that didn't happen under compulsion, because the farmer organizations were already infiltrated before Hitler's seizure of power. Now the farmers went over to the National Socialism with flying colours.

To bring the industrial organizations into line was not more deep-seizing as the "Gleichschaltung" of the labourers and farmers. They could maintain their own administrative authority thanks to their social and economic power and by using clever tactics in spite of attempts of social-radical elements of the NSDAP. The maintenance of the independence of the industrial organizations also happened with the help of the state, because the German government needed the big industry for its ambitious plans of armament especially.

Because of tactical considerations, Hitler had to discipline his SA, which had been in charge of the political street fighting as civil war's troop and had prepared the way to his power. A disciplinary proceeding had to follow, because the SA was against the conservative-monarchist-minded officer corps and aimed at as fusion of SA and German army. But the German army was just now a bulwark of conservative power in the alliance with Hitler. Therefore Hitler had unconditionally to guarantee meanwhile the weapon monopoly of the "Reichswehr" (German army), because the intention of forming a people's militia did not fit his programme of armament and his preparation for the war. So Hitler decided in favour of "Reichswehr" and against the SA. With this decision he could count on the approval of the leaders of the NSDAP, Göring, Goebbels and Heß and above all on the leaders of the SS, Himmler and Heydrich (**Rudolf Heß**: he was born on 26 April 1894 in Alexandria/Egypt and died by suicide on 17 August 1987 in the prison of Berlin-Spandau as last prisoner of the Allies. He was member of the NSDAP since April 1920 and since 1933 Hitler's deputy. – **Reinhard Heydrich**: he was born on 7 March 1904 in Halle, today a city in the German country Saxony-Anhalt. He died on 4 June 1942 in Prague by a bomb attempt on his life. He had played a decisive role in the extermination of Jews -- Holocaust)

We write the year **1934**

The political front lines were clear. The decision was accelerated by the speedy death of the German president that was to be expected soon. In case of the death of von Hindenburg Hitler aimed at the combination of the office of chancellor and the office of president. But the swearing-in of Hitler was not possible without approval of the "Reichswehrführung" (leadership of the German army). In the moment, when it was rumoured that the SA would have the intention of revolting and the "Reichswehr" was on raised alert, was cleverly put into action the intended step against the SA. Röhm, the head of the SA – Ernst Röhm was born on 28 November 1887 in Munich. He was professional officer, but 1923 he had to leave the army because of the participation in Hitler's putsch. 1925 he parted for a short time with Hitler because of differences of opinion. 1928 – 1930 he was military instructor in Bolivia. In 1931, in the meantime he had already made it up with Hitler, he became head of the SA – was with other leaders of the SA in Bad Wiessee on holiday. There Hitler took steps against him on 30 June. That was the prelude to a three-day murder action, which was not only directed against the leaders of the SA but also against other men, who had politically made themselves unpopular with Hitler and he had still to settle up with them therefore. Neither Gregor Strasser, an internal opponent, who had already retired from the politics nor General von Schleicher nor the former state commissioner von Kahr, who was Hitler's rival and adversary during the putsch of the year of 1923, nor the closest collaborators von Papen, von Bose and E. Jung had any to do with the plans and the talk of the SA. But in spite of that they were victims of the murders, which were planned by the leadership of the state and carried out with help and promotion of the "Reichswehr" (German army).

Hitler's arguments to the execution of the leaders of the SA, among them also Ernst Röhm (Röhm was shot on July 1, together with the other leaders of the SA), that he had to take action against the diffuse homosexuality within the SA, were flimsy and tasteless.

The political business and also the National Socialist seizure of power were complete when the German President, von Hindenburg, died on 2 August and Hitler took over the presidential office too. This day the "Reichswehr" was even sworn in at Hitler, who was now chancellor and Führer (= Leader – his new title; Führer was an ancient Germanic title; see Germanic History Volume 1: Teutobod, the famous Führer/Leader of the Teutonic tribe before Christ) instead of President of the German Empire. This swearing-in of the "Reichswehr" was to cause the officers of the resistance a heavy twinge of conscience later.

The page before. – Stallion of the SS to the "Groß Appell" (Great Appeal) on the Reich Party Rally Grounds in Nuremberg.

Hitler's dictatorship was now consolidated. He imagined the relation between party (NSDAP) and state as follows: "Nicht der Staat befiehlt uns, sondern wir befehlen dem Staat: Nicht der Staat hat uns geschaffen, sondern wir schaffen uns unseren Staat" (The state doesn't give us the orders, but we give the orders to the state. The state didn't have made us, but we make us our state). That was Hitler's declaration in September, by which he specified the line of the politics of the rule of his party.

We write the year 1935

On January 1, Hitler demanded in his New Year's message to the "German Nation" the "return of the Saarland", which became a separate state under influence of France after the First World War.

Also on 1 January became effective a lowering of the wage and income tax, which above all promoted families with children.

On January 3, new rules of university lecturing qualification were issued by the Nazis. According to these new rules also the certificate of Aryan ancestry belonged to the acquisition of the university lecturing qualification.

On January 13, 812,000 inhabitants of the Saarland voted under the supervision of 300 commissioners of the "League of Nations" and contingents from Great Britain, the Netherlands, Sweden and Italy on their political and economical belonging to in future.

90.8% voted for the return to Germany; 8.8% voted for the independence and only 0.4% for the union with France. The result of the voting was officially announced by the president of the voting commission and the secretary general of the "League of Nations" on January 15. After that Hitler announced with joy "die Rückkehr unserer Volksgenossen in das Deutsch Reich" (the return of our ethnic comrades into the German Empire). Two days later the "League of Nations" unanimously decided the reunion of the Saarland with the German Empire and the 1 March was fixed up as date to the return. That was also a reason for Hitler to have a talk with the Englishman Ward Price about the matter of return of Germany into the "League of Nations". Hitler said, that there should be no conditions to a return into this "People's Union", but of course the recognition of equal rights for Germany.

Saarland; "We are Germans"

On January 22, the "Amt für Volksgesundheit" (Office for People's Health) of the party NSDAP pronounced the "Gesundheitsstammbuch" (Health Studbook) obligatory on each family. This register should contain a "table of clan", which has to go back to the 1 January of the year of 1800. The German aristocrats had to present a certificate, the so-called "Arier-Nachweis" (Aryan Certificate), which showed the course of the life of the family since 1750.

On January 27, Hermann Göring started conversations about a German-Polish military alliance against the Soviet Union in Warsaw. But the negotiations, Göring had offered the Ukraine as loot of war during the talks, were broken off without result.

On 1 March at 9:30 o'clock followed the official return of the Saarland into the German Empire. The ceremony took place in Saarbrücken, the capital of Saarland. The coal mines of Saarland were bought for 900,000,000 Francs (French currency) from France, all connecting railways towards Lorraine and all mobile and real estates were taken over by Germany without payment.

On 16 March Hitler announced on the radio: "... durch diese Mitteilung an das deutsche Volk verkünde ich die Wiedereinführung der allgemeinen Wehrpflicht" (by this message to the German Nation I proclaim the reintroduction of conscription -- compulsory enlistment for state/military service) It was planned the erection of an army of 580,000 soldiers (36 divisions) till 1939. Goebbels contradicted international reproaches. Germany would not have realized the arms limitation and arms reduction according to the "Treaty of Versailles". In a press release he specified meticulously: Germany has destroyed or handed over 59,897 guns, 130,558 machine-guns, 15,714 combat aircrafts, 26 big combat ships and 315 submarines. Also many other military things were destroyed or handed over by Germany.

On April 20, it was a Saturday, Hitler celebrated his forty-sixth birthday; for this reason was hoisted for the first time the "Standarte des Führers und Reichskanzlers" (Standard of the Führer/Leader and Chancellor of the German Empire) at the "Reichskanzlei" (Reich Chancellery/building in which was the official office of the chancellor -- Hitler's office)

On 10 September was started the "Seventh Reichsparteitag" (Imperial Day of the Party) of the NSDAP in Nuremberg under the motto: "Parteitag der Freiheit" (Party Day of Freedom). For this reason was installed for the first time 10 radio stations. Four days later Hitler gave a speech at this "Party Day of Freedom". He spoke in front of 54,000 Hitlerjungens (boys of the Hitler Youth, a new organization of the NSDAP) and ordered them to be "flink wie Windhunde, zäh wie Leder und hart wie Kruppstahl" (swift as greyhounds, tough as leather and hard as Krupp steel) – Then, on September 15, the "Reichstag" of Nuremberg passed the following laws: "Flaggengesetz" (Law on the National Flag), "Reichsbürgergesetz" (Law on the German Nationality/The Reich Citizenship Law) and the "Gesetz zum Schutze des deutschen Blutes und der deutschen Ehre" (Law for the Protection of German Blood and German Honour). Germany had two flags now: the "Reichsflagge" (Flag of the Empire) with the colours "black-white-red" and the "Nationalflagge" (National Flag) with the black swastika (swastika is an ancient symbol; a symbol of the sun but also two crossing flashes of lightning: Thor's hammer – Thor was a Germanic God. – This symbol was known since more than 2,000 years in Asia and Europe). – According to the new "Reichsbürgergesetz" German citizen could only be who was from "German or related blood". By the law "Gesetz zum Schutze des deutschen Blutes und der deutschen Ehre", the so-called „Rassegesetz" (Race Law), it was prohibited the marriage of Germans or people with German-related blood to people of the Jewish race. That deprived the Jews of their civil rights (it was the first step to the holocaust)

On September 26, 51 Germans had a meeting with Heinrich Mann in the chair in Paris, in the hotel "Lutetia". It was a meeting of opponents of the National Socialism. The discussions of this so-called "Lutetia-Circle" served to prepare a German people's front against the Nazis. Four days later was held election to the regional parliament of Memel (territory of Nemunas, in those days a part of Lithuania). The result of this election was that the German population received 81% of the parliamentary mandates.

On 21 October took place in Teplitz-Schönau (a little town in Bohemia/Czechoslovakia) a mass rally of the ethnic Germans, the Sudeten. At this mass rally the leader of the "Sudeten Party", Konrad Henlein, demanded the union of Sudetenland with the National Socialist German Empire.

On 7 November began the persecution of the Jews. The leader of the "race-political office" of the NSDAP announced in Cologne: "The Jews must leave Europe, not because they had made outrages, but because they are Jews". One week later the "Minister of Propaganda", Goebbels, announced at the second annual meeting of the "Reichskulturkammer" (Chamber for Culture of the German Empire) in Berlin: "Die Kammer ist judenfrei, im deutschen Kulturleben ist kein Jude mehr tätig" (The chamber is without Jews, in German cultural life no longer a Jew is active)

On 9 December was made obligatory a "Decree for the Empire" of the Nazis. German officials and their marriage partners had to show an "Aryan Certificate". If an official or his marriage partner was non-Aryan, he had to leave his post immediately. Then, four days later, the "Reichserziehungsministerium" (Reich Ministry of Education) in Berlin forbade non-Aryans to study theology. Now such measures increased from day to day.

We write the year **1936**

January 1, Hitler gave his speech to the New Year. In his message to the "German Nation" he designated the fight against the Bolshevism for the most important goal of German politics.

On 7 January was opened a new manufacturing plant of the company Opel (today a subsidiary company of the Freench Group PSA/Peugeot Société Anonyme – before Opel belonged to the American Group GM) on the Havel (river). Up to now autos/motorcars had made the following German companies: Hanomag, Mercedes (Daimler) and DKW (Deutscher Kraft/Wagen; successor of this car manufacturer is Audi). The "VolksWagen" (VW = People's Car), which Hitler let make for the German people (therefore People's Car), had not yet left the planning phase. The designer of VW was Ferdinand Porsche. (Porsche was born on 3 September 1875 in Maffersdorf, a little town in Bohemia/today Czech Rep. He died on 30 January 1951 in Stuttgart. He was designer of many racing cars for Daimler in Stuttgart. Then, in 1931, he founded an own design office in Stuttgart; since 1950 he made own sports and racing cars there)

On 4 February was the leader of the "Swiss group" of the NSDAP, Wilhelm Gustloff, murdered by the Yugoslav citizen David Frankfurter in Davos/Switzerland. David Frankfurter was a Jew. Gustloff became a martyr to the Nazis, therefore a known ship bore his name later (The sinking of the "Wilhelm Gustloff!!!" – Later more about this tragedy) … The mortal remains of Wilhelm Gustloff were transported from Switzerland to Germany. Then, in Schwerin (today capital of Mecklenburg), his dead body was cremated during a national mourning.

On 6 February was the Winter Olympic Games inaugurated in Garmisch-Partenkirchen/Bavaria. 28 nations took place. Germany had with 148 sportsmen the biggest team. The games were broadcasted daily and transmitted into 18 countries. – One day later a Protestant pastor was sentenced to six months in prison only because he had forbidden his candidates for confirmation to greet with "Heil Hitler" during the lessons. "Heil Hitler" (Wellbeing Hitler") was the new obligatory greeting of the Germans. During the greeting the Germans had to stretch the right hand to the air.

On 19 February got the German diplomacy into hectic activity. Göring travelled to Poland, another German diplomat to Danzig. Hitler discussed with the German ambassador for Italy, von Hassell, the probable attitude of Mussolini, the Italian dictator, in case of the military occupation of the Rhineland. This occupation of the Rhineland, which was a demilitarized zone, had meant a breach of the "Treaty of Locarno". Hitler told the French newspaper "Paris Midi" two days later, saying that he would correct the opinion on his book "Mein Kampf" (My Fight – Everyone in Germany had to own this book in those days, the Bible of the Nazis) in so far as he intended to do peace politics to France. But they would see the Bolshevistic (red) peril to the world. – In February the NSDAP also founded the first "Ordensburgen" in Vogelsang (Eifel), Crössinsee (Pomerania) and Sonthofen (Allgäu/Bavaria). In these "Ordensburgen" (Order Castles) a pure "Germanic human race" should be bred, tall fair-haired men (the people of the great Germanic Empire/Great Germania of the future). – In those days many Germans were denaturalized. They could not plead Nazis' cause; therefore they had to leave Germany and to go into exile.

On March 7, the German army marched into the Rhineland; that happened under breach of the "Treaty of Versailles" and the "Treaty of Locarno" as already said. Hitler justified this step in front of the members of the "Reichstag" (German parliament), who were convoked in a hurry, with the right of all Germans to live within the own and safe frontiers, with the increased number of fortifications at the east frontier of France and with the French-Russian security treaty. At the same time he announced seven proposals for the "European securing of peace" and the dissolution of the "Reichtstag" for the 28 March. But previously it should be held a new election to the German parliament (Reichstag). Hitler had also achieved a great internal success in the shadow of the conflict of Abyssinia (today Ethiopia; Abyssinia was occupied by Italian troops in those days). Other successes were following to his medium-term goals. Mussolini, who needed the support of Germany for his politics of expansion in the Mediterranean region, had signalled that he agrees to concession regarding the problem "Austria"; 1934 he had stood up for the sovereignty of Austria, now he had changed his opinion. Hitler reacted with a German-Austrian agreement, which showed a friendly relationship, but by its wording also a certain intervention in Austrian politics. The way to the annexation of Austria was traced out.

Hitler could finally win over Mussolini to his side by his intervention in the "Spanish Civil War" (1936 – 1939). The reason for a military intervention of Germany was mainly a political matter. Germany, that prepared for the fight against the Soviet Union, was afraid of a "Volksfrontregierung" (Popular Front government = a people-oriented government) in Spain, like the "Volksfrontregierung" in France and feared that behind its back could come into being a group of states, which take sides with the Soviet Union for ideological reasons. So the military intervention in Spain fit well with the anti-Communistic propaganda, which was intensified at the same time, and the foreign orientation of the "Third Reich". Only when these political motives had led to the decision for a military intervention, also economic activities of Germany developed in Spain. These activities supported Germany's political way that was taken here, like the military reflection to test the new German weapons system in the event of a war.

Nazi Placard of the "Worker's Front"

In the summer time of this year Hitler had made preparations for the event of a blitzkrieg in the east. That happened by a secret memorandum after the Summer Olympics in Berlin. These Summer Olympic Games were inaugurated by the Minister of Propaganda on July 31. During the Olympic Games Hitler had still played on the "Friedensschalmei" (Peace Shawn – Shawn = a woodwind instrument of herdsmen, the previous form of the oboe) – 49 nations had taken part in these Olympic Games; it were not present athletes from the Soviet Union and from Spain, because of the civil war there.

This summer was also completed Hitler's second residence on the mountain Obersalzberg near Berchtesgaden/Bavarian Alps. The construction of the residence was begun in 1933. Obersalzberg was a tourist destination since the second half of the 19th century. This small mountain village was also a holiday home of Hitler since 1923. In the summer of 1933 he acquired the by him in 1928 already rented house named "Haus Wachenfeld", which he had rebuilt in two phases. It became his prestigious residence, which was called "Berghof". – After expulsion of the indigenous population in 1933 became the former resort the "Führersperrgebiet" (Führer Restricted Area) now, the second switching of power next to Berlin, where important political decisions were made, where war, peace and the holocaust were also planned. – The Nazis took advantage of the magnificent mountain backdrop for effective media productions. There Hitler appeared as close to the people politician, children's and nature lover, a good neighbour, a great statesman and lone visionary. – On 25 April 1945 bombed British long-range bombers the terrain and destroyed a large part of the buildings. Then, in 1952, the ruins of the "Berghof", the homes of Göring and Bormann and the SS barracks were blown up. Obtained were only a few buildings, among others the "Kehlsteinhaus" (Eagle's Nest) and the bunker that was built between 1943 and 1945. On 4 May 1945 occupied U.S. forces a part of the Obersalzberg. From 1947 the American forces used the Obersalzberg as a recreation area. Only a small part was opened to tourism since 1952. Only in 1996, after the American withdrawal, Bavaria, since 1946 owner, received the complete control over the Obersalzberg. Now, Bavaria established a documentation centre on the Obersalzberg, which was opened on 20 October 1999.

Back to the year 1936. On 25 October made Hitler the treaty with Mussolini on the axis "Berlin-Rome". Then, on November 25, was signed the "Anti-Comintern Pact" with Japan (Comintern = the union of the Communistic parties of the world, 1919 – 1943; Com- = communistic, -intern = international). By this pact Germany took clearly sides with Japan in its conflict with China. This pact was above all directed against England and the Soviet Union.

The world politics experienced a considerable acceleration by the increase of the international centres of conflict. That was an advantage to Hitler's calculation, but strengthened also his feeling to be pressed for time.

Vierjahresplan (Four-Year Plan) of the year of 1936:

1) *The German army must be operational within four years*
2) *The German trade and industry must be fit for war within four years.*

For example: petrolgasoline and butter were manufactured from coal short time later.

We write the year **1937**

This year became not only turning point of the internal politics of the "Third Reich/Empire", but also of the foreign politics. Hitler held on to his great goal, the "Lebensraum-Krieg" (Habitat War), and he had more and more the feeling to be under time pressure in view of the constellation of the international politics. He changed his intentions to alliances at the same time, since he had wooed England without success. By the National Socialist foreign policy was now developed the Triangle Alliance "Berlin-Rome-Tokyo" under clear anti-Communistic sign by way of compensation. This Triangle Alliance was the extension of the axis "Berlin-Rome".

On 17 January supported the German press the French intents, to look for a new space for Jewish settlements in no-European countries (The state Israel was not yet born): The French minister for colonial affairs took into consideration Madagascar, New Caledonia and French-Guinea as new regions for Jewish settlements.

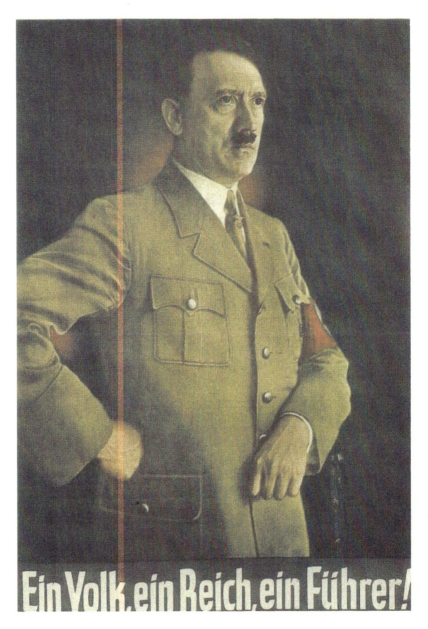

One People, one Empire, one Leader!

On 26 January was the space of the mouth of the Elbe (river) redefined by law. It was founded Great-Hamburg. The Prussian cities Altona, Wandsbek and Harburg-Wilhelmsburg were incorporated and became districts of Hamburg.

On 12 February, the German ambassador Ribbentrop and the British permanent secretary Lord Halifax negotiated in London about colonial wishes of Germany. There was also talked about a "West Pact", that could be realized perhaps. But the negotiations, which dragged on for a long time, were brought to an end without result. Some days later became the Swiss professor Carl Jacob Burckhardt Commissioner of the "League of Nations" for the "Free City of Danzig". That was a job for three years. He tried to intervene in the conflict between the German Empire and Poland because of Danzig, but he was unsuccessful. During those days Hitler inaugurated the "International Motor Show" of Berlin. The new car, the "Volkswagen" (VW/People's Car), was the focus of interest of this show.

On 1 March, the German ambassador of London (England), Joachim von Ribbentrop, gave a fundamental speech of economy at the "Spring Trade Fair" of Leipzig. There he tried to give reasons for the German right to own colonies in Africa and for the right to the military armament.

The persecution of Jews was continued in the days of this year. The holocaust approached. On 19 March were Jews expelled from the "Reichsarbeitsdienst" (Reich Labour Service - a new institution of the Nazis), half-castes (half Jew, half German) were dismissed from the leadership of this organization. On 8 April were also Germans, who were married to Jews, dismissed immediately.

On 20 April was Hitler's birthday celebrated by a great parade. At the "Königsplatz" (King's Square) of Munich gave Rudolf Heß a speech to the swearing-in of 743,000 new political leaders and party officials of the NSDAP; the celebration was transmitted by the German broadcasts. Also Fritz Todt's new book was published to Hitler's birthday, the title was: "Deutschlands Autobahn – Adolf Hitlers Straßen" (Germany's Highways – Roads of Adolf Hitler). Fritz Todt was inspector general for the German road traffic.

On 5 May, it was a Wednesday, was launched the "Wilhelm Gustloff", the "fate ship". Hitler was present at the launching. The "Wilhelm Gustloff" was with 25,000 Gross Registered Tons (GRT) the fifth largest ship of the German fleet. It was sunk by a Soviet submarine in February of the year of 1945. (Later more about this catastrophe; a catastrophe that was more terrible than the sinking of the Titanic).

On May 6, the largest German zeppelin, the "Hindenburg", went up in flames on the aviation base of Lakehurst/USA. The "Hindenburg" had 97 passengers on board; 32 passengers were killed by the flames, as result the German "Luftschiffdienst" (Airship Service) cancelled all air traffic to the elucidation of the cause of the accident. One day ago Göring had opened the exhibition "Schaffendes Volk" (Working People) in Düsseldorf; at this exhibition was showed above all the synthetic process for the production of petrol (gasoline) and **buna (bu**tane + **natri**um/sodium = synthetic India Rubber)

On 7 July presented Heinrich Focke (designer of aeroplanes; 1890 – 1979) the first helicopter of the world, which was constructed by him. The presentation took place at the airport of Bremen. The helicopter of Focke bore the name FW 61 and was already capable of doing a long-distance flight.

Since 21 October all emigrants, "Jews or Aryans", had to be sent to an ideological training's camp after their return to Germany. That was an order of the **"Gestapo"** (**Ge**heime **Sta**ats**po**lizei/Secret State Police) to prevent especially Jews from coming back to Germany. On 21 October ordered the police president of the "Free City Danzig" to liquidate the party "Zentrum". From now the NSDAP was the only party in the new state "Danzig". One day later Adolf Hitler welcomed the Duke of Windsor, the ex-king Edward VIII of England - who had abdicated -, on the "Obersalzberg" (Hitler's private palace) ... It was a friendly meeting; Hitler therefore thought that the ex-king of England would be a sympathizer of the Nazis.

On 5 November signed Poland and the German Empire a minorities' statement; by this statement guaranteed both sides right's protection and privileges (own language, cultural and ecclesiastical clubs, own schools) for foreign people, who were living within their frontiers. After the signing, Hitler conferred with the Polish ambassador, Josef Lipski, about the possibility of an agreement regarding Danzig. Late in the afternoon commented Hitler on his plans of war in plain terms in front of the Foreign and War Minister and the commanders-in-chief of the army, marine and air force; he spoke of a blitzkrieg, of the occupation of Czechoslovakia, of his "unalterable decision" to extend the German habitat in direction to the east of Europe and of an internal argument in France, which would be favourable to Germany. This secret speech became known as "Hoßbach-Protokoll" later.

On 6 November acceded Italy to the Anti-Comintern Pact that was made between Germany and Japan on November 25, 1936

The measures against the Jews were tightened up in the meantime. On 29 December were Jews excluded from the possibility to work in trade and industry. That was the reason that the Jews entrusted Aryan representatives with the business now. 7,155 Jews left Germany in this year. This year 504,093 persons were also arrested for political reasons.

We write the year **1938**

In this year it seemed to be taken the first step to "Great Germania"; the events followed hot on each other's heels, but it was not comparable with the following year.

The first blow of the impatient dictator, Adolf Hitler, was directed against Austria. On 12 February he forced the Austrian chancellor, Kurt von Schuschnigg, to give the (Austrian) Nazis a share in the government in Vienna. According to his own concept of seizure of power in Germany he demanded the taking over of the ministry of the interior by the (Austrian) Nazis and so the disposal of the police. Schuschnigg tried to resist this blackmail only by seeking refuge in attack. He fixed a public opinion poll on Hitler's demands onto the 12 March. The manipulations, by which this rescue action should be influenced, were a pretext for Hitler to threaten to intervene militarily in case Schuschnigg should not hand over his post to the National Socialist Seyß-Inquart. Also the relenting of the Austrian president, who had rejected the appointment of Seyß-Inquart up to now, in the last minute (in the night between 11 and 12 March), could not stop Hitler's step. Now another reason for Hitler's action supplied a telegram with an alleged request for help addressed to Germany. But this request for help was arranged by Göring. On 12 March, early in the morning, marched German troops into Austria. All over they met with a friendly reception, the people of Austria shouted for joy, Austria was a part of Germany again.

Heim ins Reich (back home) – Hitler is enthusiastically received by the population in Austria. – Hitler's motor- cade in front of the Burgtheater in Vienna.

The majority of the Austrians had wished the annexation by Germany and therefore cheered. The annexation of Austria meant another increase in popularity for Hitler. The name "Österreich" (Austria) was effaced now; the new name was "Ostmark" (East Mark). The "Ostmark" was divided into "Gaus" (provinces), for example: Upper and Lower Austria belonged to the "Danube Gau" now, Tyrol, Carinthia and Styria to the "Alpine Gau". But the annexation of Austria was only the condition for the next strategic goal, the encirclement of Czechoslovakia. Short time later Hitler said that he had to solve the "Czech matter" now. As vehicle of his intentions of conquest served this time the "Sudetendeutsche Partei" (Party of the ethnic Germans in "Sudetenland"/territory of the Sudeten in Bohemia and Moravia, today Czech Rep.), of which leader, Konrad Henlein, was commissioned by the "Great Brother" in Berlin to make always high demands to the Czech government, demands, which Czechoslovakia cannot meet. Hitler could not more clearly document, how he used the right of self-determination as bare means to an end.

The Czech and English reaction to the crisis "Sudetenland", which was steered by Germany, let arise the impression of resolute resistance, what Hitler used inversely to increase the crisis. The German army received the order on 30 May to prepare for a military action on 1 October. England had to make a decision now, but England ignored all warnings of the German resistance to Hitler and held on to the political compensation with him.

The background of England's "policy of appeasement" was the worry of the English Prime Minister, Chamberlain; who pleaded for a political compensation with Germany more than his predecessor, because he thought, that a European conflict would shake heavily the European status quo and would endanger England and its swaying empire too. Therefore Chamberlain travelled twice to Germany (to Berchtesgaden/Bavarian Alps and Bad Godesberg/today a district of Bonn/Rhineland). There he offered Hitler "Sudetenland" to save the core of the Czech state and to avoid a European war. But during the second meeting in

Bad Godesberg, 22 to 24 September, Hitler increased his demands and insisted not only on the right of self-determination of the Sudeten, but also on the invasion of the remainder of Czechia.

After termination of the negotiations in Bad Godesberg, a war seemed to be inevitable. But England was ready again to relent and asked Mussolini for mediation. On 29 September presented Mussolini his proposal at the conference of Munich. The conference members were Great Britain (England), France, Italy and Germany. The proposal was played into Mussolini's hands by the "Auswärtige Amt" (Department of State/German Foreign Ministry) and Göring's "Vierjahresplan-Stab" (Staff of the Vierjahresplan/Four Years Plan)

The government of Czechoslovakia, which did not take part in Munich, was obliged to hand over the "Sudetenland" (territory of the Sudeten) to the German Empire till 1 October; also Czechoslovakia had to meet the territorial demands of Poland and Hungary. For it Czechoslovakia received the guarantee on the preservation of the remainder of the state. The world could breathe again. By the additional German-British "nonaggression treaty" Chamberlain found himself confirmed in his policy of appeasement. Hitler was at the height of his popularity and power. He had achieved great foreign successes without war. But after the conference of Munich he gave still the immediate vicinity to understand his annoyance at the planned military action, which was messed up by the result now. Therefore he wanted to reach from now the next stage of his politics, which were directed above all against Russia, by military means.

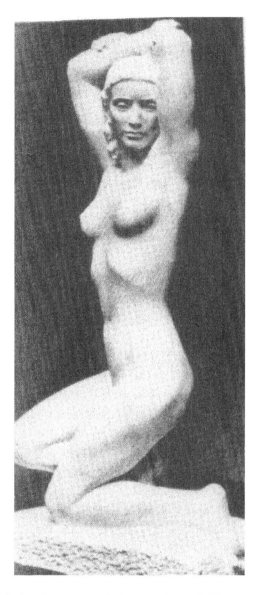

Naked female bodies as sculpture or in paintings were popular with the Nazis.

Not only the will to war was stronger, but also the policy against the Jews underwent a new radicalization. Race policy and conquest's policy crossed more and more and tightened up in batches. They followed on the one hand the programmatic goals and received on the other hand new loads by such crises. So Hitler demanded, one day after the "Reichskristallnacht", that the gossip of peace must have an end and that the war must be prepared psychologically and programmatically now. – The "Reichskristallnacht" was the occasion of concerted violence by Nazis throughout Germany against Jews and their property – more some lines further.

Another decision of the conference of Munich had far-reaching aftereffects. The fact, that the Soviet Union was excluded from the conference, made Stalin, the dictator of the Soviet Union, doubt the own foreign politics of collective security and had increased his fear of a common western-capitalistic assault on the Soviet Union under anti-Communistic omen. Therefore he looked for a rapprochement between the Soviet Union (Russia) and Germany to break this front.

There were already indications of the socalled "Reichskristallnacht" in the year of 1935 when the agitation against the Jews intensified, for example by putting up of signs at the beginning of places, villages, cities and also shops, restaurants and so on with the following words: "Juden unerwünscht" (Jews undesirable). The agitation against the Jews was also intensified by the newspaper "Stürmer", a newspaper, which was published by the "Gauleiter" (Head of the Gau) of Nürnberg/Nuremberg, Julius Streicher. Early on was published a "Ritualmord-Sondernummer" (Ritual Murder-Special Issue). The Jewish representation to Germany protested against this issue impressively. "Vor Gott und den Menschen erheben wir gegen diese beispiellose Schändung unseres Glaubens in feierlicher Verwahrung unsere Stimme" (3 May 1934: Before God and the humanity, we raise our voice against this unprecedented desecration of our faith in solemn custody). But the climax of this phase was the laws, which were passed by the "Reichstag" at the "Party Day of Freedom" on 15 September 1935 in Nuremberg. These laws regulated the relations between Germans and Jews, marriage and intercourse with Jews were prohibited, Jews were forbidden to hoist the German national flag. Jews were no citizens of the German Empire.

There were still other serious measurers in this year (1938): charges to assets which were in Jewish hand, introduction Jewish first names, for example Israel, Sara and son on, and then in November it happened upheavals, which destroyed every illusion of a further living together.

The murder of an employee of the German embassy in Paris (Ernst von Rath) by a young Jew of Polish descent led in the night from 8 to 9 November, which was cynically designated as "Reichskristallnacht" (Empire's Crystal Night), to the arrest of tens of thousands of Jewish men in Dachau, Sachsenhausen and Buchenwald, to the destruction of hundreds of synagogues, to the devastation of Jewish shops and the imposition of fines of 1,000,000,000 **RM** ((**R**eichs**M**ark/German currency of those days) for Jews. That was an enormous sum for the people of that time. Now the Jews knew that only the emigration, to Great Britain, America, Palestine or Shanghai, could save their existence.

From these pogroms of November, at which were killed Jews in large numbers and the majority of the Jewish houses of God were destroyed, increased the anti-Jewish measures. In many cities the Jews had to live in own residential districts, the ghettos, and from 1941 they were forced to wear the "Judenstern" (Star of David)

Sudetenland/Territory of the Sudeten

Sudety is a Polish/Czech word that designates the highlands in the northern Czech border area. Because there were predominantly living (ethnic) Germans, the whole of the Czech border area was called "Sudetenland"; also the southern Czech border area, at the frontier to Austria, and the western Czech border area, at the frontier to Bavaria, was called "Sudetenland" in the 20th century. The Sudeten settled since some centuries there. It was the German territory of Bohemia and Moravia. The ancestors of the Sudeten come from Thuringia, Franconia (North Bavaria) and Saxony. In 19th century they were put under pressure of the Czech national movement, but they found support by the Austrian monarchy. In November 1918 formed spokespersons of the Sudeten an own German-Bohemian government in Reichenberg (town in Sudetenland). Then they declared the union with the new state "German-Austria". But they were integrated into Czechoslovakia against their will. There they were exposed to impediments, especially in the sphere of economy and culture. Their demand for autonomy was ignored, although Germans were ministers of the Czechoslovakian government since 1926. The Sudeten-German Party and H. Henlein, the leader of the Sudeten, came more and more under the influence of Germany after the year of 1935 and demanded finally, at Hitler's insistence, the separation of "Sudetenland" from Czechoslovakia.

Two known men of those days

Konrad Zuse

Konrad Zuse was born on 22 June 1910 in Berlin. He was engineer. 1934 he developed a program-controlled calculating machine and constructed test models since 1936. Then, in 1941, he made this first program-controlled calculating machine. It was the relay calculator with the name "Zuse Z 3". That relay calculator was the first computer of the world. So Konrad Zuse was the inventor of the computer. Today the first computer (relay calculator) you can see in Hünfeld, a little town in Hessen (Zuse Museum) -- Konrad Zuse died on 18 December 1995 in Hünfeld.

Otto Hahn

Otto Hahn was born on 8 March 1879 in Frankfurt. He died on 28 July 1968 in Göttingen. Otto Hahn found out the radioactive elements and 1938 the decay of uranium into middle-heavy elements in case of irradiation by neutrons. The decay happens under release of a lot of high energy. Otto Hahn received the Nobel Prize for Chemistry in the year of 1944 and 1949 the "Max-Planck-Medaille" (a German Award)

The Second World War

We write the year **1939**

On 1 January 456,000 men had still no job in the former German Empire, in Austria there were 150,000 men without job and in Sudetenland (territory of the Sudeten) 218,000 men. – Some days later were all Jewish organizations, also the Zionist Association and the "Central Association of German Citizens of Jewish Faith", liquidated. Then, on March 7, the Jews were expelled from the military and working service. This day Hitler invited the commanders-in-chief and commanding generals of the German army to a dinner in the new "Reichskanzlei" (Reich Chancellery/Hitler's office in Berlin). Everybody could foresee that the talks during the dinner were only a preparation for war. Already three days later the German press started a campaign against Czechoslovakia by messages about unrest in the Carpathian Ukraine. As a result the Czechoslovakian President Hacha removed the rebelling Slovakian (regional) government under Prelate Tiso from office.

On 14 March marched German troops into the Czech city of "Mährisch-Ostrau" (Ostrava) and Hitler ordered that Hacha, the Czechoslovakian President, has to come to Berlin with his Foreign Minister whilst in Preßburg/Bratislava was proclaimed the independence of Slovakia and the Carpathian Ukraine. Now Hungarian troops invaded the Carpathian Ukraine.

On 15 March, early in the morning, signed Emil Hacha, now Czech president only, under pressure the "Abkommen über den Schutz des tschechischen Volkes durch das Deutsche Reich" (Agreement about the protection of the Czech people by the German Empire). After the signing Hitler immediately gave the order to invade (also) the remainder of Czechia. Already at 9 o'clock reached German troops the Czech capital Prague. The Czech soldiers stayed in their barracks by order of the Minister of Defence, whilst the Czech people of Prague had to watch with bitterness the occupation of their city. At 22 o'clock in the darkness, Hitler arrived at the Hradcany, the old castle of Prague and seat of the Czech government. He took note with delight of the non-reaction to the invasion of France, Great Britain and the Soviet Union. On 16 March von Ribbentrop, the Foreign Minister of the German Empire, proclaimed the foundation of the "Protectorate Bohemia-Moravia." This protectorate became a part of the "Great German Empire" with "autonomous" self-government. Germany took over the foreign representation and the military protection of Bohemia-Moravia and a German "Reichsprotektor" (Reich Protector) resided in Prague, it was Konstantin Freiherr von Neurath. The grasp at Prague was an open violation of the "Agreement of Munich" and to Chamberlain's (the British Prime Minister) "Appeasement Policy" a hard blow; but the British government still didn't change the political course for the moment. The occupation of Czechia (the Czech part of Czechoslovakia) was Hitler's step to the encirclement of Poland, which he wanted to defeat by a localized campaign. Thus he was not only interested in Danzig and the matter "Korridor" (the Polish land corridor between the German/Prussian provinces Pomerania and East Prussia in the east of Germany), but also in the occupation of the whole of Poland, about that he didn't let be his generals in the dark.

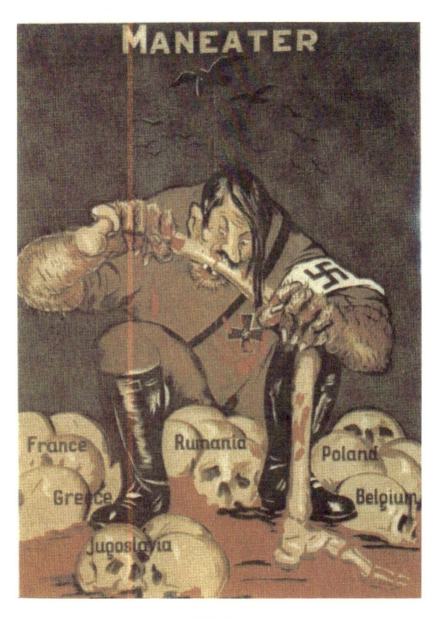

British Poster

England was still willing to come to a balance with the dictator Hitler, who was addicted to conquests, but now Hitler had the better hand because also Stalin, the Russian dictator, tried to get an arrangement with Hitler. The affair "Poland" was an invincible obstacle during the negotiation between England and the Soviet Union, because the Soviets laid claim to Poland that England couldn't accept, so presented itself the possibility to a German-Soviet (Russian) rapprochement, which was a deal of two ideological deadly enemies. But the pact was only of tactical nature for both European powers. It was a detour for Hitler's realization of his program, which designated the destruction of the Soviet Union and was still effective without reservation.

The nonaggression treaty with Stalin – Hitler informed the leadership of the German army about this treaty on 22 August – meant the death sentence to Poland. By an additional secret agreement was defined the spheres of interest and Poland's fourth partition projected.

This political coup to confuse friend and enemy, prompted Hitler to make his ideal partner England a last "generous offer", he propose a differentiation of interests to England for the time after the conquest of Poland by German troops. But the both moves in August, the pact with Stalin and the offer to England (Great Britain) with the hope of an English reserve in the Polish matter, turned out to be a "grandiose wrong speculation".

In March Ribbentrop, the German Foreign Minister, had still explained the German demands in the "question of Danzig and corridor" to the Polish ambassador, whilst in London the French Prime Minister Daladier and his Foreign Minister Bonnet discussed with the British government the changed political situation in Europe. Now, in London, they came as first reaction to an agreement on the help each other in case of a German attack onto the Netherlands or Switzerland.

On 21 March had the former Czech president, Hacha, dissolved the last Czech "Nationalversammlung" (parliament); now the "Ausschuss der nationalen Volksgemeinschaft für Böhmen und Mähren" (Committee of the National – Czech – People's Community of Bohemia and Moravia) took the place of the "Nationalversammlung". One day later Lithuania was forced Memelland (Region of Nemunas) returned to Germany. Ribbentrop and the Foreign Minister of Lithuania signed a corresponding treaty in Berlin. On 23 March Hitler started off his navigation, accompanied by many ships of the German navy, from Swinemünde (little town in Pomerania, today a town of Poland named Swinoujscie) to the city of Memel. He signed the "Gesetz über die Wiedervereinigung des Memellandes" (Law on the Reunification with the Memel) with the German Empire on board of the cruiser "Deutschland". Memel/land was now incorporated into the country "Prussia" and became a part of the administration district Gumbinnen (East Prussia). On the same day German troops marched into the country on the river Memel.

On 25 August, after the nonaggression treaty between the Soviet Union and the German Empire and the German-Russian agreement on the partition of Poland, the American President Roosevelt made an appeal to the German Empire and Poland to refrain from doing hostile steps and to enter into negotiations, whilst Hitler met the British and the French ambassador in Berlin. He suggested a guarantee to the British World Empire to England, but demanded only a solution of the German-Polish problems and the return of all former German colonies too. During the political talks in Berlin Great Britain and Poland made an alliance treaty over five years, which designated a mutual military help. One day later announced Hitler that the German Empire assured the Netherlands, Belgium, Luxembourg and Switzerland of having respect for their neutrality in case of war. Some days later it came to a head of the situation.

On 31 August happened an attack on the radio station Gleiwitz/Silesia (today Gliwice), which was directed by German officials and carried out by former Polish prisoners of a concentration camp. On 1 September at 10 o'clock declared Hitler war on Poland during a special session of the "Reichstag" (parliament): "Seit 5.45 Uhr wird jetzt zurückgeschossen" (Since 5:45 we shoot back). The German cruiser "Schleswig-Holstein" had begun with the fire at the "Westernplatte" of Danzig (Western Board of Gdansk). Now Hitler informed the German nation about his strategic targets in the war against Poland, to solve the problem "Danzig and the corridor (Poland had rejected the construction of a German autobahn/highway from Pomerania to East Prussia through Polish territory some days ago) and to take care of a change of the relation between Germany and Poland, which guarantees a peaceful living together. In his telegram to Mussolini he refused a military help by Italy, "it wouldn't be necessary".

On September 1, "Gauleiter" Albert Forster also enacted the law "Staatsgrundgesetz der Freien Stadt Danzig" (Organic Law of the Free City Danzig), which designated Danzig's immediate merger with the German Reich/Empire (In Germany the people spoke always from the German Empire) The high commissioner to Danzig of the "League of Nations", Carl Jakob Burckhardt, left Danzig with his commission at 10 o'clock. In the evening the British and the French ambassador demanded in Berlin that the German troops had to leave the Polish territory immediately.

Then on 3 September, in the morning, the British and the French government handed over the ultimate demand for the cessation of the war against Poland, but the German government rejected this ultimatum. At 14:30 spoke Hitler on the radio "the war against Great Britain and France has begun". Also on 3 September the German submarine "U 30" sank the British passenger ship "Athenia" by mistake, whilst in London was appointed a new "war cabinet": Prime Minister remained Chamberlain, First Lord of the admiralty became Churchill. At the western frontier of Germany was not yet combated this day, because there were (only) 33 German divisions facing 110 divisions of the Allies. Whilst in the west was not yet combated, were some thousand ethnic Germans killed by the Polish population in the town Bromberg (Since the end of the First World War a Polish town -- Bydgoszcz). That was the "Bromberger Blutsonntag" (Bloody Sunday of Bromberg).

On 4 September advanced German troops through the corridor (Polish land corridor between the both German countries Pomerania and East Prussia) towards East Prussia and thus established a connection of East Prussia with the German Empire again. Also this day declared Belgium, Norway, Finland, Spain, Japan, Argentina and Brazil their neutrality, one day later did the United States the same. Then, on September 7, the Polish soldiers of the Westernplatte, which was located near Danzig/Gdansk, capitulated. Five days later came the first big battle of this war to an end. Near to Radom/Poland were captured 60,000 Polish soldiers after a bloody pocket battle.

On 16 September conquered German troops the citadel of Brest-Litovsk and German units that had advanced from East Prussia in the north and from Upper Silesia in the south shook hands near Vlodava in Poland. By it West Poland was in German's hand. One day later also the Soviet Union attacked Poland from east, whilst the German submarine "U 29" had sunk the British aircraft carrier "Courageous".

German soldier fighting at the front in Poland

On 18 September announced the leadership of the German army the soon end of the war against Poland, whilst Soviet troops conquered the Polish city of Wilna (Vilnius, today capital of Lithuania) and met the German troops by "shake hands" close to Brest-Litovsk. The same day the German east frontier of the year of 1914 was still declared as new customs border by the German government. Two days later was Poland partitioned between the Soviet Union and the German Empire (the fourth partition of Poland), but the remainder of the Polish army had not yet capitulated. On 21 September there was still a big battle on the Vistula (Weichsel). The Polish troops suffered a crushing blow; more than 170,000 Polish soldiers were taken prisoner.

On 27 September offered Poland the unconditional capitulation. Hitler gave immediately order to form a military government for Poland. One day later, Ribbentrop and Molotov, the Russian Foreign Minister, made a "German-Russian border- and goodwill treaty". On 30 September the SS started off the first mass shooting of Polish Jews. Soon was to be reached the climax of the holocaust.

German soldiers shortly after the conquest of Poland

On 6 October surrendered the last Polish soldiers, by it the campaign against Poland came to an end and Hitler made Great Britain and France an offer of peace, but France rejected this offer on 10 October and Great Britain did it on 12 October, whilst the first Jews from Bohemia, Moravia and Austria were transported into the extermination camps.

On 14 October was the British battleship "Royal Oak" sunk by the German submarine "U47" in the Bay of Scapa Flow.

On 17 October began the first gunfight between French and German soldiers at the west frontier of Germany. The French soldiers, who had already occupied German territory, withdrew again. One day later permitted Hitler only restricted operations of reconnaissance patrols on the western front, great attacks should still be avoided.

On October 25, Hans Frank took over his post as head of the new "General-Gouvernement" (General Administration District of Poland) in Krakau (Cracow). By it was finished the German military administration of Poland. But that was also the end of Poland.

On 3 November signed the Soviet Union and Germany an agreement about the resettlement of ethnic Russians and ethnic Germans. The ethnic Germans, who were still living in the Baltic States and Russia, should now find a new domicile in the German part of the former Polish state and the ethnic Russians, who were still living there, should find a new domicile in the Russian part of the former Polish state. Now began also the persecution of the Jews in all Polish provinces of the German Empire. They found their end in the extermination camps in the east, the climax of the holocaust was reached and that was to last for some years.

On 8 November, it was a Wednesday, was made the first attempt on Hitler's life. Hitler made a speech on the eve of ceremony in memory of the putsch of November 1923. That he made in "Münchner Bürgerbraükeller" (cellar/basement of the brewery Bürgerbräu in Munich). He left immediately after his speech the basement of the brewery, when some minutes later exploded a bomb to the pillar where he was standing. Seven men were killed and 63 injured. Then, on 22 November, was caught the assassin, it was a 36-year-old man.

On 28 November the former Polish city of Gdynia renamed Gotenhafen. This city was to play a great part in the "great escape" of the Germans (more later). Two days later attacked the Soviet Union Finland. The Russian-Finnish (winter-) war has begun by it.

On 3 December attacked British bombers for the first time German positions (on the island Helgoland) Then, two weeks later, an air battle was between British and German tactical aircrafts; during this battle were 12 British aircrafts brought down by the Germans.

We write the year **1940**

Hitler needed bases for an Atlantic naval battle against England. On 1 April therefore he ordered to attack Denmark and Norway. Also England had planned an occupation of the Norwegian seaport Narvik, via which Germany got the essential shipments of ore from Sweden. Whilst Denmark didn't offer military resistance, because the Danish king called upon his nation to offer passive resistance, the Norwegians put up resistance and were militarily supported by British landing troops: But Norway was nevertheless defeated by quick advances and landing operations in rapid succession. Now Norway was governed by a vassal of Hitler, Vidkun Quisling; now "Quis" became a Norwegian invective to politicians, who make compliant receivers of orders of foreign powers of themselves.

On 10 May, early in the morning, invaded German troops without declaration of war the Netherlands, Belgium and Luxembourg, of which neutrality the Germans had expressly admitted shortly before. The Dutch army must already surrender after five days; on 16 May were overrun the Belgian fortresses and Brussels and Antwerp occupied. This west offensive was based on the plan of operations of von Manstein, who became field marshal later. This plan called Churchill later "sickle cut". The Allies counted on the repeat performance of the "Schlieffen-Plan" (see German History) in view of the invincible "Maginot-line", therefore they set their main armed forces against the advancing German flank in Belgium. But the centre of the German attack was surprisingly in the middle of the front. The rapid units of tanks of the army group "Rundstedt" advanced through the hills of the Ardennes and broke through the front on the Maas (river) and reached soon the Channel coast, so that the adversary was encircled and pressed against his own defensive line. The "sickle cut" was successful. German tanks encircled already the British expedition army and French divisions. Their fate seemed to be already sealed, but Hitler gave surprisingly the order on 24 May, to stop the advance of the tanks. The heavily strained units of tanks should be saved for the next battle; the annihilation of the adversary should be left a matter of prestige for the Air Force. But Göring's Air Force couldn't achieve this triumph. (Göring was the commander-in-chief of the German Air Force). By help of

887 war ships, fishing boats and many little ships could 200,000 British and 100,000 French soldiers escape and cross the Channel on 4 June. Did Hitler want to let escape the English soldiers for political reason, to build them a golden bridge for an agreement? This "Miracle of Dunkirk" is controversial to date in the research of the history. The English celebrated that as first victory, which preserved the defensive force of their country.

On 13 June marched German troops as victor into Paris. The whole of the French front had broken down without great resistance. Three days ago Mussolini, the Italian dictator, had still declared war on France. He wanted to get war loot at Hitler's side by this rapid step, without to be in military action. Now followed the signing of the German peace conditions in the famous dining car in the forest of Compiègne, in which Germany had to accept the conditions of armistice of the Allies in the year of 1918. France had to let Germany have Alsace and Lorraine again, now the new "Gau Elsaß-Lothringen". Hitler let celebrated himself as the "Greatest General of all times". He had not only defeated the hostile armies by a blitzkrieg, but also carried off the victory over his hesitating and unwilling generals.

North France, the Channel- and the Atlantic coast and also Paris, the French capital, were occupied by German troops. The old marshal Pétain, who was the victor of Verdun during the First World War, established an authoritarian regime over the non-occupied part of France in Vichy, a health resort in the south of France. He agreed to cooperate with Hitler. So France was a divided country. Now the French general de Gaulle collected from London the forces to a resistance against the collaborators. This split of the French nation remained after the war a bitter experience of the French.

In front of the parlor car of Compiégne, in which on 23 June 1940 the French surrender was signed. The men from left to right: Ribbentrop, Keitel, Göring, Heß, Hitler and Brauchitsch

Hitler now hoped that England would agree to a peace after three victorious campaigns.

On 10 May Winston Churchill had succeeded Chamberlain. He announced in his speech: "I can offer nothing but blood, trouble, tears and sweat". He was convinced that this war must not be settled in Europe but amongst the continents and at ideological and economical level. Therefore he firmly counted on the intervention of the United States, which helped England by supplies of weapons and material in spite of their formal neutrality. So Churchill didn't see a reason for giving up. Should England be compelled to yield by force of arms, Hitler had to take rapidly action then. But he didn't have a convincing plan of operation for a campaign against England. On 16 July he ordered to prepare a German invasion (Unternehmen Seelöwe"/Operation Sea Lion) ... The absolute air supremacy was the condition. On 13 August began Göring's Air Force the offensive. The offensive applied not only to the airports, radar stations and traffic routes, but also to London and the industrial centres. A full-usable radar system and the tactical superiority of the "Royal Air Force" decided the air war – the battle for England – in favour of England. The realization of the landing operation was out of the question now.

The German navy and its commander-in-chief at that time, Großadmiral Raeder (Grand Admiral Raeder), suggested the conquest of Gibraltar, Malta and Suez to Hitler by German operations in the Mediterranean Sea; so should be compelled the English empire to yield. The new plans took aim at the vital nerve of the English position as world power, the influence over North Africa and the Near East. On 23 October met Hitler Franco, the Spanish dictator, to win the "Caudillo" (Spanish title of Franco) to an attack onto Gibraltar. But Franco didn't want to go over to Hitler before the defeat of England. He kept cool, also in the moment when Hitler began to shout and became irascible. Also a meeting with Marshal Pétain came to nothing although Hitler had promised him English colonies in Africa. Some days later mixed news from Rome all plans up.

Franco, the Spanish dictator, visits Hitler in Germany

On 28 October Mussolini surprisingly attacked Greece, it happened without consultation with Hitler. The ambitious "Duce" (that was Mussolini's title in Italy) wanted to realize his vision, the change of the Mediterranean Sea into an Italian "mare nostro" without German help. But short time later; the Italians were driven away from Greece again. That happened by English troops. Now the Italians had also to leave Somalia and Egypt, then Abyssinia (Ethiopia). All these countries found military support by England (Great Britain). Now it seemed that Italy would also lose the remainder of North Africa. To prevent that, German troops of the "Afrikakorps" under General Erwin Rommel invaded North Africa some months later. But Hitler's dream, to extend the German living space in the east, had priority for the time being.

In the meantime, Italy, Japan and Germany came to an agreement about the spheres of interests, so belonged Europe to the spheres of influence of Italy and Germany and Asia to the influence's sphere of Japan. On 17 November also Bulgaria acceded to this treaty. On 22 November Hitler met the Romanian 'Conducator' (leader) Antonescu, who also acceded to this pact one day later, also Slovakia followed then on 24 November. Now also the Soviet Union showed interest to join the pact of the three powers, but the Soviets demanded for it the withdrawal of the German troops from Finland. There the Germans had supported the Finnish troops in their combat against Russia. The Soviets demanded also the influence over Bulgaria, bases at the Strait of Dardanelles (Turkey) and the cession of the southern part of the island of Sakhalin by Japan. But all that was rejected by Italy, Germany and Japan.

At the end of November began General Paulus with schedules for a campaign against Russia (Soviet Union). On 18 December issued Hitler the "Weisung Nr. 21" (Directive No. 21), the so-called "Fall Barbarossa" (Operation Barbarossa/Barbarossa = Emperor Friedrich I, 1152 – 1190, see German History). By this "Weisung" the German army was prepared for the war against the Soviet Union. The Soviets had occupied in the meantime Lithuania, Latvia, Estonia and Bessarabia (today Moldavia). From now belonged these countries to the Soviet (Russian) Empire. Only many, many years later they became independent states again.

In the last weeks of this year the British Air Force attacked many German cities, whilst the German "Luftwaffe" (Air Force) bombed the English cities of Coventry and London. On both sides were killed several thousand people by these attacks.

Concentration camp of Dachau close to Munich.

It served as a model for all later concentration camps and as a school of ciolence for the men of the SS, under whose rule it was. In the twelve years of its existence, more than 200,000 people from all over Europe were imprisoned here and in numerous outdoor facilities.More than 43,000 of these people died. On April 29, 1945, American troops liberated the survivors.

We write the year **1941**

On 1 January bombed the British (Royal) Air Force the German seaport of Bremen for three hours. Then, on January 10, Germany still signed an economical agreement with the Soviet Union although the preparation for the war against Russia was already going on.

After the defeat of the Italian troops in Libya, they had lost several battles against English and Australian troops there, General Erwin Rommel arrived in the Libyan city of Tripoli, where he took over the command of the "Deutsche Afrikakorps" (German Africa Corps) Two days later the first German troops landed in Tripoli. During this time began the extermination of Jews in Germany. In Vienna were 10,000 Jews arrested and then deported into the extermination camps in Poland. Few days later, there was a wave of extermination of Jews from Amsterdam (Netherlands), who were deported into the concentration camps of Buchenwald and Mauthausen. – In these days the German battleships "Scharnhorst" and "Gneisenau" have sunk several British ships in the Atlantic Ocean. On 3 March England took revenge for it. Five British destroyers attacked the Norwegian archipelago of the Lofoten Islands. There they destroyed fishing factories and sank one German outpost boat and seven trading vessels and captured 215 German soldiers. Few days later was also sunk the German submarine "U 47" by the British navy, whilst the Royal Air Force bombed the German cities of Kiel, Berlin and Mannheim. The German Air Force took revenge and bombed first the English city of Birmingham and then Plymouth, whilst the German navy sank 16 ships of the Allies.

On 24 March conquered the German "Africa Corps" under General Rommel the Libyan city of El Aqeila, which was defended by English and Australian troops. – Yugoslavia joined the pact of the three powers one day later. But on 27 March was already the pro-German government under Prime Minister Dragiša Cvetković overthrown and Prince Regent Paul went into exile whilst Prince Peter became king of Yugoslavia. General Dušan Simović became new head of the Yugoslavian government. Now Hitler ordered the attack on Yugoslavia consequently, also Greece should be attacked. – On 31 March started off the German-Italian units with the big offensive against the English and Australian troops in Libya.

On 2 April the German troops, who were at the Hungarian-Yugoslav and Romanian-Yugoslav frontier, were concentrated and in Libya German troops conquered the city of Benghazi two days later, whilst the English and Australian troops fell back there. – On 6 April began the war against Yugoslavia and Greece. On 9 April the Greek city of Thessaloniki was already conquered by German tanks, whilst Rommel conquered the Libyan city of Bardiya. Then, only one day later, German troops occupied the Yugoslavian city of Zagreb and Ljubljana (Laibach). Now the leader of the radical Ustasha-movement, Ante Pavelić, proclaimed the independent state "Croatia". That happened by help of the Germans. Croatia had to give up a part of its Dalmatian coast, which got Italy, but for it became Bosnia and Herzegovina Croatian provinces. The remainder of Yugoslavia was now occupied by Italian and German troops. On 17 April surrendered the last Yugoslav units. The Yugoslav king Peter and the Yugoslav government went into exile to London. Then, few days later, Bulgarian troops occupied the Yugoslav province Macedonia (today Republic Macedonia).

German troops in Yugoslavia

On 30 April was the whole of the Greek mainland occupied by German troops. Now Hitler fixed the time for the beginning of the assault on the Soviet Union (Operation "Barbarossa"). The date should be: June 11.

At the end of May German paratroopers conquered the Greek island Crete, there they wanted to win a strategic-favourable position and to secure the southeast flank against English landings. Short time before Germany had still tried to convince England of the senselessness to continue the war. Hitler wanted to keep clear the back to attack the Soviet Union. Rudolf Heß, Hitler's representative, had jumped off by parachute over Scotland and then contacted the British government directly. Whether this was a real wish of Hitler that could never be clarified. Heß's enterprise went wrong, he was taken prisoner and Hitler let pronounce him mentally ill.

The campaign against Russia (Soviet Union) was now prepared as racial-political extermination fight. By the notorious "Kommissarbefehl" (Commissioner Command) of June 6 was a crime against the Russian civilian population set out of persecution. All political commissioners of the "Red Army" (Soviet army) should be immediately executed after their capture. The administration of the conquered Russian regions was entrusted to Himmler and his task forces. The Slav "subhuman creatures" should be exposed to brutal exploitation and extinction; the east should be colonized and become a part of a "Germanic Empire".

German bombers; Messerschmitt: Rotte Me 262

The attack on Russia (Operation "Barbarossa) was started off on 22 June, as planned. Russia (Soviet Union) took surprisingly this attack, although Stalin was warned before. In few weeks already succeeded the three German army groups – North, Middle and South – in winning enormous areas of Russia by the well-tried strategy (in Poland and France) of the assault wedges of tanks and forming of pockets. In the middle of July was reached the first assault goal, the Dvina-Dnieper-Line (Dvina and Dnieper are Russian rivers). Also this time Hitler seemed to defeat his adversary by a "blitzkrieg". But the "Operation Barbarossa" failed because of excess of operational goals. The general staff suggested, as it did Napoleon once, to advance towards Moscow directly. But Hitler wanted to advance towards Leningrad (today St. Petersburg) and also towards Ukraine at the same time, to seal off Russia's access roads to the Baltic Sea (Ostsee) and to secure the access to the rich cornfields of the Ukraine.

On 31 July followed a cruel order: "Reichsfeldmarschall" Göring (Reich Field Marshal Göring) put Himmler, who was SS group leader, in charge of the preparation of the "Endlösung der Judenfrage" (Final Solution of the Jewish Question = extermination of the Jews).

On 21 August Hitler gave the order to encircle the bulk of the "Red Army", which was between the German army groups Middle and South in the Pripet Marshes. The Russian army was defeated in its greatest battle of all time, 665,000 Russian soldiers were captured by the Germans. Also a huge lot of matériel fell into German hands. Hitler spoke of the "greatest battle of the world history", but this battle of Kiev (Ukraine) proved to be an operative mistake. This battle slowed down the advance towards Moscow for several weeks. Now set in the mud period by heavy rainfalls, it followed – earlier than expected – the winter;

but the German troops had not prepare for the winter and therefore neglected to see to the supply, because Hitler had counted on a quick victory. In Germany was collected winter clothing and ski articles, but that did not change the despairing situation of the German soldiers in Russia. More than 1,000,000 German soldiers froze to death or were killed in action or were captured by the Russians during this winter period. The German advance was finally stopped early in December. In the south was the city of Rostov on Don (river) conquered, but then given up in a hurry again, in the north was Leningrad (St. Petersburg) encircled and then besieged for three years. It was a destructive fight there. The Russians provided the population of Leningrad with foodstuffs and other essential articles over the Lake Ladoga. The German generals demanded to take back the exceptional length of the front, but Hitler gave the order on 16 December: "hold the front line" and "offer fanatic resistance". Three days later he deprived the military leadership of its power and took over the supreme command of the army personally.

In the meantime the Russian counteroffensive got under way. Stalin called a "Great War of the Russian native country" against the German invaders. His appeal to the national feeling showed effect, caused by the clear unmasking of Hitler's anti-communism, which had so far found sympathy in a great part of the Russian population but showed its real face by the terror of the National Socialist racial policy now in the occupied Russian regions. In April the Soviet Union – also before the beginning of the German campaign against Russia – had already made a non-aggression treaty with Japan. That happened for Hitler surprisingly. Japan and Russia kept to this treaty to the capitulation of Germany, so that Russia had never to fight at two fronts during the war against the German Empire. On 12 July had Great Britain made a treaty with Russia about a war alliance against Germany and the United States volunteered to supply matèriel into the Soviet Union, so that became reality, what Hitler had always criticized as reason for the German defeat in the First World War, a two-front-war against several hostile super powers, which could rely on the potential of the world power U.S.A. Now the anti-Hitler-coalition disposed of 75% of all personal and material reserves of the world.

The U.S. had declared their neutrality with the beginning of the war, but then left this course step by step, because it became more and more clearer that Hitler's supremacy in Europe also threatened the own security. In March the American President Roosevelt could enforce the "hire and lease law"; by this law the U.S. was declared "arsenal of the democracy" and arms depot of all adversaries of Hitler. By this law was also allowed to provide the adversaries of Japan and Germany with weapons and material. In August Roosevelt and Churchill signed the "Atlantic Charta" (Atlantic Pact). The U.S. took their place in the war front of the democracies now. Then it came to a decision on joining in the war by the incidents in Pacific. When the war began in Europe, Japan was already at war of aggression since two years in China. According to the Japanese phraseology it was aimed at a "great Asian sphere of prosperity" there in the whole of Southwest Asia and China; this region should be welded together to a bloc, which was culturally and economically dominated by Japan. The U.S. saw threatened its trade interests and its strategic apron in the Pacific region and Roosevelt reached that it was put an oil embargo on Japan that was dependent on import. In this situation Japan wanted to negotiate, but Roosevelt stood firm. He refused to defuse the conflict. Did he that only to lead the reluctant American people into the European war by using the Pacific "back door"? Or did he only reacted to Japanese repression? It was clear Roosevelt was a strong adversary of totalitarian states. The raid on the American Pacific navy in Pearl Harbour hit the U.S. unprepared, although the Japanese plans of the attack on Southwest Asia had been become known by the American secret service. In the morning of December 7, Japanese bombers attacked the American naval base on Hawaii without declaration of war before. As a result the United States and Great Britain declared war on Japan. On 11 December followed Hitler with the declaration of war on the United States. So he gave Roosevelt the wished opportunity to be at war against him. Also Italy now declared war on the U.S. Hitler's speculation America would concentrate its forces in the Pacific region now, turned out to be wrong. The Allies agreed to defeat Germany first.

A German woman and a Jewish man; a picture of degradation

We write the year **1942**

On 2 January capitulated the encircled German-Italian garrison in the Libyan city of Bardia. Four days later disembarked Soviet soldiers at two places of the Crimea (east front), that happened on the west coast and on the east coast near at hand of Yalta. Then, one day later, evacuated General Rommel during a sandstorm the city of Ajdabiya in Libya (North Africa). The sandstorm offered him cover, so that he could withdraw unnoticed. On 8 January attacked strong Soviet units the German positions off the fortress of Sevastopol, so that the German troops had to withdraw. On 17 January conquered British troops the Pass of Halfaya, the last base of the German-Italian troops in Egypt. 5,500 German and Italian soldiers were captured by the British. Three days later was decided, at the so-called "Wannseekonferenz" (Wannsee Conference) of Berlin, the systematic extermination of the Jews and the "Endlösung der Judenfrage" (Final Solution of the Jew's question = holocaust). That conference took place with Reinhard Heydrich in the chair. Heydrich was the head of the "Reichssicherheitshauptamt" (Reich Security Main Office) -- On 21 January followed in Africa, in the Cyrenaica (a part of Libya), the German counteroffensive of the "Africa-Corps"; by this offensive the German troops could recapture large areas. Then, on 8 February, was stopped this offensive by British troops near El Gazala, 60 km to the west of Tobruk.

On 13 March, it was a Friday, deported the Romanians 110,000 Jews into the extermination camps of ex-Poland. With it was also started off the extermination of the Jews who didn't live in the German Empire.

On 8 May began the great summer offensive of the Germans on the Crimea. One day later the "Red Army" under Marshal Timoshenko tried to recapture the city of Charkov (or Kharkiv) in the south sector of the east front. This city was occupied by German troops. Then, on 19 May, the Germans started off the counteroffensive there. The leader of the German troops was Field Marshal von Bock. This offensive was only the prelude to some great battles of this year.

On 22 May had the "Kreisauer Kreis" (Kreisau Circle) the first time a meeting. This circle was a group of resistance fighters, who had given themselves the name of the landed property of Helmuth James Count von Moltke, the estate Kreisau in Silesia. Two days later succeeded the German troops in encircling of large units of the Soviet army to the south of Charkov. The battle came to an end by the victory of the Germans. 220,000 Russian soldiers were captured.

On 27 May there was an assassination attempt on Heydrich, who was protector of the German Empire in Bohemia, in Prague. Seven Czech resistance fighters, amongst them Josef Vaclic, Jan Kubiš and Josef Gabčik, who came from London, were the assassins. They were caught after the attempt and shot dead immediately. Reinhard Heydrich died of his injuries on June 4. Then, on 9 June, it was followed the command to a retaliatory action against the Bohemian village Lidice. 199 men of Lidice were placed on the wall and shot dead by SS units. 184 women were deported into the concentration camp Ravensbrück, 7 into the prison of the police in Theresienstadt, 4 pregnant women were taken to a hospital. 98 children were taken along for "Eindeutschungszwecke" (purpose of Germanizing). All that had directly nothing to do with the attempt; it was a pure arbitrary act, which Hitler was still filming. The village Lidice was razed to the ground then.

The remnant of Lidice

In the east of Europe and in North Africa loomed the German catastrophe already. Hitler's armies stormed once more in Russia and North Africa. A German army group hoisted the German war flag on Elbrus/Minghi Tau (the highest mountain in the Caucasus, 5,590 m high) and advanced through the Caucasus whilst the sixth army under General Paulus reached the large Russian industrial city of Stalingrad (today Volgograd). In July Rommel's troops reached El Alamein after the victory close to Tobruk. El Alamein was the last British position before Alexandria/Egypt. Hitler's empire had reached its largest extension, now began the decline. The Russian winter brought about again a stop of the German advance. In the burning city of Stalingrad raged a fierce houses' combat, because the "Red Army" didn't give up. And also for Hitler was Stalingrad, the city with Stalin's name, a matter of prestige long ago. Instead of giving up Stalingrad and the Caucasus, Hitler gave the order to hold the position. On 22 November encircled the Soviets the sixth German army in Stalingrad completely. 260,000 German soldiers and more than 30,000 Romanian soldiers with 100 tanks, 1,800 heavy guns and more than 100,000 vehicles were in the trap without supplies. General Paulus wanted to break out in direction southwest, but Hitler took Göring at his word, who promised to supply the sixth army from the air. Göring couldn't hold this promise this time too. An attempt of help by the tanks' divisions of von Manstein failed; they couldn't break through towards the encircled German troops in Stalingrad.

German troops close to Stalingrad

The battle in front of Stalingrad

General Erwin Rommel; he was called "Desert Fox"

There was also no better situation in Africa. On 3 November were the British tanks successful close to El Alamein, they broke through the German-Italian lines. Then, one day later, the German-Italian units withdrew after 12 days of lasting land- and air fights, they withdrew towards western part of the desert (Sahara). On 8 November landed the American invasion troops under the command of General Eisenhower in French-North-Africa (Operation Torch). The goal was the occupation of Casablanca, Oran and Algiers. General Eisenhower wanted to bar Rommel's way of withdrawal. In the hours of the evening Algiers capitulated to the Americans. By it came into being a second front against the German troops in Africa. Now the encircled German-Italian troops capitulated by Mersa Matruh (Egypt). But the non-encircled German-Italian troops there could escape.

On 11 and 12 November German troops also occupied the remainder of France, the new Vichy-France in the south, whilst Italy occupied the French island Corsica. The whole of France was under foreign rule now.

We write the year **1943**

At the beginning of this year the operations of the Allies, which were already started off by storming the "fortress" Europe in the second half of the year of 1942, set the tone of the situation in the theatre of war, there in the Soviet Union, North Africa and on the Pacific. The year 1942 had brought the zenith of success for the German navy in the naval war of the Atlantic. But by the air war that was led more and more intense by the United States and Great Britain the Germans had to suffer.

On the Eastern Front, the events focused on the battle for Stalingrad (Volgograd). Here the Sixth German Army was stuck. The attempt to rescue the encircled Sixth Army failed. The troops, which were led up by Field Marshal General Erich von Manstein, couldn't break through towards Stalingrad because the resistance of the Russian troops was too fierce. So his attack was stopped some kilometres before Stalingrad and the encircled German soldiers were waiting in vain for help there. Also on the other front lines in the east the Soviet troops had taken the offensive.

On 8 January rejected "Generaloberst" (Colonel General) Friedrich Paulus, who kept occupied 90% of the city of Stalingrad, the Soviet demand to capitulate, as a result began the "Red Army" with the offensive to shatter the pocket of Stalingrad.

**The defeat of the German army by Stalingrad
General Paulus was cacptired**

On 12 January began the "Red Army" the great offensive against the Second Hungarian Army and the Eight Italian Army in the area of the upper reaches of the river Don by the city of Sloboda (today: Liski/Ukraine) Both armies were defeated within some days. 30,000 Hungarian soldiers were killed and 50,000 Hungarians were taken prisoners by the Soviets. The Red Army advanced through the gap, which came into being now, and marched along a broad front line towards west. Now in Russia originally fought 200,000 Hungarian soldiers. After many casualties there it was formed two new corps from the remainder of the Hungarian army, which were put into action in back areas.

On 18 January, the city that bore the German name Schlüsselburg and is located on the mouth of the river Neva into the Lake Ladoga, was reconquered by the Red Army. Since 1944 this city bears the name Petrokrepost. It happened in the part of the renaming of all places in Russia that bore German names. The name Petrokrepost was derived from the name of Peter the Great, the Russian Tsar. – Now the Red Army succeeded in making a landed connection with 8 – 11 km in breadth towards Leningrad that was besieged by German troops since 8 September 1941. But the hills of Sinyavino, by which was controlled the environs of Leningrad, could hold the Germans. Only more than one year later was finally brought the encirclement of Leningrad to an end.

On 23 January informed the German leadership of the army that the German-Italian tanks' army had withdrew after hard combats, according its plan, in Tripolitania (a part of Libya). By this movement Tripoli was evacuated without combat after the destruction of the harbour by the own troops (German and Italian soldiers) that had also removed all stock and the whole of the matériel before. Now the German-Italian tanks' army rolled towards west and British troops occupied Tripoli.

In Stalingrad the combats came more and more nearer to the end. On 31 January capitulated the south group of the Sixth Army under the command of Friedrich Paulus. The battle in the hell of Stalingrad was decided by it. In the night before there the German air force had still dropped supply material for the encircled soldiers. In the south pocket were 17,000 German soldiers, amongst them were only 3,000 men fit for action. In the night Hitler had still ordered Paulus by radio message to endure, whilst the first German soldiers already surrendered, because they had shot off their last ammunition. But the battle of Stalingrad was continued. General Karl Strecker, who was in command of the north group in Stalingrad, continued the combat for this Russian industrial city. But he capitulated then on 2 February too. Germany had begun the battle for Stalingrad with 364,000 soldiers (22 divisions). During the encirclement of the Sixth German Army there were still 260,000 soldiers on 22 November 1942. The end of the battle in the hell of Stalingrad had only survived one third of the original German soldiers there. Now the remainder of the German "Stalingrad Army" was taken prisoner. That was the end of the former proud Sixth Army. The last 91,000 German soldiers, amongst them 2,500 officers and 23 generals, were taken prisoner. Many soldiers died during the march into the assembly camps of Beketovka (close to Stalingrad), Krasnoarmeisk and Frolov. There died of epidemic typhus other German soldiers by the thousands. Now the transports in the POW camps in Siberia were following. These transports were lasting several weeks during the winter time. During these transports died thousands and thousands of German prisoners of war again. Who reached the POW camp had hard to work there, so didn't survive many Germans. In 1956 the remainder of the soldiers of the Sixth German Army could leave the POW camp in Siberia. Only 6,000 German soldiers of the "Stalingrad Army" arrived in Germany now, 6,000 out of 364,000 of the great Sixth Army and the remainder, they had lost their lives in Russia.

German soldiers and Polish nurses in Łowicz/Poland

In Russia and North Africa were continued the combats. On 18 February gave the "Reichspropagandaminister/Reich Minister of Propaganda" (Goebbels) a speech to the German nation in the "Sportpalast" (Sport Palace) of Berlin; during this speech he called upon the population of the German Empire to mobilize the last reserves to the war. The invited audience was a cross-section of the German population, so Goebbels could give the impression that it would be a plebiscite.

**Goebbels gave his famous speech in Berlin, he asked:
"Do you want the total war?" The answer of the crowd: "Yes!"**

After his speech, which had whipped up the people, he asked the audience in the "Sportpalast" ten questions, which culminated in the request to say "yes" to supreme efforts for the war. The fanatic crowd answered the question "Wollt ihr den totalen Krieg?" (Do you want the total war?), with an enthusiastic "yes". After the last words of Goebbels broke out a thunderous applause that was broadcast on the radio till a half hour after the end of his speech. Goebbels made later the following note in his diary: "Diese Stunde der Idiotie! Hätte ich gesagt, sie sollen aus dem dritten Stock des Columbus-Hauses springen, sie hätten es auch getan!" (This hour of idiocy! Had I told them to jump from the third floor of the Columbus Building, they would have done it too).

The terrible Nazi court of Berlin

This day, the 18 February, were also arrested Hans and Sophie Scholl in front of the university of Munich. They belonged to the resistance group "Weiße Rose" (White Rose). They had distributed leaflets with criticism about the Nazi-regime. On 22 February, they had just an age of 21 and 24 years, they were sentence to death together with their friend Christoph Probst, who was 23 years old. After the condemnation they were immediately executed.

Hans and Sophie Scholl with a friend

In February the German armies in Russia and North Africa could still achieve some successes, which were still lasting early in March too. But the Germans also had to register some defeats. In the middle of February they lost the important city Charkov in the Ukraine. Then, on 1 March, the army group "Middle" began with the evacuation of the front bow of Rzhev; that led to a shortening of the front for 230 km. This day was also introduced the German right in Elsaß-Lothringen again; up to now there was still effective the "Code civil", the French right. One day later German troops conquered the city of Slavyansk and Bogo-rodichno in the south sector of the east front and formed a bridgehead on the river Donets. On 3 March followed a big transport of Jews from Romania into the extermination camp of Treblinka (Poland); there they were killed by gas.

On 6 March competed the Fourth German Tanks' Army under the command of Colonel General Hermann Hoth and the army detachment "Kempf" against the units of the "Red Army" in the area to the west of Charkov. After the destruction of a part of the Third Soviet Tanks' Army, Charkov was occupied by SS-troops on 14 March. On 21 March recaptured German troops also the city of Belgorod, which was liberated by the Fortieth Soviet Army before.

By these successes of the army group south under Field Marshal General Erich von Manstein was stopped the Russian offensive in this front sector. Before, there the Russians had also con-quered the cities of Rostov and Kursk. But after the recapture of Belgorod the German attack subsided; now began also the mud period, so that another advance was impossible.

On 6 March also followed a new German offensive in North Afri-ca. Field Marshal General Erwin Rommel began with the Third

Tanks' Division, two light divisions and parts of three Italian divisions the last offensive against the Eight British Army. It was an offensive without success. The German army lost 55 tanks by the attack from the position of the Mareth Line towards Médenine. Now the Germans had fewer than 100 tanks in Africa. During the battle were also 500 German soldiers killed in action.

On 9 March was Rommel relieved from his office in Africa and took the command of the army group B in Italy; the leadership of the army group "Africa" took over Colonel General Hans-Jürgen von Arnim.

In the night between 19 and 20 March began the Eight British Army with a great offensive against the First Italian Army and the remainder of the German army in Africa at the Mareth Line; so the last battle for Africa had begun by it, in Tunisia. The Italian army could offer resistance for the present with success, but for a prolonged time the British soldiers were victorious. In the middle of April the last German-Italian units were encircled in the Gafsa-Gabés area, the remainder of the former 13 divisions attacked 500,000 British and American soldiers now. The Germans had only 48 tanks and 300 guns. Then, on 13 May, the German and Italian troops capitulated in Africa. Colonel General von Arnim was already captured by the British one day ago in the airfield of Sainte Marie du Zit, to the west of Hammamet/Tunisia. The war in Africa cost the life of 35,500 British soldiers, 16,500 American soldiers, 13,700 Italian soldiers and 18,600 German soldiers. 130,000 German and 180,000 Italian soldiers were taken prisoners. The war in Africa came to an end, but in Europe (but also in Asia, the war between Japan and the U.S.A. and Great Britain) was the war continued. At the east front occurred several bloody battles, whilst the British air force and the American air force bombed many German cities and little towns, thousands and thousands people were killed.

Auschwitz, the gate to the death camp

Another bloody event began on 19 April. In the ghetto of Warsaw, from here were already more than 300,000 Jews deported into the extermination camps, broke out a rebellion against the German oppressors, who intended to close this ghetto. As a result marched two battalions of the "Waffen-SS" (Arms-SS = a detachment of the SS; each member of this detachment was half soldier and half security officer; it was a special unit of hard men) into the Jewish ghetto of Warsaw to transport the last 60,000 – 70,000 Jews, who were still living in the ghetto, into the extermination camps. But the Jewish underground movement under the leadership of Mordecai Anielewicz offered fierce resistance.

The rebels the German troops under the command of the SS-Brigade's Leader Jürgen Stroop could force to withdraw for the present. They had pelted the Germans with projectiles from the roofs. Few hours later the SS-units came back with guns and began with the bombardment of the ghetto. Then, one day later, they put flame thrower into action. Now it was systematically set fire to each house; many Jews died in the flames and many jumped through the window into the death. Who could escape and hid in an air-raid shelter or in the sewage system, was killed by grenades or was driven to the open air, where SS-members were waiting for them to let them march off immediately. The survivors were taken away to the Jewish cemetery, which was on the outskirts of the ghetto, there they gathered for the transport into the extermination camp of Treblinka. Then, in Treblinka, the gas chamber was waiting for them. But some Jews survived this terrible action in the ghetto. They continued their combat against the Germans. On 16 May the combat of survival of the Jews of Warsaw came finally to an end. After the rebellion the synagogue was now destroyed. The leader of the SS-brigade (Jürgen Stroop), who had put down the Jewish rebellion, reported on the rebellion few days later, that during the combat were killed 56,065 Jews, but the Jews, who died in the sewage system or were killed by fire, he couldn't count. Then on 23 May were the last Jewish rebels shot dead.

German terror in Warsaw; Jews were deported into the exter-mination camps

THE ILLUSTRATED LONDON NEWS,

SATURDAY, MAY 22, 1943.

GENERAL VON ARNIM, ERSTWHILE LEADER OF THE GERMAN ARMIES IN TUNISIA, IS POLITELY ESCORTED BY OFFICERS INTO THE BARBED-WIRE ENCLOSURE SURROUNDING HIS NEW QUARTERS—IN ENGLAND.

Gerneral von Arnmim, leader of the German army in Tunesia is escorted by officers into the barbed wire enclosure surrounding his new quarters in England.

In June began the invasion of the British and American army in South Italy. On 11 June capitulated 11,000 Italian soldiers on the island of Pantelleria and one day later also the Italian troops on the island of Lampedusa.

On 5 July was started off the German operation "Zitadelle" against the Soviet front bow of Kursk; it was to be the final large-scale offensive of the German army on the Eastern Front. The army group "South" and "Middle", supported by the army detachment "Kempf" and the Fourth Tanks' Army should encircle the units of the "Red Army" by a movement like a pair of tongs, but the Germans failed because of the Soviet resistance, which was immediately put in action. In the south of the front sector the German army could only win a terrain of 18 km, in the north of 10 km. As a result the "Führer und Reichskanzler", Adolf Hitler, stopped the operation on 13 July.

The planning of the operation "Zitadelle" was already started off early in March; but the planned beginning of the attack for the middle of April had to be postponed to another date over and over again, because of a delay of the deployment and an insufficient concentration of the armed forces. On 15 April Hitler issued the "Operation Order No. 6" for the carrying out of the operation. The text of the issue is as follows to read: "Ich (Hitler) habe mich entschlossen, sobald die Wetterlage es zuläßt, als ersten der diesjährigen Angriffsschläge den Angriff 'Zitadelle' zu führen. Diesem Angriff kommt daher ausschlaggebende Bedeutung zu. Er muß schnell und durchschlagend gelingen. Er muß uns die Initiative für dieses Frühjahr und diesen Sommer in die Hand geben ... Die besten Verbände, die besten Waffen, die besten Führer, große Munitionsmengen sind an den Schwerpunkten einzusetzen. Jeder Führer, jeder Mann muß von der entscheidenden Bedeutung dieses Angriffs durchdrungen sein. Der Sieg von Kursk muß für die Welt wie ein Fanal wirken" (I - Hitler - have decided, as soon as the weather situation permits, to lead as most of this year's attack blows the attack „Zitadelle". Therefore, this attack plays crucial importance. It must succeed quickly and striking. It must give in our hands the initiative for this spring and summer. The best military units, the best weapons, the best leaders, large quantities of ammunition are to be used at the focal points. Every leader, every man must be convinced of the crucial importance of the attack. The victory of Kursk must act as a beacon for the world.)

On 5 July were so facing an enormous crowd and a huge quantity of matériel. On German side were combating in the southern front sector 7 infantry divisions, 11 tanks' divisions and 3 brigades with storm guns, the northern group had 2 "Panzer Grenadier Divisions" (Special troop; an escorting division of the tanks, the soldiers are equipped with hand grenades and hand guns), 6 tanks' divisions and also 7 infantry divisions; additional to it there were supporting units of the German air force. 900,000 German soldiers were combating against 1,340,000 Russian soldiers in this battle. On both sides were put in action 6,000 tanks and more than 4,500 aeroplanes. Then, on 12 July, there was the largest tanks' battle of the world history close to Prokhorovka. During this battle of 12 July more than 1,200 tanks came into action, supported by more than 1,000 aeroplanes. This tanks' battle came to an end without victor. Then, one day later, Hitler stopped the offensive. 500,000 German soldiers were killed in action or were captured by the Russians. Germany lost 1,500 tanks and 1,500 aeroplanes by the combats of Kursk. Also the "Red Army" had a big loss and many casualties, so the "Fourth German Tanks' Army" could capture 32,000 Russians and the Russian army lost a total of 4,000 tanks. Few days later the "Red Army" attacked the German army on the edge of the area of

Donets (river) close to Izyum and Mius. But the Germans were victorious this time. 18,000 Russians were captured and 700 Russian tanks destroyed.

The hell for women, the concentration camp in Ravens-brück

General Montgomery, victor of Alamein, now leading his famous Eighth Army into Europe.

On 10 July landed the troops of the Allies under the leadership of Dwight D. Eisenhower on the island Sicily. This operation was carried out by five divisions of the "Eighth British Army", four divisions of the "Seventh U.S.-American Army" and units of the Canadian army. It were in action 280 war ships, 320 transport ships, 900 big and 1,225 small landing vessels and 3,680 aeroplanes. This invasion army was too strong, so that the Italian military units could not offer much resistance. On 13 July joined together all invasion troops by Ragusa and on 22 July occupied American troops Palermo. On 16 July were the German troops, which were still on Sicily, concentrated under one leadership in the north of the island, at the Strait of Messina. It was the tanks' division "Hermann Göring" and the 15th "Panzer Grenadier Division". On 29 July were the German positions by Nicosia (Mount Etna) conquered by the Allies.

The American President Franklin D. Roosevelt designated the landing operation as "the beginning of the end of Hitler's Germany".

In the night between 24 and 25 July the "Royal Air Force" started off the heaviest air raids on Hamburg. 740 British bombers dropped 2,300 tons of bombs onto the city. To 3 August two air raids happened every day and four air raids every night. 30,500 citizens of Hamburg were killed during these air raids and 60% of the city was destroyed.

The
face
of a
woman
that
reflects
horror
of an
air raid.

Whilst the combats were continued at the east front, with reciprocal successes, the Italian troops surrendered on 20 July on Sicily. Only five days later the "Duce", Benito Mussolini, was deprived of this power and arrested. Marshal Pietro Badoglio formed a new government and King Victor Emanuel III became commander-in-chief of the Italian army. The new Italian government assured Germany of the continuation of the war on Germany's side.

Whilst the Allies were successful in the south of Italy and the "Red Army" at the east front, the members of the resistance movement "Kreisauer Kreis" discussed for the first time the possibility of an overthrow of Hitler's regime. Only two days later, the German army was successful once more during the pocket battle of Kalach (east front). But by the battle for Charkov, the industrial city in the Ukraine, the German army suffered a big defeat at the end of August again.

Whilst the Soviet armies were also successful early in September, Pietro Badoglio announced on the radio on 8 September in Italy that he had agreed upon a cease-fire with the Allies, because for Italy it would be impossible to continue the war. One day later he informed Hitler about his step. Now German troops occupied Italy, because Italy had retired from the alliance with the German Empire. Also the German soldiers immediately began to disarm the Italian army. The Italian navy tried to escape towards Malta, but the Italian battleship "Roma" was sunk by the German air force while attempting to escape.

BESITZZEUGNIS

DEM

Paul Herings, Panzer grenadier

(NAME, DIENSTGRAD)

1.Pz.Gren.Rgt.11

(TRUPPENTEIL, DIENSTSTELLE)

IST AUF GRUND

SEINER AM 31. Juli 1943 ERLITTENEN

1. MALIGEN VERWUNDUNG – BESCHÄDIGUNG

DAS

VERWUNDETENABZEICHEN

IN Schwarz

VERLIEHEN WORDEN.

Lozitsch DEN 2. Sept. 194 3

(UNTERSCHRIFT)

Oberstabsarzt u.Chefarzt

(DIENSTGRAD UND DIENSTSTELLE)

Wounded in a senseless war, wounded for a madman!

Why?

On 10 September German troops occupied the Italian capital Rome, whilst the German soldiers withdrew from the Sea of Azov (part of the Black Sea/Russia). On 11 September took place hard combats between German troops and troops of the Allies in the south of Italy, close to Salerno. The victors of this battle were the Allies. One day later Hitler ordered to free Mussolini. A SS-special unit under the command of SS-Hauptsturmführer (Main-Storm-Leader) Otto Skorzeny carried out the order and freed Benito Mussolini, who was kept prisoner on the Gran-Sasso-Massif in Abruzzo. Mussolini was immediately taken to Vienna after his freeing. During this action the Allies in South Italy advanced towards north. Taranto and Brindise were occupied.

Early in October the Russian troops broke through the German front lines at several places. Therefore the Germans had to withdraw more and more, they had many casualties. Now also the new Italian government under Prime Minister Pietro Badoglio declared war on the German Reich/Empire. Thus the Italian government drew the conclusions from the encroachment on the Italian army by the Germans after the capitulation of Italy.

On 14 October took place the largest air battle over Germany. During a day attack of the Eighth American Air Force on Schweinfurt (town in the north of Bavaria) were 60 out of 291 American bombers brought down, after the battle other 17 bombers plunged into the North Sea and 121 bombers were so much damaged that they could no longer be put into action. Germany lost 50 aeroplanes during this battle. The American Air Force could start off with the next attacks only few months later because of the large number of lost aeroplanes.

On 3 November caused Heinrich Himmler a massacre. He had 40,000 Jews shot by machine-guns in prepared ditches in the concentration camp of Lublin/Poland. The SS designated this massacre as "Aktion Erntefest" (Action Harvest Festival). That was a terrible word for this crime.

On 28 November met the American President Franklin Delano Roosevelt the British Prime Minister Winston Churchill and the Soviet dictator Josef W. Stalin in Teheran/Iran. It was the first common meeting of the three heads of state. Till 1 December they discussed on the coordination of the military operations of their states and the new territorial division of Europe after the end of the war. Roosevelt made the suggestion to liquidate the German Empire and to found five new states: Prussia; Hannover (with Northwest Germany); Saxony; Hessen-Darmstadt (with Hessen-Kassel and the region to the south of the Rhine); and Bavaria (with Baden and Württemberg). Churchill wished an independent state Prussia and a new state "Austria-Hungary" with the countries Bavaria, the Palatinate, Baden and Württemberg. Stalin tended more towards the suggestion of Roosevelt, but there came no decision in the end.

In December the combats were continued in Russia and in Italy too. During these combats was also the German army successful, but in spite of that the withdrawal could not be prevented at both fronts.

We write the year 1944

On 1 January Field Marshal Rommel took command of the army group B in France. Thus Rommel had the command of all German troops to the north of the Loire (river). This day Count von Moltke and Count Yorck von Wartenburg were also arrested, they were the leading heads of the resistance movement "Kreisauer Kreis".

On 3 January reached the "Red Army" the former Polish frontier by Olevsk. The German front was broken down along a broad line in the north sector. Two days later began the Fifth American Army the offensive against the German winter line (Gustav-Line) in Italy. On 15 January American soldiers conquered Monte Trocchio, the last hindrance before Cassino. By it the operation against the German winter line came to an end.

Short Report from the Russian front lines

"South"Strong units of the Red Army, which had pushed back the troops of the German "Army Command South" from Dnieper to the south west until the end of December 1943, continued their attacks in early January. That happened in the large Dnieper bend north east of Krivoy Rog. – In mid-January the German Ninth Panzer Division still supported with some units the 15th Infantry Division, which had to take with the Panzer Division the section to west and east of Sofievka, 45 km north-east of Krivoy Rog. The largest part of the Division remained at the disposal of the 6th German Army; that was 20 km behind the front near Maryevka. As on 2 February superior forces of the Red Army could break into the German front along the railway line from Dnepropetrovsk to Kherson, there was a 25 km wide gap. After heavy fighting near Jekaterinovka, Mikhailovka, Wolnoye, Kamenka and Marienfeld, the Division separated from the enemy on 6 February. The Division took immediately a bolt position 50 km southeast from Krivoy Rog; that happened between Shesternya on Ingulez and Novo Woronzovka on the Dnieper.

From here it succeeded in lossy battles for Marinskoye, Bolshaya Kostromka and Petrovsky, to push back the enemy behind the rail hub of Apostolovo (Petrovskoye) Because of the favourable development of the situation the Ninth Panzer Division had to dodge behind the river Ingulez and to take positions between Arkhangelskoye (Kronau) and Annivka. – In early March, the Red Army continued its offensive and drove back the German forces from Ingulez. Then, on March 6, the Soviet units broke into the defence area of the Ninth German Panzer Division near Mirovka, 55 km south-west of Krivoy Rog. A little later the Soviet armies succeeded in the encirclement of several German divisions in the area southeast of Novy Bug. Also the Ninth Panzer Division came into the encirclement at the places Vladimirovka, Kristofo-rovka and Novo Sevastopol. On 14 March began the battered German forces to break out to west over the railway line Novy Bug – Nikolayev. In the courtyard Trawen several units of the Division were wiped out. The remainder could escape via Bashtanka and Privolnoye to the Bug River, which they crossed near Vosnessensk end of March. During these battles many German soldiers of the Ninth Panzer Division were missing. Many soldiers have fallen in battle, many fell into Soviet captivity. Many who were taken prisoner died on the way to the prison camps. Especially who was sick or wounded was not able to endure the arduous march to the camps. Insufficient clothing and food, as well as the epidemics caused by the inadequate sanitary conditions occurring there through the camps, led to numerous deaths.

On 20 January conquered the Russian troops the old town Novgorod and bared German troops' way towards Gulf of Finland to the west of Leningrad (St. Petersburg) Two days later landed the Fifth U.S.-American Army surprisingly by Anzio and Nettuno, to the south of Rome, and formed a bridgehead there.

On 24 January conquered the Russian troops the city of Smolkova in the north and interrupted by it the railway line from Narva (Estonia) to Leningrad, which was important for the German troops. Then, on 27 January, Russian military units drove out the German soldiers from the area of Leningrad, whilst in Italy the American troops advanced towards Rome. On 1 February British and American troops broke through the German Gustav-Line. One day later crossed Russian soldiers the frontier of Estonia by Narva and on 8 February conquered Soviet soldiers the centre of manganese of Nikopol and pushed back the Germans from the east bank of the river Dnieper on a length of 1,100 km. Then, on 14 February, the Soviet troops encircled the Germans by Cherkassy in the bend of the Dnieper River. But on 17 February the German soldiers could break through the encirclement, but they had also many casualties by breaking through the Russian lines; during these combats the British Air Force bombed Berlin and dropped 2,500 tons of bombs within only a half hour. Two days later the British and American air forces were flying wave after wave and dropped bombs onto the German cities. Main objective was the German aircraft industry; the German superiority in the air over the European continent should be broken. Germany lost more than 500 aeroplanes during these air battles. In revenge for the air raids of the Allies the German Air Force bombed the British capital London on 19 February. It was the heaviest attack since May 1941. During these days the Soviet army advanced more and more and recaptured town after town.

Feldpost

26.1.44

The page before: The last letter from Russia, the last letter before his death! He was killed in action for Hitler's Empire, killed for a madman and his Reich. Somewhere in Russia is his grave, but where exactly, it knows only the wind.

On 1 April were started off the mass transports of Jews from Southeast Europe into the extermination camp of Auschwitz in Poland, whilst the Soviet troops invaded Romania. On 4 April reconnaissance planes of the Allies took for the first time pictures of the extermination camp of Auschwitz. In the following days recaptured the Soviet troops the whole of the south of the Soviet Union and reached also the frontier of Slovakia.

Düsseldorf; like the most German cities, a landscape of ruins that was Germany in those days!

On 1 May the German troops could once more achieve a success by Anzio in Italy. A heavy attack of the Germans on the bridge-head forced the British troops there to withdraw. On 7 May attacked 2,000 British and American bombers Berlin and 1,000 bombers Bucharest, the capital of Romania. On 13 May left the last German soldiers the Crimea (Black Sea), whilst the Russian army continued to advance towards west. Also in Italy American and British troops could continue to advance towards north.

On 20 May bombed 6,000 British and American aeroplanes roads and bridges along a line of 250 km between Belgium and the Bretagne. By it should be prepared the invasion of the Allies in this area. Then, on 4 June, General Dwight D. Eisenhower gave the order to start off the operation "Overlord" (landing in the Normandy/North France) on 6 June. On 5 June broadcast the BBC a line of Paul Verlaine's poem "Chanson d'automne" as password to the French resistance for the beginning of the invasion; but in the year of 1943 the German counterintelligence under the leadership of Admiral Canaris had already deciphered the code at the first broadcasting of another line of this poem; now Germany knew, that the invasion was started off, but Rommel expected the invasion on the narrowest spot of the Channel, therefore the German troops in the Normandy were not warned. At 0:15 landed the first paratroopers of the 101st American Air Division on the Contentin Peninsula and by St.-Germain-de-Varreville. Then, at 6:30, the first military units of the 1st American Infantry Division landed on the "Omaha Beach", there they had many casualties caused by the German resistance. But British, Canadian and American soldiers could form several bridgeheads. At 15:00 Hitler gave the order to the counteroffensive. The landing operation of the Allies in the Normandy was unprecedented in the war history up to now: **D-Day**. The landing heads became one bridgehead till 10 June, a bridgehead of 90 km in length and 23 km in the width. It is true that the Germans could hold the town Caen (but only till 19 July) by putting a tanks' division in action, but the situation of the German troops worsened day by day. The Allies disembarked more than 600,000 soldiers for the bridgehead in two artificial harbours, "Mulberry A" and "Mulberry B", till the middle of July. Both harbours were mainly formed by swimming components. "Mulberry A" was already destroyed by storm on 19 June, but the advance of the Allies could not be stopped by it. Then, on 27 July, the American army succeeded in breaking through the German lines by St.-Lô.

D-Day. The landing of the Allied troops in Normandy on June 6, 1944.

At the end of June began also the great summer offensive of the "Red Army" against the German troops in Russia. On 2 July the Russian troops conquered Minsk, today capital of Belorussia. Few days later was conquered Vilnius, the capital of Lithuania and then at the end of July the Polish towns Brest-Litovsk and Przemyśl.

On 20 July was made an attempt on Hitler's life in his headquarters "Wolfsschanze" by Rastenburg in East Prussia. The culprit was Colonel Claus Graf/Count Schenk von Stauffenberg. Hitler should be killed by a bomb, which was in a bag and was put beside to him, during a meeting. The bomb exploded, but Hitler survived miraculously. After the failure of the occupation of the headquarters of command in Berlin and in the empire by units of the resistance fighters in the course of this day the military offices of the plotters in the Bendlerstraße (name of a street in Berlin) were occupied by regime-loyal troops in the evening. Stauffenberg, General Friedrich Olbricht, Colonel Albrecht Mertz von Quirnheim and First Lieutenant Werner von Haeften were shot dead by order of a court martial, also Colonel General Beck, who was designated for the post of the new head of state, was shot dead after an attempted suicide. Only in Paris and Vienna were the SS and the security service eliminated for a (very) short time. In Paris happened that under the command of General Carl Heinrich von Stülpnagel. But at midnight the rebellion broke down all over. Many high officers like Field Marshal General von Witzleben or officials and diplomats like Ulrich von Hassell, Count/Graf von der Schulenburg, Adam von Trott zu Solz and former politicians like Goerdeler, Leuschner, Leber and the Jesuit father Alfred Delp were sentenced to death by the "Volksgerichtshof" (People's Court), others like Field Marshal General Erwin Rommel were driven to suicide or were murdered in the concentration camps like the head of the counterintelligence,

Canaris, or General Hans Oster and the theologian Dieter Bonhoeffer. After the attempt on Hitler's life were 7,000 men arrested, 5,000 of them were executed, many in a horrible way.

Men of the German resistance

Julius Leber, Worker Union, executed in 1944

Claus Graf Schhenk von Stauffenberg, executed in1944

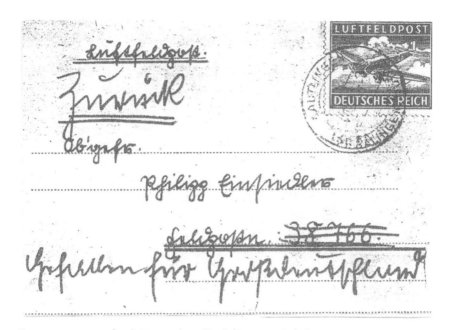

Return to sender! Note: he died (in Russia) for Great Germany! – Where are the German boys, where in Russia? Nobody knows it, only the wind! Many soldiers were missing anywhere in Russia, for ever!

On 1 August was cancelled the gipsy camp of Birkenau; before were taken 4,000 gipsies to the extermination camp of Auschwitz, there they were gassed. This day also broke out a rebellion in Warsaw. It was a rebellion of the Polish resistance movement against the German occupation troops. This rebellion was put down by SS-troops under the leadership of "Obergruppenführer" (Head Leader of the Group = a title of the SS) 'von dem Bach-Zelewski' (that was his complete name!). The Russian troops, which were already before Warsaw, didn't help the Polish rebels. The rebellion was lasting till 2 October, but then it broke down finally.

The Holocaust; execution of Jewish women in Latvia

On 17 August attacked 1,200 aeroplanes of the Allies the cities of Kiel (Schleswig-Holstein) and Stettin (Pomerania/today a Polish city -- officially since 1990, according to the peace treaty by which the territories that were occupied by Poland after the Second World War, have been recognized by Germany as Polish territories), they dropped 70,000 incendiary bombs. Both cities were only a sea of flames with thousands and thousands of dead bodies. This day had also the leading men of French Vichy-France, Marshal Pétain and Pierre Laval, to leave Vichy by order of Hitler. Now they tried to govern Vichy-France from Sigma-ringen (town in Baden-Württemberg), but in realty Vichy-France had come to an end. This day conquered the Second Canadian Division also the town Falaise in the north of France. Also Dreux, Orléans and Chartres were occupied by the troops of the Allies. The German troops, which were encircled since 13 August there, were wiped out and Vichy-France (South France) formed the Allies a bridgehead of a length of 75 km. This day the "Red Army" also crossed the first time the German frontier in East Prussia.

On 19 August reached the troops of the Allies under the command of General Patton the river Seine in France. One day later General Charles de Gaulle (few years later President of France) set foot on French ground and went immediately to General Eisenhower. From now also French troops combated again against Hitler-Germany. On 18 August a general strike had broken out in Paris, which had spread to struggles against the German occupation forces. As a result General Eisenhower sent the Second Tanks' Division of General Philippe Leclerc to Paris. In Romania Marshal Antonescu was arrested one day later, after that there was formed a new government. This new government immediately ceased fire against the Soviet Union and declared war on Germany on 24 August.

On 25 August marched French troops into Paris. The German troops had already left the city without combat before. With the French troops also came General Charles de Gaulle to Paris. Some days later also in Slovakia broke out combats against the German occupation forces and in Hungary the pro-German government was brought down whilst the Red Army invaded Romania and occupied Bucharest, the capital of this country.

On 1 September conquered Canadian soldiers the French towns Dieppe and Rouen, whilst the U.S. –American troops occupied Verdun and crossed the Belgian frontier. Only three days later British troops occupied the Belgian capital Brussels and the seaport Antwerp, whilst American troops advanced up to Lüttich (Liége). Then, on 8 September, the Belgian government in exile returned to Brussels, whilst the Germans the first missile of the world (V2) launched towards London. This so-called "wonder weapon" should still bring about the "Endsieg" (final victory) of the German Empire; that was Hitler's dream. On 8 September marched the Soviet troops into Bulgaria and formed immediately a communistic government, which declared war on Germany some days later.

On 12 September crossed U.S.-American soldiers the first time the German frontier by Aachen (the town of Charles the Great). Two days later the (new) Polish army and Russian troops got into Warsaw.

On 17 September was the offensive of the Allies forced. The British general Montgomery let strong airborne troops dropped by Grave, Nimwegen/Nijmegen and Arnheim/Arnhem (cities in the Netherlands), what happened behind the German front line, to take the bridges over Maas, Waal and Rhine (the main rivers in the Netherlands). Then, by Nijmegen, the British could form a corridor, but by Arnhem failed the operation. There the Allies met with stiff resistance of the 9th and 10th SS-Tanks' Division (The famous movie of this event: The Bridge of Arnhem). Two days later the Finnish and the Soviet (Russian) government arranged a cease-fire in the east. Finland lost a large area (Karelia) and Germany was now missing an important ally in the east.

On 25 September signed Hitler a decree to the creation of the "Deutscher Volkssturm" (German People's Storm = Germany's last reserves). According to this decree were to put into defensive action all men who were between 16 and 60 years old (the so-called "Kinder- und Greisenarmee"/Children and Old Man Army). Martin Bormann, Hitler's secretary, had the job to organize these last reserves now.

On 26 September withdrew the British troops over the Rhine by Oosterbeek (town in the Netherlands) again. They had lost the battle for Arnhem. The operation "Market Garden" cost the life of 17,000 soldiers of the Allies. During the combats in the Netherlands advanced the "Red Army" more and more towards west. Then, on 29 September, the first Russian soldiers reached the Czechoslovakian border; they had advanced in a breadth of 270 km. On 5 October began the "Red Army" the offensive against the German Memel-Land (in the northeast of East Prussia). One day later crossed units of the Russian army and the (new) "First Czechoslovakian Corps" the Hungarian frontier. On 7 October tried prisoners of the extermination camp of Auschwitz in vain to blow up the crematories. All rebels were shot dead by the SS-guard.

The horror of the Holocaust. Jews are victims of an SS-Einsatztruppe in Poland.

On 9 October was the German town Memel encircled by the "Red Army", the German resistance was to break down soon there. Only two days later Hungary and the Soviet Union agreed on a cease fire. Now Germany was without an ally in Europe. In Asia Japan combated against the U.S.A. only. On 2 November left the last German soldiers Greece, only the island Crete was left in Germany's hand. On 2 November were also stopped the gassings in the extermination camp of Auschwitz. Three days later were the German troops successful once more in the east; they could recapture the German town Goldap in East Prussia.

On 8 November began the American troops under the command of General Patton with the offensive towards Saarland. Then, ten days later, the "Third U.S.-American Army" crossed the frontier between France and Germany.

On 20 November left Hitler his headquarters "Wolfsschanze" in East Prussia because the "Red Army" had already advanced too near. Now he moved into the "Reichskanzlei" (Chancellor Office) of Berlin, his last headquarters, whilst the "First French Army" recaptured Belfort and Metz and advanced to the Rhine River. On 23 November was occupied Straßburg by French soldiers. From now on, this city bore the name Strasbourg again; it was the name that it had borne in the French period.

On 2 December crossed American soldiers the "West Wall" (the so-called Siegfried Line/Siegfried = the hero of the Germanic legend) by Saarlautern (today Saarlouis/Sarrelouis) Two weeks later started off General Model with the German "Ardennes' Offensive" (Ardennes = the Belgian part of the Eifel, the ranges between Belgium, Luxembourg and Germany). The offensive began in the area between Monschau (little German town at the Belgian frontier) and Echternach (little town in Luxembourg), it was the so-called "Operation Herbstnebel". Also that was a "blitzkrieg" again, because the Allies didn't know it and were therefore taken unaware. But after one week the surprise offensive was brought to a stop because the German army was lacking in fuel. This offensive was Hitler's last military success in the west. On 27 December were the German troops pushed back again in Belgium. One day later also Hungary declared war on

Germany. It was a terrible war for both sides with much suffering. But Hitler was still dreaming of the "final victory". Who ever hung his hopes upon so frail a twig? The war was continued with thousands and thousands of casualties and the horror for the German population in the east was to be following.

Late summer 1944, on the border in the east the Soviet armies were waiting for the invasion of Germany. On 16 October they began with the great offensive. Their aim was Königsberg, the great Prussian city in the German province East Prussia. From August to the middle of October East Prussia and Silesia were quiet regions, but the inferno was to be not long in coming, more than 2 million Russian soldiers forced even the extermination of Hitler's Germany, the extermination of a nation of beasts in their eyes. The terrible end of an ancient empire was approaching, an end full of cruelty. The great flight of more than 12 million Germans, mostly women and children, led off. Also the family of my wife had to have first-hand experience of the horror end of the war and the German nation, a nation that was led into the abyss by a fanatic man. The family of my wife lived in Königsberg, the proud city of Prussia in the east. Before the storming of East Prussia the Russian author Ilya Ehrenburg called upon the Russian soldiers to start the great slaughter. "The Germans are no human beings; they are animals, therefore notice soldier! There in Germany a beast hides; this beast has killed your child, has violated your wife, your bride and sister, has shot dead your mother and father, has burnt down your home. Go and hate this beast and wipe out this enemy; that is your holy duty, your duty to go into the hell of this beast in order to take revenge for the blood of your comrades, killed in action, for the agony of our people, revenge for the murder victims and the raped women."

The family of my wife had no presentiment of the hatred of the Russians against the Germans. My mother-in-law had the good luck to leave East Prussia; she had to do it according to an order of the authority, but many other members of the family did not have this luck, they had to have first-hand experience of the Russian hatred against Germans. – Women with 4 and more children were evacuated, had to leave all regions in the east of the empire, they were intended to be out of harm's way during the big storming that was now expected. The other women were ordered to stay, to defend their home against the "aggressor" from the east; Hitler's slogan was namely: "The final victory is certain, our proud armies defend home and country, after that they march back, defeat the armies of our enemies. Therefore the east of Germany cannot be depopulated." That was an error of the Nazi-regime; the great flight began few weeks later, the flight of the 12 million Germans.

My mother-in-law was on the platform of the station of Königsberg, on her side her four children, also her parents were with her, but they could not leave East Prussia, what they did not want too. My father-in-law fought at the western front in those days. Now, on the platform in Königsberg, the engine driver called upon the people to board the waggons and the few carriages. My mother-in-law said goodbye to her parents. "We'll soon see us again, therefore don't be sad. We'll come back. But the Russians, what will they do unto you?" "Don't worry, we did not harm them, therefore they will also not harm us." But that was a terrible error; they suffered the fate of thousands and thousands of other German women, children and old men there in the east, killed by Russians who were in murder intoxication. Nobody knows whether they were killed or died during the flight of the last Germans there in the east. But one can be certain that they were hurriedly buried, there somewhere in the east of the former German Empire. Now so many Germans had to suffer for what criminals of the Nazi regime had done to the Jews. It was the revenge of the history, the sorrow of innocent persons.

Before my mother-in-law had said goodbye to her parents and boarded one of the carriages, she had embraced her mother and father, whilst tears were running over her face. After that her parents could not let go of their grandchildren. "We are so missing you." More they could not say because there was the last call for boarding. "Till later, in Königsberg, our home." Everybody could now hear when the train left the station. People who were waving their relatives burst into tears and watched as the train disappeared in the distance.

Now an odyssey began, which brought my mother-in-law to Dresden. There she stayed for several weeks. She lived with her children and some other persons in one room and slept on a wooden board together with her children. An administrative body of the city had to take care of them. But the hygienic conditions were catastrophic. She was happy when she got the possibility to leave this city that was already overcrowded with fugitives. Thus she did not see the big catastrophe, the terrible fire attack by British and American bombers, the complete destruction of the baroque city with thousands and thousands of killed persons, mostly women and children.

The next aim of the odyssey was Lower Bavaria. There they found the next place of refuge. In an old farmer house they were allowed to move into two rooms. The farmer was not enthusiastic about the new occupants (or tenants? But they had no money, the country Bavaria had to pay!) The farmer himself had children who needed place and now the Prussian woman with four children; that he did not want indeed, that he could not accept, but he had it to do, it was order of the government. So there was tension enough. Some months later both sides accepted the awkward situation and my mother-in-law could be happy because many other people did not have rooms, they were living in ruins, stables, cowsheds, corrugated iron huts or simply in the streets, sleeping on blankets there if they had.

Königsberg is now called Kaliningrad and is located in the eponymous Russian exclave.

The last heads of the German Empire

		Title
Friedrich Ebert	1919 - 1925	Reichs-präsident
Paul von Hindenburg	1925 - 1934	Reichs-präsident
Adolf Hitler	*1934 - 1945*	*Führer*
Karl Dönitz	*1945*	*Reichs-präsident*

The Great Escape
and
the end of the German Empire
(forever!)

We write the year **1945**

The east front came nearer; the first Russian soldiers had already passed the German frontier. The appeal of the Russian general Ivan D. Chernyakhovsky from October 1944: **"There is no mercy – to nobody, as there was also no mercy to us. There is unnecessary to demand from the soldiers of the Red Army that they have to have mercy on Germans. They are full of hatred and vindictiveness for them. We must make a waste land from the country of fascists like they did it with our country".** So Russian soldiers had full of hatred conquered the little German village Nemmersdorf (today the Russian village "Mayakovskoye) in East Prussia and killed all women and children there. The campaign against the "German pigs" had begun by it in the east. Few weeks later also began the great escape of the Germans.

On 1 January attacked the German Air Force once more the airfields of the Allies in North France, Belgium and in the Netherlands. The result: 800 aeroplanes of the Allies were destroyed. But the Allies hit back already one day later, 1,000 aeroplanes bombarded the German cities of Ludwigshafen, Nürnberg (Nuremberg) and Berlin.

The NS leadership did not hesitate to send children into battle as the last contingent of the Reich. Their end was death or imprisonment. – American soldier and German boys.

On 3 January was started off also the great offensive of the "First U.S.-American Army" in the Ardennes (Belgium). The Americans advanced towards Houffalize now.

On 6 January the Germans could achieve a success in the Southeast. In Hungary they broke through the Russian lines and could advance 200 km towards east. One day later German soldiers conquered the Hungarian fortress Esztergom, which was occupied by Russian soldiers in the meantime. Esztergom is situated on the Danube, in the north-west from Budapest.

Germans on the run. The march through the ruins of a little town in East Prussia. Temperature: - 25° C!!! A march into the death!!?

On 8 January Hitler gave the order that the German troops had to withdraw towards west. The new front line should now be the line Dochamps-Longchamps.

On 12 January the Soviets started off the great offensive on all fronts in the East. That produced the mass escape of the German population towards west; the greatest escape of the world history began. This day East Prussia was befallen by the catastrophe. Early in the morning roared everywhere the Russian guns and crushed the German positions. The Russian armies succeeded in advancing to the Baltic Sea coast within some days; by it they barred the landed escape route of the German population. From Tilsit to Johannesburg, from Goldap to Elbing (those were towns in East Prussia) were 2,500,000 Germans in the trap now; these were women, children and old men, who couldn't be evacuated in time before because Hitler had prohibited that. Now they were encircled from three sides, their only escape route was the way over the Baltic Sea. The despairing people fled, panic-stricken, to the seaports. Nothing was prepared, the German government had failed; the plans of evacuation lay still in the drawers. The people were waiting in many places for an order to escape. There were often members of the Nazi-party who first fled helter-skelter with their families in view of the menace. They burnt files and papers in a hurry and left on the quiet their offices. Their wards like women, children and old men, who were prohibited on penalty of death for months any preparation for the escape, had to see alone how they could save their life.

Now, in the middle of January, all people of East Prussia were on the run. Wagons, carts and carriages of the fugitives lined up without end. The big treks moved through the whole of East Prussia towards west, but where exactly to, nobody knew it. The temperature had sunk in the meantime onto - 25° C. Deep snow and heavy snow flurry obstructed the flight. The wheels of the wagons got stuck in the mass of snow, the axles broke. On the icy roads slipped the horses over and over again, wagons placed themselves crosswise and hindered the following wagons. The country roads and avenues, which were very narrow, were divided in halves: one side had to be kept clear for the German army, which forced its way towards main front line. That led often to accidents, the army trucks and tanks pushed the fugitives aside, swept along them and damaged heavily their wagons. But the soldiers didn't have time to take care of the fate of the fugitives. The military situation was a catastrophe; everywhere were the German lines broken through, were overrun by the Russian superiority. The German soldiers struggled for their own life; they endeavoured to hold the front till the moment of a certain security for the civilian population. In spite of that it happened often that they stopped their vehicles to share a warm soup with the exhausted fugitives or to give old and weak persons a lift in their military trucks for some kilometres. Many long-serving soldiers, who had already seen much grief on the way through Russia, had pity on fugitives and their misery. "Wir in unseren Militärfahrzeugen waren meist gegen Witterung geschützt, aber die Flüchtlinge waren ihr hilflos ausgesetzt. Diese armen Leute, die mit den Trecks flüchteten! Hinten am Wagen hingen vielleicht eine, zwei Kühe, vorne zogen ein paar magere Pferde. Ach, das war wirklich ein Elend!", remembered a former tank driver. (We were mostly protected against the weather in our military vehicles, but the fugitives were helplessly exposed to it. These poor people, who fled with the treks! At the rear of the wagon hung perhaps one, two cows, in front of the wagon were lean horses pulling it. Oh, that was a real misery!)

The grim coldness demanded soon the first sacrifices. Some few hours after their departure were many fugitives already freezing through and through and very desperate. The coldness was above all to the little children and old men a mortal danger. The little children died first because of missing of sufficient clothing, weakening by the strains of the flight and a lack of food: babies froze to death in the arms of their mothers, who had pressed them desperately against the own body. By the warmth of their bodies they tried to protect the babies against the icy coldness. But when the nappies were drenched and there was no dry article of clothing for changing, then the babies had no chance to survive. A trail of misery showed the ways in East Prussia: there were left baby carriages with stiff-frozen little bodies on the edge of the roads, dead babies, who were wrapped in rags, rose out from the snow-drifts. The mothers had seldom time enough to bury their babies. The hard frozen ground also made it impossible to dig a grave. Each attempt failed.

The sight of dead bodies became soon a cruel matter of habit to the fugitives. The people became insensible by each step on the agonizing way towards west, pity and solidarity came more and more to grief. The own existential menace often blinded the grief of the others. Food and hot water were not shared. Everybody thought of himself only. At many people the provisions already run short after few days. Circumspect persons had only reckoned with a long march over some weeks, perhaps lasting many months. With the coldness also came the hunger. Some few succeeded sometimes in milking a cow, since all over moved huge cow flocks through the country in the east; also they were on the run from the Russian troops or were bellowing in the snow-covered meadows and fields. Many farmers had to leave their cows behind during their flight and so to leave them to their fate. Because the cows couldn't be milked, swelled their udders, suppurated and hurt. The bellowing of the cows was uncanny for many fugitives. Now and then was a cow milked by the fugitives, but the mass of them didn't have time for that. But also that little bit milk couldn't help, the lack of food generally led to faintness and stomach and bowel complaints. Especially old persons weren't up to the strains of the flight. Squatted down under blankets they died silently and unnoticed in the horse-drawn vehicles, at the back. The relatives had no choice but to bury scantily in hurry the dead bodies in the snow and to speak a short prayer, then they were swallowed again by the endless stream of fugitives.

When on 23 January leaked the news out that the Russians had already reached the coast near Elbing and so barred the way of the fugitives, decided many of them to return; but that was a return into the death, a return into the arms of the Russian soldiers who were full of hate. Also fugitives, who didn't return, were often overrun by Russian tanks. When ever there was a rattling noise by Russian tanks then always broke panic out amongst the fugitives within the trek. If they weren't successful in leaving the road in time and didn't find cover in a ditch, they were mercilessly rolled down by the tanks. The heavy tanks buried under themselves carts and horse-drawn vehicles, crushed persons and horses. It was a horrible sight.

Since the escape route by land was barred, some hundred thousand people tried to escape over the ice of the "Haff" (lagoon) to march then on the "Frische Nehrung" (Vistula Spit, the name of a sand bar in East Prussia) for reaching the seaports Danzig and Pillau. In the last weeks of January was the ice still thick enough to carry the heavy load. But in February decreased the coldness and to the fugitives arose a new danger. The ice, that covered the "Haff", became day after day thinner and thinner. Behind the back of the fugitives combated the "Fourth German Army" desperately against the Russians to win space and time for the poor people who were marching towards coast in long treks. In the meantime, a merciless fortress combat had broken out in Königsberg, the beautiful capital of East Prussia. This beautiful city was besieged by Russian troops since the last days of January. The life got more and more worse each day for the inhabitants there, they frighteningly squatted in the cellars of the house ruins, which arose to the sky after the heavy air raids of the summer of the year of 1944 like black stumps.

The last trains towards west had left Königsberg at the end of January. At the stations, there were going on dramatic scenes. The people despairingly crowded on the platforms to get into the few railway carriages. Mothers hugged tight their children to close them not in the surge of people. When the train finally started to move, panic broke out on the platforms; the mothers, whose children were already in the train, despairingly tried to get still into the train, they clung from outside to the railway carriages and climbed to the roofs of the travelling train. But many people failed the strength on the long way through the icy coldness and heavy snowstorms – their blue-frozen fingers slipped off; they lost the hold and fell from the running boards or the roofs of the carriages. The most fugitives didn't survive that. Russian fighter bombers also fired over and over again at the trains. Then the trains had to stop between the stations and the people burst screaming out the carriages to look for cover somewhere in the white landscape, but there they didn't often find a cover and became fair game for the Russian fighter bombers, which started off the hunt for the "German pigs" now.

On the run in East Prussia

Whilst the East fell into the catastrophe, U.S.-American soldiers conquered Houffalize and advanced towards St. Vith (East Belgium). By it the German offensive failed in the Ardennes. In Hungary the last Hungarian soldiers capitulated to the Russian soldiers of the "Red Army". Now the new (communistic) Hungarian government declared war on Germany on 18 January. On 29 January crossed Russian troops, from East Prussia coming, the frontier of Pomerania and advanced to Waldenberg, there they were 190 km before Berlin only.

The last days of East Prussia were the saddest days, which had ever seen this nice and proud country. 2,500,000 German women, children and old men were on the run there, were caught in the endless stream of the treks, were crowded together in the seaports Danzig and Pillau. Who reached the "Frische Nehrung/Vistula Spit" and had the good fortune to get on board of one of the overfull ships, thought to be saved. Many people swallowed hard: "the life is going on, that's not yet the end". But the people were very much mistaken there. Their way of suffering did not yet reach the end. After they had abandoned their homes in East Prussia, they were caught in the merciless mills of the war to the west of this country; they were taken hold of Russian troops or died of hunger and typhoid in the camps. But when they were on board of the fugitive's ships they thought to be safe, that was a mistake too.

Cows on the run; cow trek in East Prussia

During those days of the great flight also the "Wilhelm Gustloff" rode at anchor in the seaport Gotenhafen (today: Gdynia). There this ship seated fugitives now. On 25 January had the first big convoy of ships started with fugitives from Pillau towards west; now other fugitives, whose way was barred by the "Red Army", forced their way towards the ships, which still rode at anchor there. Also in Gotenhafen, that had the longest ship's landing place in the east, the pier was more than 14 km long, crowded thousands and thousands of fugitives in those days. Many smaller ships, coming from Pillau and Memel, arrived with other fugitives now there. So the landing place of Oxhöft (a district of Gotenhafen/Gdynia) filled more and more with other masses of fugitives, who were also waiting for bigger ships, together with the first thousands and thousands. All wanted to leave as quickly as possible the hell of East Prussia.

On 21 January "Grand Admiral" Dönitz/Doenitz, who was commander-in-chief of the German navy, had already given the order to transfer the "Submarine-Teaching-Division" and the "female helpers of the navy", both were stationed up to now in Gotenhafen, to west. But the ships to this transport should pick up also fugitives, so the "Hansa" 3,000 fugitives – the "Hamburg" 5,000 fugitives – the "Deutschland" 6,000 fugitives and the "Wilhelm Gustloff" also 6,000 fugitives. Also some smaller ships should transport fugitives, but all together not more than 30,000 persons. But in Gotenhafen were 90,000 fugitives. When the news was spread that the last ships with fugitives would soon leave the seaport, everybody of the fugitives knew that there was not enough space for all of them. And when now the ships opened their gates, all fugitives forced onto board. On 25 January so also the "Wilhelm Gustloff" opened their gates. The captain of the "Wilhelm Gustloff" let fugitives go first, who had an orderly ticket. But the sailors and female helpers of the navy couldn't bring themselves to reject the persons without ticket, persons, who were all frozen stiff. The "Wilhelm Gustloff" had the order to transport above all mothers with their children. But where was the limit? At the pier were also waiting women with their fourteen or fifteen years old sons, some looked like older persons after the strenuous flight. The mothers despairingly declared that their boys would still be children and that they would need them urgently for the care of the younger siblings. If the sailors and female helpers of the navy would let enter the teenagers the ship now, then they risked annoyance with the "Feldjäger" (Field Hunters = Military Police), who were looking for young men for the "total war" in the crowded city of Gotenhafen.

The "Wilhelm Gustloff"

The belly of the ship (Wilhelm Gustloff) slowly and systematically filled with people. At the pier piled up the sleighs and pieces of luggage, which were left behind. Some prosperous fugitives had to be energetically convinced of missing of space for several bags or projecting wardrobe trunks. Everybody could soon hear that all cabins were taken. But the people continued to push their way over the wooden gangway of the "Wilhelm Gustloff". Each one was registered by name and confronted with the question, who should be informed in case of a misadventure. Many people couldn't answer the question because their relatives and friends were also on the run or were killed on the front or were missing. The fugitives always had to clear the way, when a new transport of wounded soldiers was arriving from the front or female helpers of the navy hurried into the "Wilhelm Gustloff".

Inside of the ship the crew began to improvise. The furniture of the music hall, of the banqueting hall, of the cinema and theatre was removed and was replaced by mattresses. Quite near of the sickroom was established a delivery station for pregnant fugitive's women.

On 28 January reached the big ship "Wilhelm Gustloff" its limit of capacity. The last cabin was taken – it was kept clear for the family of the leader of the NSDAP of the "District Gotenhafen". Now the passageways had to serve as whereabouts for the stream of fugitives. The crew had to watch with uneasy feeling how the fugitives blocked up the emergency exits by mattresses and pieces of luggage. Also the indoor pool was converted into a dormitory. Here, on the deepest deck of the ship, the female helpers of the navy found their accommodation – some metres under the surface of the water.

It was still necessary to assign space to the fugitives. The most fugitives don't care where they found accommodation. They were glad to have really found a space on board; they thought also to have found a safe refuge there and so to have escaped the hell.

The crew of the "Wilhelm Gustloff" tried to help the exhausted people according to their possibility. The crowded ship was loaded with a gigantic lot of foodstuffs, whilst the female Navy assistants (Marinehelferinnen) took care of the children. Some little girls and boys had lost their mothers or other persons of their company during their expedition through the ship. So everybody on board of the "Wilhelm Gustloff" could soon hear the first search reports by loudspeakers.

The "Wilhelm Gustloff" had only 12 lifeboats for 700 persons. The remaining lifeboats were in need of foundations of fog throwers, which were in action in case of air raids. But now thousands of fugitives crowded on board of the "Wilhelm

Gustloff". The captain had still can muster Marine boats and cork rafts for some 5,000 persons with difficulty. The Marine boats and rafts were loaded in hurry on the sun deck and moored there. On each raft could take seat 2 – 10 persons in case of emergency. So the most passengers had a seat in case of emergency, the remaining persons had to help themselves by life jackets. That was enough to the official passengers, who had registered, but there were more, because the careful registration of the fugitives was stopped late in the afternoon of January, 29. The remaining pages of the scribbling pads of the "Marinehelferinnen" were full-written; on the registration list was written the last number: 7,956. That was the number of the fugitives who were already on board 20 hours before the departure of the "Wilhelm Gustloff". A "Marinehelferin" estimated that more than 2,000 persons went still aboard after the registration, so there were more than 10,000 persons on board of the "Wilhelm Gustloff" when this ship finally left the seaport of Gotenhafen on 30 January. At 13:00 the "Wilhelm Gustloff" left the harbour of Gotenhafen-Oxhöft and put to sea. The captain didn't know where he has to navigate his ship to. Only at sea he should be informed about his way: perhaps Kiel or Flensburg. Not more than two days would be lasting the journey.

Some nautical miles to the west of the "Wilhelm Gustloff" the Russian captain of the submarine "S 13" tried to keep the crew happy. It was Alexander Marinesko, an alcoholic, who should resign his job on "S 13" after a boozing tour, but his crew interceded with the commanders for him and could prevent his removal. Marinesko now needed a success to rehabilitate his ruined reputation. Since 11 January he was looking for a great success. There was to expect that the German ship traffic towards west increases strongly in the next few days. Marinesko's mission wasn't harmless. The convoys from the Bay of Danzig had a massive escort at their disposal and the waters weren't deep but were strongly mined. Whilst the "Red Army" stormed forward more and more in East Prussia, the "S 13" was waiting for the first contact with the enemy, till January, 30.

The "Wilhelm Gustloff" was already received by rough sea out of the harbour basin. Many seasick passengers needed help. During the lashing snowstorm fell the temperature more and more and showed already considerable degrees below zero in the afternoon. The upper deck of the "Wilhelm Gustloff" was soon covered with a thick ice layer. The bad weather caused above all the escorting boats trouble; the little ships couldn't keep up by the high waves. After a voyage of a half hour the captain of the "Wilhelm Gustloff" had already to notify to the control station of Gotenhafen that he had sent back the little torpedo boats and that he would now expect a new escort. When the "Wilhelm Gustloff" passed the Hel Peninsula (Hela) some minutes later, the "Hansa" (name of this ship) was already waiting for the "Wilhelm Gustloff" here. The "Hansa" should now be the escort of the "Wilhelm Gustloff". The "Wilhelm Gustloff" didn't get speed. Soon the captain of the "Wilhelm Gustloff" received the following radio message: "Hansa manövrierunfähig – Maschinenschaden" (Hansa unable to manoeuvre, – machine damage). This message the crew of the "Wilhelm Gustloff" had feared. The captain had to make a decision now. Should he wait for a new escort and risk that on board a tumult breaks out or should he expose the ship to the attack from the air? He couldn't expect support, because also the torpedo boats, which he had sent back, had machine damages. So the "Wilhelm Gustloff" was only escorted by the little torpedo boat "Löwe", which forced its way through the waves in front of the bow of the "Wilhelm Gustloff". "Ein Hund führt einen Riesen durch die

Nacht" (A dog guides a giant through the night) sarcastically commented the captain of the "Wilhelm Gustloff" on that.

At 18 o'clock the radio mate notified that some (German) mine-sweepers approached the "Wilhelm Gustloff" directly and that by it the "Wilhelm Gustloff" would run the risk of a collision. Because the "Wilhelm Gustloff" sailed as a precaution without lights in the darkness, the captain now decided to set position lights to avoid to be rammed by the minesweepers. A member of the crew, who had survived the catastrophe, was puzzled to date, that none of the radio operators of the "Wilhelm Gustloff" or "Löwe" had received any radio message about the approaching minesweepers. The "Wilhelm Gustloff" didn't really meet minesweepers in this night. From where the message about approaching minesweepers came, was never settled. Was it sabotage or only a misunderstanding? It's a fact, definitely: the position lights were the decisive link in the line of incidents, which led to the tragedy of the "Wilhelm Gustloff".

When the lights of the "Wilhelm Gustloff" were switched on, some members of the crew couldn't believe their eyes, a bright-illuminated ship within enemy waters, impossible.

Around 19 o'clock was sounded the alert by the sailor of the lookout of the Russian submarine "S 13". There was anything, a ship or a convoy of ships, he would see lights, which didn't belong to the coast. Captain Marinesko put on the alert his radio station. A Russian radio operator remembered: "I could hear the rotation of two screws of a ship. It might be a big ship in front of us". The crew of the "S 13" was electrified. Was that the chance that they were waiting for? Marinesko had hurried through the submarine and said: "We take the offensive, but I cannot promise, whether we'll survive here".

"S 13" sailed on the water surface. Marinesko had quickly given up the idea to dive, because he had only a chance to hit the bow of the enemy ship from the water surface. The position lights of the ship also did not suggest that there was particular vigilance on board. Marinesko decided to sail around the sea giant and its little escorting boat in a big curve and then to approach from the land side. From here would nobody guess an attack and the submarine would be invisible against the dark background of the coast, but the manoeuvres were still risky, because the waters offshore were mined and the depth was only 30 m there; so there was no possibility to dive. But Alexander Marinesko took the risk.

During these minutes the fugitives on board of the "Wilhelm Gustloff" prepared for the night. The last days were coined by mad rush and dread, now they needed rest; they also felt out of danger. – The Russian submarine "S 13" had finished its manoeuvres of encirclement at 20:45. Now the "S 13" was on parallel course between "Wilhelm Gustloff" and the coast, about 2,000 metres from this giant ship. Alexander Marinesko instructed his crew to make ready the torpedoes for the launching. 21:05, the beginning of the catastrophe, the "S 13" approached the "Wilhelm Gustloff" up to 700 metres. Then it happened. At 21:15 the "Wilhelm Gustloff" was shaken by a deafening bang; then it followed the second explosion before the passengers could realize what happened. In this moment came the commando from the bridge of the "Wilhelm Gustloff": "Maschine stopp!" (stop ship engine) and the lights went out. After that followed the third detonation, still louder than the both before, then there was silence. The crew of the "Wilhelm Gustloff" knew, that were torpedoes.

The female helpers of the navy, who were in the swimming room of the E-deck, were already beyond all hope. The first torpedo had smashed into the front of the ship and had hit the living section of the crew there. The second torpedo detonated just under the swimming room (baths); that was the death warrant for the girls there. The third torpedo hit the centre of the ship, quite near of the machine-room, and burst open the boarding wall up to the rail. Tons of water got through the hole into the ship now and shot up with enormous force to the upper decks. Within some minutes the bow plummeted several metres. When the captain burst to the bridge, the front of the "Wilhelm Gustloff" was already under the rolling breakers. On the lower decks had broken loose all hell. From there the passengers tried panic-stricken to find a way to the upper decks. But after some minutes the gangways were hopelessly jammed up. One who remembered, said: "Tiere in Not sind schlimm, aber Menschen in einer solchen Situation sind schlimmer als Tiere. Es hieß nur noch: Rette sich, wer kann"(Animals in trouble are bad, but people are worse than animals in such situation. It said only: Every Man for himself) Many persons, who moved towards the upper decks, were trampled to death by other persons, who tried to push past them. It was a chaos, no discipline. Discipline had maybe saved the life of many persons. On upper deck had broken out the combat for the lifeboats. A great part of the life rafts was frozen to the boards and the fastening of the lifeboats was coated with ice of some centimetres. The sailors could the metal eyes only break off by force from the deck. The frightened fugitives built up in front of the lifeboats. The sailors endeavoured with pistols, the safety catches of them were realized, to cover the incensed crowd. When old men tried to get hold of a seat in the lifeboats before women and children, were fired the first shots.

Fugitives, who had survived the catastrophe, said later that the evacuation of the people on board was a hopeless chaos. But the command of the "Wilhelm Gustloff" trusted in the illusive safety of the ship. The rescue efforts have been made even difficult by the accommodation of a great part of the crew in the front of the ship, where the first torpedo hit in. The bulkheads were immediately shut to hamper the water to penetrate more in the ship. The men, who knew extremely well the ship and could help therefore, were already dead some minutes after the first detonation.

Whilst the crew succeeded in evacuating at least some fugitives from the upper deck, a drama was developing inside of the ship. In illusive faith to reach the upper deck, some hundred passengers had thronged into the glazed lower promenade deck. A sailor saw to his dismay, how one passenger after the other thronged into this deck, which turned out to be a deadly trap. He reported later: "Whilst I ran past the people, I yelled at them: Turn around because there you have no possibility to get out! But it isn't possible to placate the crowd or bring this mass of persons to senses". It was presented to the passengers, who were in front of the glass partition of the promenade deck, a horrible sight. The "Wilhelm Gustloff" sank more and more. Behind the glass front were persons, who gasped for breath, whilst the water was rising higher and higher. Some sailors tried to break the safety glass of the promenade deck from outside by ice picks, but in vain. Military security officers shot at the glass from inside, but the glass didn't break. The people were imprisoned in a coffin of glass. The "Wilhelm Gustloff" inclined about 30 degrees now. The fugitives slipped helplessly on the icy upper deck. Who could hold himself climbed hand over hand along the rail. Who stayed behind in the exits could see to his horror, how the "flak" (antiaircraft gun), which was positioned on the bridge deck of the "Wilhelm Gustloff", loosened by the increasing angle of inclination of the ship and then rushed loudly towards the rail and tore the people away there, into the depth of the Baltic Sea.

The loudspeakers of the ship implored the passengers over and over again to keep quiet, the "Wilhelm Gustloff" would never sink and rescue would be already on the way. But who could believe that in view of the icy waves, which were breaking over deck at regular intervals!? There happened cruel scenes on board. – A scene like many other scenes: A little boy had reached the upper deck with his family in the meantime. His mother had to take care simultaneously of three children. She held the boys tight and close to her side, one child on her arms. When she found a frozen life raft at the rail now, she said to her youngest son: "Sit down in this raft and do not move from the spot." That was the last time that he had heard the voice of his mother. When the "Wilhelm Gustloff" inclined again, loosened his raft and slid crosswise over deck. The boy had asked himself over and over again the question later, what was going on in the thoughts of his mother when she saw, how her youngest son was sliding towards the waters of the sea. She was always worried and had paid attention to her children that no child got lost. The raft crashed against the rail of the other side of the ship and the boy fell into the sea. There he was immediately drawn into another life raft. Some minutes later approached the torpedo boat "Löwe", rope ladders were hung down and all tried to climb up, but the little boy was drawn back by anybody and some minutes later he was alone. More than a half hour later he saw a drifting lifeboat and he cried for help, but nobody answered. Then short time later he became aware of a companion, who hung in the stop lines of the raft. It was a young soldier. Now the little boy tried to pull the helpless soldier into the life raft, but he was too weak, he was just few years old. Still some time later he saw that the soldier was dead, but his dead body accompanied the little boy through the night. – The little boy was rescued later, but the other members of his family found their graves on the ground of the Baltic Sea.

The moment, in which the passengers of the "Wilhelm Gustloff" dived into the water, had put out the reminiscences of many of them, who had survived. The most of them had only survived few minutes in the cold water. The air temperature had minus 18° C and the water temperature had just 0° C. Many people of the "Wilhelm Gustloff" were taken by surprise by the torpedo hit whilst they were sleeping; therefore the most of them were only dressed with a nightie or a thin jacket. Many fugitives had used their life jackets as pillows and they didn't make it somehow possible to put on the swimming helps, which had saved their life, within the seconds which they had only. Around the sinking ship the cries of the drowning persons reverberated. The persons, who had got hold of a seat in a lifeboat, tried to row rapidly away from the "death ship". They feared to come into the suction of the ship whilst it was sinking. The "Wilhelm Gustloff" held still, but its bow inclined deeper and deeper. Inside of the ship the furniture, which was screwed off in Gotenhafen, became independent and crushed the huddled crowd there.

The most of the fugitives, who had survived the catastrophe of the "Wilhelm Gustloff", answered the question, what are you first remembering about if you are thinking of this catastrophe: "That was the moment, when the ship sank". The ocean giant had got the worst hit at the bow. Minutes after minutes the bow had sagged, then suddenly, the stern rose into the air by a gigantic jolt. The "Wilhelm Gustloff" seemed to be growing stiff for a short time, but then, it was only a moment, this ship sank bow first. The shipwrecked fugitives on the water paused for a moment, because all lights of the giant went on and the sirens of the "Wilhelm Gustloff" wailed, but few seconds later they became silent again and the ocean giant vanished for ever into the waves of the Baltic Sea.

Time was 22:15 when the "Wilhelm Gustloff" sank. The feared suction failed to come, it wasn't deep enough. There were some minutes of silence; you could then hear the cries of drowning people again.

The "Wilhelm Gustloff " took thousands and thousands of persons into the depth of the sea, but more than thousand passengers were floating in the waves, only few were sitting in the lifeboats or on rafts, the most clung to wreck's pieces or hung helplessly in their life jackets. Who was still in a position to reach a boat or raft, tried to do that. But there was no rescue for the helpless victims of this catastrophe. Many children were floating in the water, they wept or were speechless with shocks or were already dead.

The "Wilhelm Gustloff" couldn't transmit SOS, because the transmission tower was considerably damaged by the torpedo attack. So the crew could only let rise flares as distress signal. But the torpedo boat "Löwe", which was only some metres away from the scene of the catastrophe, transmitted distress signals immediately. The "Wilhelm Gustloff" was on the "Zwangsweg 58" (enforced way 58), which was also taken up with other convoys from the Bay of Danzig. That was to have a favourable effect. The first ships, which received the distress signals of the "Löwe", were the cruiser "Admiral Hipper" and its escort vessel, the torpedo boat "T 36". Both had left the harbour of Gotenhafen few hours after the "Wilhelm Gustloff", but they had considerably more speed, so that both ships were only 30 minutes away from the "Wilhelm Gustloff" during the tragedy. When the "Admiral Hipper" reached the scene of the tragedy, the "Wilhelm Gustloff" was still holding just above water. The "Admiral Hipper" had many fugitives on board, but it could accommodate several hundred other passengers still. But the "Admiral Hipper" turned away and gave hurriedly full speed towards west. Nobody, who was in the water and fully conscious, could that understand. But the captain of the "Admiral Hipper" feared that the enemy was still near and so the cruiser was an ideal target for another attack. He didn't want to put at risk the life of the fugitives on board of his ship.

Together with the "Admiral Hipper" the torpedo boat "T 36" had also reached the scene of the tragedy. The captain of "T 36" was just 27 years old. 250 fugitives crowded on board of the little ship, amongst them the mother of the captain. The "T 36" approached the sinking "Wilhelm Gustloff" cautiously. The captain of "T 36" knew that every unconsidered turn of the ship could cost the life of the passengers on board. It was presented a horrible sight to the crew of "T 36". The "Wilhelm Gustloff" was brightly illuminated. People fell from the ocean giant or jumped from this ship. The ship was surrounded with hundreds of persons, who wanted to be saved, but also with hundreds of dead people, who were floating in the water. The captain of "T 36"tried to approach nearer the sinking "Wilhelm Gustloff". But it became quickly clear that the "Wilhelm Gustloff" would sink within few minutes. The captain of "T 36" had no choice but to keep his distance from the "Wilhelm Gustloff" and to prepare himself for salvage from the sea. Then, after some minutes, the "Wilhelm Gustloff" sank too. Now the both little boats, the "Löwe" and the "T 36", were the only hope of several thousands of shipwrecked persons. The crew of "T 36" did all now, what was possible. It was a hard slog for the rescuers of "T 36". They rotated in the front line during the rescue operation; they lifted and pulled the people from the water. The clothes of the people were soaked, so all of them were wet to the skin and were also very heavy by their wet clothes. So it was a hard work to the sailors of "T 36" to lift the wet bodies. When a shipwrecked person was heaved over the boarding wall, he was immediately undressed by the sailors or other fugitives and rubbed down. Then the mother of the young captain of "T 36" saw to it that the shipwrecked persons had got hot tea or schnapps to call these poor persons, who were rigid with fright and coldness, back into the life.

At 0:25 was suddenly heard the cry on board of "T 36": "Torpedos auf Kollisionskurs" (torpedoes on collision course). The Russian submarine "S 13" had really launched still some torpedoes and had ducked to disappear towards east then. The young captain could turn the "T 36" hard starboard and so get away from the attacking torpedoes. It was high time to leave the scene of tragedy. With 564 shipwrecked persons on board the "T 36" left the place of catastrophe now and followed the "Admiral Hipper". The torpedo boat "Löwe" stayed alone behind now, in the middle of a field of dead bodies and fragments of the "Wilhelm Gustloff". But soon disappeared the "Löwe" too, it had 470 shipwrecked persons on board, and the persons, those still alive and were still swimming in the cold Baltic Sea, had to watch how the last lights of the searchlights went away. Now an endless time of waiting began for them. Many were still in lifeboats around them were swimming people, who were crying for help. But soon it got quiet, because the last persons, who were swimming in the water, were dead; they died of exhaustion. But also in the lifeboats shipwrecked persons died of hypothermia and exhaustion; they were thrown over board.

There were four torpedoes that the Russian submarine fired. As if to emphasize Soviet retribution, each torpedo has been painted with a dedication:

Torpedo 1: For the Motherland

Torpedo 2: For Stalin

Torpedo 3: For the Soviet People

Torpedo 4: For Leningrad

At 2:30 the "Löwe" had left the place of catastrophe, but three other ships had arrived in the meantime there, the motor ship "MS Gotenland" with its escorting boats "M 341" and "M 387". They continued the rescue operation. The "MS Gotenland" had already 3,300 shipwrecked persons on board, in spite of that the captain let down lifeboats. In the sea were still found living persons in lifeboats or on fragments of the "Wilhelm Gustloff". But in course of time the sailors in the lifeboats of the "MS Gotenland", "M 341" and "M 387" received no answer, when they shouted to shipwrecked persons.

The rescue ships took the shipwrecked persons to Kolberg, Swinemünde (today the Polish border town Swinoujscie) and Saßnitz. All ships could save together only 1,239 persons of the "Wilhelm Gustloff", more than 9,000 dead persons were left behind; they found their graves in the Baltic Sea. Till beginning of April the German navy was by sea able to evacuate 2,500,000 persons; more than 33,000 persons died on the way over the sea route, since not only the "Wilhelm Gustloff" suffered such a cruel fate. The wreck of the "Wilhelm Gustloff" is in the Baltic Sea even today, just 60 metres under water, close to Stolpmünde (today a Polish seaside resort with name Ustka).

Russian tanks in Mühlhausen (East Prussia); on the streetside you can see the remainder of a trek of fugitives

At the end of January the "Red Army" had also reached Silesia. There were living 4,600,000 Germans. Here the Russian troops had advanced at a breadth of 90 km towards west. On 26 January the Russian army had reached the German Baltic coast, close to Tolkemit (today a Polish town with name Tolkmicko). By it the connection between East Prussia and the remainder of the German Empire was cut off. Only some days later the extermination camp of Auschwitz was freed by Soviet troops. Thus Russian soldiers were the first foreigners, who saw the cruelty of such a camp. That increased naturally the hatred of the "German pigs".

The "Volkssturm", Germany's last reserves, children and old men

Whilst the Russian advanced more and more in the east, the Americans and British continued to bomb the German cities; so on 3 February they dropped 2,266 tons of bombs over Berlin. On 6 February Russian soldiers crossed the river Oder (Drina) in Silesia and established a bridgehead of 80 km breadth on the western side of the river, whilst the stream of fugitives towards west went on. Only few days later a Russian submarine sank a German ship in the Bay of Danzig again, it was the German hospital ship "General Steuben" with 3,400 passengers. 3,000 passengers drowned. Whilst the "General Steuben" was sinking the Soviets conquered the East Prussian seaport Elbing (today a Polish city with name Elblag). Soon was the Silesian capital Breslau the next goal of the Soviet army. Breslau (today a Polish city with name Wroclaw) had 600,000 (German) inhabitants in those days.

Many fugitives from the Silesian country, but also from East Prussia and Poland, had sought refuge here, so that this city had more inhabitants now. Many of them intended to go soon home again, because the Nazis had always promised, that the Soviet offensive would be stopped and the Russian soldiers would be chased away from German ground. But it was a departure without return for the fugitives. When on 21 January treks of fugitives still reached the capital of Silesia, this city was already overcrowded with other fugitives. Panic and chaos reigned in Breslau, because there was given already an order to evacuate the city, which had unexpectedly hit the inhabitants. Overnight some hundred thousand should leave Breslau.

The inhabitants of Breslau had taken no notice of the war up to now. Only in November 1941 one air raid happened by the Russians. 10 persons were killed by it. The inhabitants of Germany looked enviously upon the "air-raid shelter of Germany" (Breslau). All towns and cities of Germany suffered from the bomb's attacks of the Allies, especially in the west, but not Breslau (and Dresden). Therefore many people were also evacuated from West Germany into this city. Also administration, cultural assets and important manufacturing plants of armament were transferred to Breslau. Breslau was accepted as safe city, therefore there were also taken no military measures to defend the city.

In July 1944 Joseph Goebbels had announced in front of 12,000 people in Breslau, that a Russian soldier would never cross the Silesian border. But in August Hitler had already declared Breslau "fortress" by a secret order. Strong attack's and siege's forces of the enemy should be bound to stop the advance of the "Red Army" towards Berlin as long as possible. But that was a death sentence to many old German towns in the east, like Königsberg, Kolberg (today a Polish seaside resort with name

Kolobrzeg), Glogau (today a Polish town with name Glogów) or Breslau. They were sacrificed for a war, which was a losing battle for quite some time now.

The inhabitants of Breslau didn't know that their city was already a fortress. On 17 January were all replacement's troops put on the alert in Breslau; German soldiers of wiped out troops and other soldiers, who were available, were united in four regiments and reinforced by the "Volkssturm" (People's Storm = military reserve unit of young persons, who were 16 – 18 years old and men older than 60 years). Thus this armed force to the defence of Breslau had 50,000 men, but the Russian superiority had more soldiers.

On 20 January the inhabitants of Breslau should be evacuated. At the stations of Breslau crowded thousands and thousands of children and women. A mass panic broke out, some hundred persons were trampled to death; the most of them were children. Also treks were formed, which left the city now. In spite of that some hundred thousand civilians stayed behind in Breslau.

On 21 January Breslau was officially declared fortress, too. A placard showed the sheer scorn: "Männer von Breslau! Unsere Hauptstadt Breslau ist zur Festung erklärt worden. Die Evakuierung der Stadt von Frauen und Kindern läuft und wird in Kürze abgeschlossen sein ... Für die Betreuung der Frauen und Kinder wird gemacht was möglich ist" (Men of Breslau! Our capital Breslau was declared fortress. The evacuation of women and children was already started and will be completed shortly ... It will be done all what is possible for the care of women and children). But many people left Breslau without food in reality; they left this big city in icy coldness, without chance of survival to babies. The mothers couldn't nurse their babies, because they were exposed to the icy wind. It was the march of death for many mothers; 18,000 mothers from Breslau lost their life during this march of death towards west. The dead bodies remained lying on the roadsides or edges of ways. Search parties were made up later to recover the dead bodies and to bury them hurriedly in mass graves.　　Many women and children were also overrun by Russian tanks. German soldiers, who often crossed the way of the fugitives, related what they saw: "We crossed just a road, when we saw the remainder of a trek. Then we saw a destroyed Soviet tank at a distance, perhaps 500 metres. That tank had overrun the whole of the trek before it was destroyed. It was a cruel sight. Dead human bodies, dead animals, beds, household effects, hay, straw, oats – all that was mixed up and steamed, was still warm. They (the Russians) had shot at all, also at horses, at all what moved. Some persons, who had survived the tragedy, were standing on the roadside, they trembled and wept and couldn't realize what was happened" A fugitive related: "Wir waren fassungslos, als dann auf der linken Seite der Straße die NS-Parteibonzen mit ihren Autos und Lastwagen, vollgepackt mit allem Möglichen, ihre Frauen in Pelzmänteln, an uns vorbeifuhren. Wenn mal ein Fuhrwerk im Weg stand, haben die Begleitkommandos gleich zur Waffe gegriffen. Sie haben die armen Leute gezwungen, Platz zu machen – richtig radikal. Wir hatten eine unglaubliche Wut" (We were stunned, when we saw how the Nazi-bigwigs drove past by their cars and lorries on the left side of the road, full-packed of all sorts of things, their wives in fur coats. When there was a horse-drawn vehicle or cart in their way, then the escorting soldiers have immediately drawn their firearms. They have forced the poor people to make room for them – really radically. We were seething with rage).

Whilst the Nazis had already run away, the first executions followed in Breslau. Persons, who had made public that the defence of Breslau wouldn't make sense, were immediately shot dead.

Early in February were still 200,000 civilians in Breslau, whilst the Red Army encircled this city. At the same time began the conference of the "Three Greats", U.S. President Roosevelt, Prime Minister of Great Britannia, Churchill, and the Soviet dictator Stalin, on the Peninsula Crimea. This conference, the Conference of Yalta, concluded on 11 February. The heads of state came to an agreement about the time of the beginning of the war of the Soviet Union against Japan, about the maintenance of (Outer) Mongolia as independent state and about the annexation of the southern part of the island Sakhalin and the Kuril Islands by the Soviet Union. The Soviet Union should also get the eastern part of Poland. The "Three Greats" also prepared for the unconditional surrender of Germany and the division into four occupying zones. But the three rulers could not reach an agreement about Poland's western border. Stalin intended to give Poland the eastern part of Germany.

The Great Three: Churchill, Roosevelt and Stalin at the Yalta Conference on February 11, 1945

The bombardments by the Allies were continued in the German Empire. Some large cities in the east of Germany, like Breslau and Dresden, weren't destroyed up to now. But that was to change soon. The catastrophe of Breslau and Dresden is connected with the tragedy of the fugitives. Early in February many fugitives sought refuge in Dresden, above all fugitives from Silesia, thus also many fugitives from Breslau, who thought to be safe in this wonderful baroque town, because nobody would attack this old town of art. But in the night between 13 and 14 February this wonderful town changed into a sea of flames, whilst there were thousands and thousands of fugitives in the streets.

The evening performance of the circus "Sarassani" was just in full swing. The inhabitants of Dresden sought a little bit diversion after the hard days of war, but then they suddenly heard the sirens: air-raid warning. That couldn't be possible in Dresden, therefore the spectators kept calm. Everybody knew Dresden was like Breslau the so-called "Reichsluftschutzkeller" (Air-raid shelter of the German Empire). Also the inhabitants of Dresden knew that the metropolis of Saxony was not important from military point of view. Therefore they hoped that the Allies would esteem and spare the architectural treasure of their "Elbflorenz" (= so-called Florence on the Elbe; Florence/Italy is a famous baroque town like Dresden). Also several hundred thousand refugees from Silesia, who were in the city for a few days, here felt safe. In this evening thousands and thousands people crowded on the banks of the Elbe. There were hardly air-raid precautions and air defence. Many antiaircraft guns were only dummies, because the real guns were needed at the front.

At 22:09 the radio station broadcast: "Achtung, Achtung, Achtung! Feindlicher Bomberverband über der Stadt! Suchen Sie sofort die Luftschutzräume auf" (Attention, attention, attention! Enemy bombers over the city! Go immediately to the air-raid shelters). The pilots of the 244 British Lancaster bombers were surprised when they approached their goal: no glaring spotlights that swept the sky, no roaring antiaircraft guns that mingled with the noise of the aircraft motors. The few German fighter planes, which had their air base close to Dresden, had to wait and see on what goal the British bombers flew.

At 22:10 broke out an inferno. The first two-ton-bombs detonated in the city. The sky turned crimson. Incendiary bombs kindled gigantic fires; high-explosive bombs caused a tremble of the ground. Many streets changed into a hell of fire; a hot storm, like a hurricane, was whirling through them and was carrying along everything. Gigantic jets of flame shot out of the houses. The asphalt burned, fire engines burned up on the pavement. In the cellars suffocated and burned the people. The "fire storm of Dresden" was still seen at a distance of 350 km. Many fugitives could see this inferno from the trains, which were parked outside the city. One of them reported: "Dann kam der Angriff, wir saßen dicht gedrängt in dem Waggon. Dresdner stürmten auf uns zu, Leute, die die schlimmsten Verbrennungen hatten, wollten zu uns hinein. Wir hörten nur noch Bomben und sahen das Feuer. Aber das ganze Ausmaß des Schreckens wurde uns erst klar, als wir die armen Menschen erblickten" (Then came the attack, we sat huddled in the wagon. Inhabitants of Dresden stormed towards us, people who had the worst burns wanted to come into our wagon. We heard only the bombs and saw the fire. But the whole extent of the horror became clear to us only when we saw the poor people).

Two other air raids were following, which exceeded the first raid in its violence. That was more than the fire brigades could handle. Smoke came to the devastating heat. The people didn't get a chance: who left the cellars and ran away from the dust and smoke, was killed by rubble that fell down or was burned alive.

The railway station of Dresden, which had weathered the first air raid, showed a scene of horror now. The incendiary bombs of the second air raid had penetrated the roof of glass of the waiting room. The fugitives, who were crowded waiting for trains, which they would take out of the city, were encircled by flames. Each aid came too late. The rescue party found only corpses.

When on 14 February the day dawned, the people realized the whole extent of destruction. Dresden, one of the nicest cities of Germany, was in ruins. But the work of destruction was not yet brought to an end. At 8:00 started 450 "flying fortresses" of the U.S. American Air Force. In the night before were more than 2,000 tons of bombs falling down, now followed 700 tons, which destroyed the remainder of Dresden and killed thousands of persons. The British and Americans were never ever in the right of justification for this work of horror, because they knew that Dresden was no military city, without soldiers but full of some hundred thousand fugitives. It was not important for such an air raid; it was only a senseless killing. But why? The Germans weren't "pigs" to the British and Americans; they were only a military enemy! But the British commander Arthur Harris was thoroughly convinced that he did a deciding blow to the economy and war will of the enemy. But the air raids of the German air force had already showed that such raids made only stronger the will of defence. But Arthur Harris didn't change his opinion, although he knew that Dresden was full of fugitives. In this night of horror died more than 50,000 people in Dresden, killed by bombs of the Allies. There were mainly killed women and children, but no (German) soldier!

This inferno was still in store for Breslau. The Russians conquered Liegnitz, Goldberg, Löwenberg, Bunzlau, Sprottau, Grottkau, Strehlen, Striegau and Jauer. Hitler's order was, to hold Breslau in any case; but it was held by children and few old men, who resisted bravely the Russian soldiers.

On 21 February the Soviet troops had reached the confluence of Oder/Drina and Neisse, only 100 km to the south of Berlin, whilst the German troops withdrew from the regions on the river Saar and Moselle (West Germany) after heavy U.S.-American attacks. On 23 February Turkey declared war on the German Empire and Japan, only one day later followed Egypt. During the declaration of war the Egyptian Prime Minister, Ahmed Maher Pasha, was shot dead by a pro-German Egyptian.

On 1 March marched American soldiers into the city of Monchengladbach (a city close to Düsseldorf). Three days later also Finland declared war on Germany, whilst the Soviet army reached the coast of the Baltic Sea by Kolberg in Pomerania. On 6 March U.S.-American troops occupied Cologne. One day later reached a patrol of the 9th U.S.-American tank's division the bridge of Remagen, the Ludendorff-Eisenbahnbrücke. This railway bridge over the Rhine was the only bridge, which was still intact. The German army was failed to blast this bridge, how it was done with the other bridges. So the U.S.-American soldiers could form without combat a bridgehead on the right side of the Rhine. (It was made a well-known movie about the fight for the bridge of Remagen) Then, on 10 March, the Allies conquered Wesel, the last German bridgehead on the left side of the Rhine.

March 7; Americans conquer the Bridge of Remagen

On 11 March gave Goebbels, the minister of propaganda, his last speech in Görlitz (a town in Silesia, today frontier town at the new frontier between Poland and Germany). He spoke about the heroic defence of the native country and the "Endsieg" (final victory) of the German nation. Only one day later Russian troops conquered the fortress Küstrin (today the Polish town Kostrzyn). Now they were only 80 km away from Berlin.

Goebbels; Hitler's propaganda minister while inspecting one of the last German contingents in Luban (Silesian town); March 11, 1945

On 14 March tried Ribbentrop (the German Foreign Minister) in vain to probe a separate peace with France, Great Britain and the United States. That happened by a Swedish contact. Two days later began the Soviet troops with their offensive towards Vienna. This offensive was lasting till April 14. The Austrian frontier (in those days the southeast frontier of Germany) was first reached during this offensive on 29 March.

On 17 March was the "Ludendorffbrücke" of Remagen destroyed by German combat aircraft. But the most American soldiers had passed this bridge in the meantime and had also constructed a pontoon bridge.

American soldiers in Bensheim (West Germany)

On 19 March gave Hitler the order "Verbrannte Erde" (Scorched Earth). All public utilities and industrial plants had to be destroyed during the withdrawal; they should not fall into enemy's hands. This order was observed especially in the east.

At the end of March broke down the whole front on Rhine. Seven armies of the Allies advanced from the Rhine towards east now. In the east of Germany the "Second White Russian Army" conquered together with Polish troops the Baltic seaport Danzig. On 1 April was the whole region on the Ruhr (Ruhr-Pot) encircled by the "First and Ninth U.S.-American Army". This day were also conquered the cities of Hamm and Paderborn (towns in the east of North Rhine-Westphalia, which is a new country later) by the Americans. Only two days later the cities of Osnabrück and Münster (Westphalia) fell into the hands of the Allies.

"German soldiers, hold the position, Danzig will never fall!"

Encircled by Russian troops, the (German) population in Danzig

On 9 April were the German cruisers "Admiral Scheer" and "Admiral Hipper" destroyed by bombers of the Allies. It was the "Admiral Hipper" that had left the shipwrecked persons of the "Wilhelm Gustloff" in the lurch.

In the east went on the drama of the fugitives. Since the way towards west was cut off by Russian troops, many fugitives returned, returned into the death. By a leaflet of October, 1944 the Russian soldiers were ordered: "kill, kill the German pigs!

There is nothing, what makes Germans as innocent as a new-born babe, - no German, those still alive and those are not yet born. Follow the order of comrade Stalin and trample for ever the fascist pip under your foot. Break the power of the racial arrogance of the German women! Take them as legitimate loot!" This order had effect. When the German defenders of Königsberg capitulated, they had to feel the hatred of the Russian soldiers. All women were violated and then shot dead. April 9, it's a cruel day to Königsberg, the once nice town of East Prussia. In the hour of death of this town were ringing once more all bells there, whilst the Russian soldiers violated and killed in an ecstasy of hatred. The German soldiers, who had surrendered, heard the cries of the tormented women. It was a terrible moment to them, but it was still to come a more terrible time to them, the time of their captivity in Siberia. The most of them didn't survive the years there. Whilst Königsberg was falling and disappearing for ever, Russian troops marched into Vienna. Also the inhabitants of Vienna had to suffer now; women were violated, tormented and shot dead.

On 10 April occupied the Ninth American Army Hannover and the British army crossed the Leine (river) close to Celle one day later. By it all connecting ways between Hannover and Hamburg were cut off. On 11 April the Ninth American Army had already reached the Elbe to the south of Magdeburg. – On 12 April died Franklin Delano Roosevelt, the U.S.-American President. He was just 63 years old. His successor became Harry S. Truman. On 12 April, the day of Roosevelt's death, the Allies also conquered the cities of Braunschweig/Brunswick, Essen, Erfurt, Baden-Baden and Rastatt, one day later also Jena fell and American soldiers built a second bridgehead on the east bank of the Elbe, to the south of Wittenberg (Luther's town; see the book "Germany before and after the Thirty-Years' War by E. Harings) Four days later began the final offensive of the Soviet armies against Berlin and by it the death blow to the German Empire, an empire, which was more than thousand years old.

On 17 April U.S.-American soldiers conquered Halle and forced their way also into the suburbs of the big Saxon city of Leipzig. One day later invaded the "Third U.S.-American Army" under General Patton Bohemia, whilst the last German defenders of the "Ruhr-Pot" (since many days was the whole region on the Ruhr/river encircled by the Allies) surrendered. During these days was continued the battle for Breslau. The fortress was held, although the first Russian soldiers had already forced their way into the southern suburbs of this city. They had forced their way by combats from street to street, a situation such as Stalingrad more than two years ago. Breslau should become Stalingrad for the Russian army that was Hitler's idea. A Swedish newspaper reported on the battle for Breslau: "There is not only fought for each floor, but also for each window, where the Germans have positioned machine-guns and other automatic weapons! Nobody can understand how the Germans provide themselves with foodstuffs, water and ammunition. There were only few counterparts of such a dramatic and fanatic struggle during the war. The battle for Breslau exceeds all anger and contempt of death up to now."

Any time it could hit a shell at any place of the city. The civilian population spent the most time in the cellars. When at the end of March set in mild weather, the children ventured out of the cellars to get some fresh air in the streets. There, in the streets, many children lost their life by fire of artillery now.

Days before: On 27 March appeared Soviet aeroplanes over Breslau, but they didn't drop bombs, they threw down leaflets, which denounced Hitler's terror and the slogans of holding out of the German military leadership of Breslau. Some Germans didn't see sense in continuing the defence of Breslau, therefore the followed the groups of resistance. They were considered to be traitors, who would prevent the struggle for survival of the German nation. It was the "Holy War" to the Nazis; therefore they also knew no mercy on traitors. Each day were executed traitors, the executive commandos were sometimes on piece-work.

The bombers, which appeared on 1 April over Breslau, let their lethal load drop. It was Easter. The news followed hot on each other's heels: bombardment, lasting for hours, aimed dropping of bombs at the "Dom– and Sandinsel" (Cathedral- and Sand Island). In the whole town were extensive fires. The bells of the churches, which threw down, seemed to ring during the fall of the Silesian metropolis. The most churches and houses of Breslau burned; the city was a sea of flames.

The airport Gandau in the western districts of Breslau was from the beginning a main goal of the Soviet attacks. By the loss of the airport in March was also interrupted each contact to the outside world. The NS-leadership let raze many streets to the ground now, to build a new airport in the centre of the city. The Nazis called on children, boys from the age of 10 upwards and girls from 12 upwards, to do the hard work. But also old persons, who could still "creep" and pregnant women, had to help to build the new airport in the centre of Breslau. The people came over and over again under fire of the artillery. 13,000 dead bodies piled up after few days on the taxiway. The "delusions of holding out" knew no taboo: ruins of churches were converted into defensive positions, cemeteries were flattened for the creation of a better line of fire; gravestones were pulled down and used as material of barricades. Resistance was slowly arising to the line of action of the municipality, but it was no use. The senseless battle for Breslau was continued.

"Unser auf Hitler gegründete Zuversicht wird umso größer, je länger wir uns behaupten. Denn Adolf Hitler ist mit den Tapferen, seine Stärke wird unsere Widerstandskraft sein" (Our confidence, which is based on Hitler, becomes greater, the longer we can hold our position. Because Adolf Hitler is with brave men, his strength will be our powers of resistance), praised the fanatic Nazis once more their "Führer" (Leader) on 20 April, the birthday of Adolf Hitler. But Hitler intended already his suicide in the bunker under the "Reichskanzlei" in Berlin; so he wanted to evade the responsibility for the death of some millions of persons. Three days later he removed Göring from his office and let him arrest by members of the SS. The reason to this action was Göring's question about Hitler's successor, what happened by a telegram. That was a high treason. Only one day later Himmler, the leader of the SS, handed over an offer of capitulation to the west powers via the Swedish Count Folke Bernadotte, but the west powers rejected this offer. As result Himmler was also removed from his office mow.

On April 25 the Russian troops advanced from east and the U.S.-American troops from west towards Torgau on the Elbe, there they met now. One day later the Italian dictator Mussolini was arrested together with his mistress Clara Petacci on Lago di Como (Lake Como/North Italy) and then shot dead by Italian partisans. The dead bodies were taken to Milan; there they were hung up head down at a petrol station. On 26 April the German army made its last attempt to rescue Berlin from the threat by the Russians. But Berlin was on the losing side during the battle for its existence, whilst Hitler was still living there. On April 29 Adolf Hitler got married to his "sweetheart" Eva Braun, who came from Munich to Berlin on April 15. On his wedding day he signed still a political and personal last will and testament. Göring and Himmler were not only removed from their offices, because of negotiations with the enemy, they were also expelled from the NSDAP. Now Hitler laid also down his successor, the new "Reichspräsident" should become Karl Dönitz and the new chancellor Joseph Goebbels after his death. Martin Bormann should be "Parteiminister" (Minister of the Party). These three men should then form a new government. On April 29 also the last German soldiers surrendered in Italy.

April 25, near Torgau on the Elbe, soldiers of an advanced part of the 1st US Army and the 5th Soviet Guards Army meet.

On April 30 Russian soldiers stormed the government district of Berlin, whilst Hitler, who was in the "Führerbunker" (bunker of the Führer = Hitler's own bunker), bit a poison capsule. In addition to that he shot himself into the head. Also his wife swallowed a poison capsule; so she committed suicide together with his husband. Hitler's dead body was wrapped up in a blanket and then carried upstairs into the park by Goebbels and two other helpers. Also the dead body of Hitler's wife Eva was carried upstairs into the park in front of the bunker. There were both bodies laid side by side, directly in front of the entrance of the bunker; then was poured petrol over the dead bodies. Now the helpers took a burning rag and threw it over the bodies, the mortal remains were immediately ablaze and burned.

Battlefield German cities; American tanks in the streets of Nuremberg (Nürnberg)

On May 1 the "Großdeutsche Rundfunk" (Broadcasting of the "Great German Empire") informed: "Adolf Hitler, unser Führer, ist in seinem Befehlsstand in der Reichskanzlei, bis zum letzten Atemzug kämpfend, für Deutschland gefallen" (Adolf Hitler, our Führer, was killed in action, he fought for Germany to the last gasp in his command centre in the „Reichskanzlei"). That was the last lie of the NS-regime – whilst Hitler died the battle for Breslau on the Oder/Drina was continued. Breslau was the last big city of Germany in which was still combated, but it was a senseless combat. By a short cessation of fire the Soviets gave the last possibility to the inhabitants of Breslau to surrender voluntarily. But the defenders of the Silesian metropolis were stubborn and gambled away the chance to save at least the life of some people. "Wir kapitulieren nie" (Never we surrender), was the slogan of the NS-leadership of Breslau. Now the Russian soldiers advanced more and more towards centre. Then in the night between 4 and 5 May there was a talk by pressure of some clergymen with the NS-leader of the city, Hanke, and General Niehoff. Niehoff proposed to choose the suicide in view of the threatening defeat, but Hanke, who had sent thousands and thousands of children into the death, said that he would be too young to die. Hanke found another possibility. General Niehoff had a little aeroplane at his disposal. Whilst General Niehoff stayed in Breslau and shared the fate of his soldiers, Hanke cowardly cleared off. He left a city of ruins behind. Hanke was missing after the war. Some people said later, that they had seen him in South America, but he would have another name now.

April 30, a Soviet soldier hosting the Soviet Flag on the Reichstag building in Berlin

When Hanke had left Breslau, it became eerily still there. No shots were fired. On May 6 surrendered Breslau. That was the end of this wonderful German town, for ever (today there is a Polish town, the new name is Wroclaw, as already mentioned). With Breslau disappeared many other German towns in the east, so Königsberg too. Königsberg is today a Russian town with the name Kaliningrad within the exclave with same name. Now the suffering of the German fugitives in the east was to continue for some months, although the war came to an end.

On May 1 Goebbels committed suicide with his family; that happened after his attempt to enter into an armistice with the Russians, but the Russian marshal Zhukov had rejected Goebbels' offer. Goebbels took also his six children with into the death. Whilst Goebbels committed suicide, Martin Bormann tried to escape from Berlin, but he was shot dead during his attempt to escape. Now "Großadmiral" (Grand Admiral) Dönitz, the new president of the German Empire, formed a new government under Chancellor Lutz Graf (Count) Schwerin von Krosigk in Plön (Plön is a little town in Schleswig-Holstein).

On May 2 the last German soldiers surrendered under the command of General Helmuth Weidling in Berlin. All of Berlin was occupied by Russian troops now.

On May 3 aeroplanes of the Allies once more bombarded German ships in the Bay of Lübeck. All ships were full of fugitives from the east of Germany. Why did the Allies this senseless act? The passenger ship "Cap Arcona" sank after the bombardment and dragged 7,000 former prisoners of the concentration camp of Neuengamme into the death.

On May 4 surrendered all German soldiers in the Netherlands, in the north of Germany, in Denmark, in Norway, on the island Helgoland and the islands of Friesland. On May 5 the South German army surrendered with 300,000 soldiers to the Americans in Bavaria and West Austria, whilst the east of Austria was already occupied by Russian troops. Now, on May 5, the official capitulation of the German Empire also followed. Then, on May 7, Colonel General Alfred Jodl and Admiral General Hans-Georg von Friedeburg signed the document about the unconditional capitulation of the German Empire. That happened in presence of General Eisenhower (U.S.A.) and representatives of the British, French and Soviet air forces in Reims/France. On May 9, at 0:16, was repeated the signing of the document about the unconditional capitulation of the German Empire by Colonel General Hans-Jürgen Stumpff, Field-Marshal Wilhelm Keitel and Admiral General Hans-Georg von Friedeburg. This time was also present the Soviet marshal Zhukov. On this day also Hermann Göring surrendered to the Americans. He hoped to be treated like Napoleon 130 years ago and to have the possibility to go into exile; living in exile he wished to have a quiet period of his life then. Many leading NS-politicians and officers of the German army were also arrested now.

May 7, at 2:41 – In Reims (France) Colonel General Jodl signs unconditional surrender of Germany with Colonel Wilhelm Oxenius (left) and Admiral Hans Georg von Friedeburg

On May 12 only surrendered the last German soldiers, although the war was already over since some days. 14,000 German soldiers, who had occupied the Greek island Crete, laid down their arms now. Two days later the new provisional Austrian government declared the independence of Austria.

On May 22 was still shot a 22-year-old man by a German summary court. It happened before the British put an end to the spectre. Dönitz, Jodl and Reich Minister Albert Speer were arrested. A few days later announced the US magazine 'Time': The German Reich died on a sunny morning of May 23 near the Baltic Sea port of Flensburg".

May; Benito Mussolini and his mistress Clara Petacci, hung up head down at a petrol station in Milan

On May 23 was the German government under Chancellor Graf Schwerin von Krosigk liquidated and arrested by the Allies. That was now **the end of the German Empire**, the end for ever of an empire that was more than 1,000 years old. Also this day Heinrich Himmler committed suicide; that happened after his arrest by British soldiers. Then, on May 31, the NSDAP was prohibited by the (new) American (military) government of Germany.

1945, Düsseldorf's "old town" (down town)

Düsseldorf a city of ruins like many other German cities

The war was over and Germany a landscape of ruins. The cruelties of the war came to an end in the west of Germany, but in the east of the former German Empire and in Sudetenland (Bohemia) began just the tragedy. On June 3 ordered the new government of Poland that all Germans must leave East Germany and on 5 June the four victorious powers took over the government power in the whole of the remainder of the former German Empire. Germany, the western and the middle part, was divided into 4 occupying zones. East Germany came under Polish administration, the eastern part of Prussia under Russian administration. Later the world had forgotten the eastern part of the former German Empire, many people said "East Germany" and thought really of "Middle Germany" and not of East Germany. The country Prussia was liquidated for ever. Berlin, the capital of the former German Empire, was divided into 4 sectors. Also the new state Austria was divided into 4 zones and Vienna into 4 sectors.

The terrible war was just finished and a new tragedy began in the east of Germany. The Germans were put in internment camps by the Polish militia there – often in camps, where Jews had suffered. The Foreign Office of London/England reported: "The concentration camps aren't closed, they were only taken over by a new owner" (= Poland). A (new) notorious camp was Lamsdorf in Silesia. That camp was set up by the Polish general Alexander Zawadzki in July. That camp was the "forecourt to the hell", the arrest conditions were cruel for the German women: maltreatment, forced labour, hunger, rape, murder. The Nazis did that with Jews and Poles before, now did it Poles with the German women. The Germans were without rights in East Germany, everybody could treat them like hunting bags. After the great escape were still several million Germans in the eastern part of Germany, which was under Polish administration now.

The inhabitants of Görlitz, the town on the Neisse (river), saw especially the tragedy of the Germans from the east. Fugitives from the east came still to Görlitz, whilst other fugitives, who were since some days there, wanted to go back again, back home! But the new fugitives told cruel things. "Don't go back! The Poles are horrible. They take all things away from you! You will be killed at home. They destroyed your houses". But the fugitives, who wanted to go back said: "Here is no room for us, we want to go home. There we have our field, a house, a flat".

Some fugitives went back, but the mass of the fugitives had no possibility for a return now. The Polish militia started off already to expel the Germans from East Germany in June, so also the inhabitants of the village Lissa. A woman, who was expelled, reported later: "Am 16. Juni, abends um 21 Uhr, kamen polnische Offiziere. Einer von ihnen sagte, morgen früh um sieben Uhr müsst ihr dort und dort sein. Wir sollten zu einer großen Pferdekoppel am Ende des Dorfes gehen, durften aber nichts mitnehmen, nur eine Tasche. Als wir morgens zu Koppel kamen, sahen wir, dass das ganze Dorf versammelt war. Aber niemand hatte uns vorher gesagt, warum wir dort sein sollten. Plötzlich haben sie uns aufgeschreckt – mit Maschinengewehren. Als wir alle standen, haben sie über unsere Köpfe hinweg geschossen. Wir haben uns sofort auf den Boden geschmissen und geschrien. Danach wurden wir Richtung Görlitz gejagt. Wir sollten spüren, dass wir Deutsche waren, die verhassten Deutschen, einfach nur die bösen Deutschen! (On June 16, by 21 o'clock in the evening, Polish officers came. One of them said: tomorrow at 7 o'clock you have to be there and there. We should to go to a paddock at the end of the village, but were allowed to take anything, just a bag. In the morning when we arrived at the paddock, we saw that all inhabitants of Lissa had gathered there. But no one had previously told us why we should be there. Suddenly they have startled us – with machine guns. As we were standing, they shot over our heads. We immediately threw ourselves on the ground and have cried. Then we were chased Görlitz. We should feel that we are Germans, the hated Germans; just evil Germans).

Short time later all people were called to leave Görlitz. The strict order of the Poles was, to leave this town within 48 hours. Also in other towns and villages of Silesia followed the same order. So the inhabitants of the administrative districts of Sorau, Sagan, Görlitz, Lauban, Löwenberg, Bunzlau, Hirschberg and Frankenstein, more than 200,000 Germans, had to leave their flats in two days and to march towards Middle Germany. East Germany was forgotten now, for ever; it should be Polish land, but officially only more than 40 years later! Today the towns have Polish names, like Zary, Zagań, Lwówek, Ślaski, Boleslawiec, Jelenia Góra, Zabkowice, Ślaskie.

On July 17 the conference of the victors was started in Potsdam. An official photo showed Stalin, Clement Attlee and Harry S. Truman in unanimity. But that picture is very much mistaken there! It was already emerging the contours of a new global conflict, the "Cold War". But in spite of the distrust amongst the Allies the Germans could not count on mildness. The European people hated and feared still Germany more than Russia. All German war criminals should be brought to trial and Germany should repair again all caused damage in the world. But how should look the frontiers in future in Europe? Stalin claimed East Poland, Poland should then get East Germany as compensation. The new Polish-German frontier should be the Oder (Drina)-Neisse-Line. Poland should also get the large German seaport Stettin. The British and Americans tried on the other hand to get no new frontier line in the east. The heated debate about the question of Germany's east frontier was lasting 4 days. When Churchill, who had opened the conference with the other two heads of state (Attlee became new Prime Minister of Great Britain during the Conference of Potsdam and had relieved Churchill of his job few days later), and Truman talked of the expulsion of the Germans from East Germany Stalin said, that would be fascist propaganda, nobody would expel the Germans from East Germany, they would flee voluntarily or left voluntarily their homes. The British and Americans did not really know the fate of the Germans in the east and also not the tragedy there. The final decision over the German east frontier should make by a peace treaty later, therefore Silesia, East Pomerania, the little "Grenzmark" (Frontier Area) and East Prussia officially remained a part of Germany, till 1990! But the world had forgotten that before! Soon the middle of Germany was "East Germany" in the thoughts of the people! Already now the Germans had to leave their native country, although the eastern countries were still a part of Germany. A British protest came too late, Attlee submitted himself and signed the following resolution: "The three governments ... admit, that the transfer to Germany of the German population ... who are still living in Poland (here was already named Poland and not East Germany or Silesia, Pomerania and East Prussia), must be realized. They (United States, Great Britain and Russia) agree concurrently that the transfer (??? = expulsion!!!) has to happen in orderly and human way". By that was opened the door to a complete expulsion of the German population from East Germany. Now the Germans could feel the human transfer. Nobody could also hope for an undoing of the so-called resettlement (= expulsion) by a peace treaty later. So the Conference of Potsdam, which came to an end on August 2, sealed the fate of the population of East Germany. Now the north-east part of East Prussia together with Königsberg officially came under Russian administration, the south-west part of East Prussia under Polish administration, also all German regions to the east of Drina (Oder) and the "Görlitzer Neisse (river)" was put in charge of Polish administration.

The expulsion of the German population was now carried out with violence, whilst in the Polish cinemas was weekly showed that the Germans abandoned their homes peacefully, humanly, voluntarily and cheerfully. But also the Polish population had to suffer; several million Polish people have been displaced from East Poland, which belonged to the Soviet Union now. They were now settled in East Germany (Silesia, East Prussia and East

Pomerania). Many Polish people arrived at Breslau (now Wroclaw), in a city that consisted of ruins only. Polish treks moved through the streets of Breslau (Wroclaw), it was a strange sight to the Germans, who were still living there. "What these people are doing here, why they come here? We're in Silesia and not in Poland", said many residents of Breslau. The new (Polish) inhabitants of Silesia called themselves "repatriated people"; that sounds as if Silesia would be a Polish country for many hundred years, but there were living only Germans hundreds of years ago. What happened now there is also the destiny of the history. Today are living in Wroclaw (Breslau) 650,000 Polish citizens and several hundred Germans (Silesians).

Sonderbefehl

für die deutsche Bevölkerung der Stadt Bad Salzbrunn einschliesslich Ortsteil Sandberg.

Laut Befehl der Polnischen Regierung wird befohlen:

1. Am 14. Juli 1945 ab 6 bis 9 Uhr wird eine Umsiedlung der deutschen Bevölkerung stattfinden.

2. Die deutsche Bevölkerung wird in das Gebiet westlich des Flusses Weisse umgesiedelt.

3. Jeder Deutsche darf höchstens 20 kg Reisegepäck mitnehmen.

4. Kein Transport (Wagen, Ochsen, Pferde, Kühe usw.) wird erlaubt.

5. Das ganze lebendige und tote Inventar in unbeschädigtem Zustande bleibt als Eigentum der Polnischen Regierung.

6. Die letzte Umsiedlungsfrist läuft am 14. Juli 10 Uhr ab.

7. Nichtausführung des Befehls wird mit schärfsten Strafen verfolgt, einschließlich Waffengebrauch.

8. Auch mit Waffengebrauch wird verhindert Sabotage u. Plünderung.

9. Sammelplatz an der Straße Bhf. Bad Salzbrunn-Adelsbacher Weg in einer Marschkolonne zu 4 Personen. Spitze der Kolonne 20 Meter vor der Ortschaft Adelsbach.

10. Diejenigen Deutschen, die im Besitz der Nichtevakuierungsbescheinigungen sind, dürfen die Wohnung mit ihren Angehörigen in der Zeit von 5 bis 14 Uhr nicht verlassen.

11. Alle Wohnungen in der Stadt müssen offen bleiben, die Wohnungs- und Hausschlüssel müssen nach außen gesteckt werden.

Bad Salzbrunn, 14. Juli 1945, 6 Uhr.

Abschnittskommandant

(-) Zinkowski
Oberstleutnant

July 14, 1945; Polish order: All Germans have to leave the territory between the rivers Oder and Neiße (West Silesia) — The beginning of the expulsion of millions.

During the Conference of Potsdam informed the Polish government the Allies that in the (former) German territories, which were now managed by Poland, would be living still 1,500,000 Germans. But these Germans would go voluntarily after the harvest; after they had done their work for Poland, they want to go towards west. But in Silesia, East Pomerania and (Polish) East Prussia were still living more than 4,000,000 Germans really in those days. Now it followed after the agreement of Potsdam, the so-called "secured resettlement according to the treaty of Potsdam". But that was another chapter of the horror history of the expulsion, not only the expulsion from the German east countries of today's Polish territories, but also the expulsion from Sudetenland (today Czech Rep.). In the eastern territories of Germany the German language was also banned. The surviving German population in these territories was forced to speak in public only Polish, which was a foreign language for all that they did not understand. In those days after the Second World War Poland stated always that in its western territories Germans would no longer live, although today there still live 1 million. For the Germans there was a bad time after the war. Only through contracts changed their situation after 1989. Germans speak German, their native language, in the public again in the former German territories. Particularly in Upper Silesia, German is spoken, since there is still a strong German minority, which even forms the majority in some small places again. 1963 was the last school that gave German lessons, closed. The school year 1992/93 schools were reopened that granted German lessons again, the mother tongue of their pupils.

August 1; the Conference of the victors in Potsdam. Sitting from left: Prime Minister C.R. Attlee (UK), Pres-ident H.S. Truman (USA), Generalissimo J. Stalin (Soviet Union)

In the Czech Republic there are places today, where an observer sees no noticeable things in the landscape. Only people there are who know that there also were German villages and towns many years ago. The German tracks should be blotted out for ever after the expulsion of more than 3,000,000 people from Bohemia after the war. The German population (Sudeten) had to wear armlets with a black **"N"**. **"N"** for **"Němec"** = German. Short time after the capitulation of the German army, in May, everybody could read in a Czech propaganda publication: "All

Germans are responsible for the crime of Hitler, Himmler and Henlein. Therefore they must be punished also for the crimes of these persons". That was to be no empty menace. Now in Bohemia and Moravia the Germans had to pay for that that happened under the rule of Hitler in Czechoslovakia. The suffering and the expulsion of the Germans lasted till 1952 in Bohemia and Moravia (today Czech Rep.).

Examples of the Czech cruelties showed two reports, so the report from Duppau (Doupov), a German village with 2,000 inhabitants, that village is no longer existent and another report from Prague, the Czech capital. A female witness reported on the end of the war in Duppau: "Am 7. Mai ging der Rückzug der deutschen Truppen los. Überall auf dem Marktplatz war Militär. Die Offiziere haben auf der Lindenallee Papiere verbrannt. Bei uns im Hause waren deutsche Soldaten einquartiert. Meine Mutter hat den ganzen Tag Suppe für sie gekocht. Mitten in der Nacht hat Dönitz im Radio die Kapitulation durchgegeben. Da sprangen alle auf. Es ist zu Ende! Noch in der Nacht sind die deutschen Soldaten abgezogen" (On May 7 was started the withdrawal of the German troops. Soldiers were all over on the market-place. The officers have burnt documents in the street "Lindenallee". With us at home were billeted German soldiers. My mother has cooked soup all day for them. In the middle of the night Dönitz has informed on the radio that Germany has capitulated. Everybody jumped up. The war is over! Now the German soldiers left us in this night already). The inhabitants of Duppau were alone – it began the hour zero. There was new hope when after few days an American jeep turned up in Duppau. Some inhabitants asked the American soldier a question, they just understood a little bit English, whether other American soldiers would follow, the answer was no, America would not occupy this region. Duppau remained a no man's land. The American army was in Karlsbad (Bohemia). The unloved Russians, fugitives from Silesia had only told the worst about them, did not show up in Duppau. Also Czech people didn't show up there. So the inhabitants of Duppau, who had nothing seen of the war, kept the Whitsun. But the silence was deceptive, because in other German villages in Bohemia and Moravia (Sudetenland) the happenings had already followed hot on each other's heel. Now Duppau was for it! Czech militia came into the village, plundered and violated the women. Many Germans fled, who stayed had to bear much sorrow. 1952 the last Germans had to leave Doupov, what was the new name of Duppau now, and were deported to Germany. In Prague the situation for the Germans was worse than in Duppau, they had to feel the hatred of the Czechs especially. 1945 lived more than 200,000 Germans in Prague. Prague was an "island of peace" for them during the war. The front was far away. No German was afraid in Prague; also when the end of the war came near and everybody knew that Germany will lose this war was no German afraid of the Czechs. But on May 5, early in the morning, the situation changed. In the centre of Prague flocked the Czechs together. The furious crowds of people pulled off the German street signs and painted over German placards with Czech slogans. Czech flags were hoisted. German soldiers were attacked and disarmed. Everywhere were German offices raided, were ordnance depots plundered. The situation became critical when Czech rebels occupied the radio station Prague II and used it for anti-German propaganda. **"Smrt Němcum"** (death to Germans) reverberated through the ether. Now spread unrest like wildfire from quarter to quarter in Prague.

The German soldiers in Prague were taken by surprise. They failed to put down the rebellion. The German general Toussaint had to surrender on May 8. Now began the cruelties of the Czech rebels. They raped German women, thrashed German men to death, threw German children into the Moldau (Vltava, river through Prague), where the children drowned in the trouble water. Wounded German soldiers were shot dead in the hospitals. Young Germans were tortured in public. Few days later many Germans were driven through Prague, they were only stopped in the stadium Strahov, a stadium that was to obtain sad fame now. There happened tortures and rapes, no German was spared suffering. Who survived the tortures, victim of the catastrophic hygiene was. Many Germans died of dysentery, their dead bodies piled up in the latrines of the stadium, therefore also many Germans said to themselves: "Es ist egal, ob du heute oder morgen tot umfällst. Sterben wirst du hier sowieso" (It does not matter if you drop dead today or tomorrow. Dying thou shalt here anyway.)

The rebellion of Prague was the signal, which many Czechs were still waiting. In the whole of Bohemia and Moravia the Czechs rose in arms against the German population, whilst the Soviet army, which had occupied Czechoslovakia (= Bohemia + Moravia + Slovakia) in the meantime, had kept in the background. The Russians had given the Czech rebels a free hand.

A tragic highlight of the expulsion of the Germans from Bohemia (Sudetenland) was the "Death March of Brünn/Brno" in May. The revolutionaries of Brno (Brünn) demanded the expulsion of all Germans from the city. But the representatives of the Czech government prohibited the revolutionaries from doing that. The revolutionaries ignored the prohibition and organized raids on May 29 in the whole of the city and ordered the Germans to assemble in the monastic garden of the old part of Brünn the day after. In long line assembled 25,000 Germans in the street; from all lanes flocked the Germans together. Then the revolutionaries gave the order to the crowd of women, children and old men to march towards Austria. The Czechs in the streets applauded and threw dirt, stones and all sorts of things at the Germans, who just marched past them. "You damned pigs that is the end for you", shouted many Czechs at the Germans. The march of that day in May was a torture for many women and children, soon lay the first dead bodies in the road ditches. Who could not go on, was hit by rift butts to continue the march of death. The first day of this terrible march was over and 1,700 women and children were dead.

After 30 kilometres the column reached the little town Pohořelice/Pohrlitz. Who could not continue the march, was interned here. So families were inconsiderately separated. Many old people stayed behind whilst the crowd had to continue the march. It was a parting for ever for many people. Who stayed behind was arrested in Pohořelice and vegetated without food under catastrophic hygiene conditions there. The most of them died of dysentery and typhoid now. The smell of putrefaction was soon over the little town in Bohemia and heralded wide-spread death. The Czech inhabitants of Pohořelice could do nothing to relieve the misery of the Germans, because who had pity on the Germans and wanted to help had to reckon with the revenge of the revolutionaries. Captain Bedřich Pokorný, the leader of the revolutionaries in Brünn/Brno, got later the praise from the Czech government for his "excellent line of action against the Germans".

Poholeřice/Pohrlitz was only one of many internment camps in "Sudetenland" (the German part of Bohemia and Moravia). Also here were maltreatments, rapes and plunder that what the people knew in East Germany, the order of the day. The Czechs made clear to the German prisoners, why they had to suffer. Czech guards drove them over and over again upstairs and downstairs, to the point of their exhaustion and forced them to cry old slogans: "Ein Volk, ein Reich, ein Führer. Adolf Hitler! Sieg heil, Sieg heil! (one people, one empire, one leader/Führer. Adolf Hitler! Sieg Heil, Sieg Heil!) Then they got the order to beat one another. In some villages Germans were also bricked alive in walls or other Germans had to take hoes and shovels and to dig a long pit, after that they had to go into this pit; then they were shot dead by machine-gun's volleys there. It was that that the Nazis had also done with Jews before. Now the Czechs also demonstrated Nazi's cruelties. So the Czech revolutionaries behaved like the Nazis before.

In the summer time of this year the expulsion of the German population from Czechoslovakia was legalized by law. Already on May 19 Beneš, the head of the Czech government, had issued the following decree (the notorious Beneš-Decree):

The property of unreliable persons that is within the territory of the Czechoslovakian Republic is under the charge of the "National Assembly" (parliament of Czechoslovakia) until further notice … Unreliable persons are:

   a) Persons, who have German or Hungarian nationality.

   b) Persons, who were launching into activities against the sovereignty, independence, integrity, the democratic-republican form of government, the security and the defense of the Czechoslovakian Republic.

By this decree the Czechoslovakian Republic was the owner of the property of the 3,000,000 German inhabitants of Sudetenland. The Germans had to give their property to the Czechoslovakians without compensation. The Germans in East Germany met the same fate. Also they had to give their property to the

Polish and Russian state now. The expellees from East Germany were controlled by the Poles and Russians over and over again and had to give over also their last things to the new rulers of the eastern part of Germany. In January 1946 was started the great expulsion of all Germans from Czechoslovakia. That expulsion was lasting many years. Today are living only a few Sudeten- Germans in the Czech Republic.

The expellees and the fugitives from East Germany and Sudetenland were a great problem for the remainder of Germany now. Germany was only a landscape of ruins; there were no rooms for all persons. And now other Germans came to the middle and the western part of the former German Empire, more than 12,000,000 persons, who had to leave their native country "with nothing".

A fugitive in Cologne – "Ground Zero in Germany"

In August was brought a charge against Herman Göring, Rudolf Heß and 22 other high NS-personages, whilst also in Asia the war came to an end, by the capitulation of Japan.

Two murderers after their arrest. Left: Irma Grese, she was overseer in the concentration camps of Ravensbrück, Auschwitz and Bergen-Belsen. Right: Josef Kramer, he was camp commander in Bergen-Belsen and Auschwitz.

On September 17 a guard of the concentration camp Bergen-Belsen was put on trial the first time. Two day later the military government in the U.S.-American zone of Germany ordered to form three countries in South Germany: Bavaria, Württemberg-Baden and Great Hessen. At the end of September was started the dismantling of all industrial plants in the western part of Germany. Germany should be never again an industrial state; it should only be farmland in future. During those days were also founded the first new parties; the NSDAP was prohibited in the meantime in Germany. Early in October were also trade (labour) unions registered in West Germany again.

On November 5 Lieutenant General Lucius D. Clay reported to Washington (U.S.A.) that there is a lack of food in the U.S.-American zone of Germany because of the mass of fugitives from East Germany.

On November 17 were passed the first sentences on guards of the concentration camp of Bergen-Belsen and Auschwitz. Some SS-men were sentenced to death amongst them was also Josef Kramer, the commandant of the concentration camp of Bergen-Belsen.

On November 20 began the "International Military Court of Justice of Nuremberg" with its job, the reading out of the bill of indictment against 24 main war criminals. This "Court of Justice" laid down the rules for the proceedings and made available counsels for the defence or accepted the counsels, who were already determined by the defendants. The trial was lasting till October 1946.

On December 13 were 36 guards of the concentration camp of Dachau (close to Munich) sentenced to death by an U.S.-American court. Then, on December 20, the governors of the 4 occupying zones in Germany (French Zone, British Zone, U.S.-American Zone, Soviet/Russian Zone) were authorized by the (new) "Control Council of the Allies" in Germany to carry through the trials against the war criminals independently.

On December 28 was hanged Paul Hoffmann, a SS man who was on the staff of the concentration camp of Majdanek/Poland. That happened in front of the former crematorium of the concentration camp of Majdanek. Paul Hoffmann was responsible for the murder of more than 2,000,000 Jews.

In the last months of this year were also removed all public swastikas of the former German Empire (the so-called "Third Empire", the last German Empire) in the occupying zones of Germany.

Chronology

1914 Archduke Franz Ferdinand of Austria is murdered;
the begin of the First World War

1915 Battles of the World War in Europe and South
Africa

1916 Russia against Turkey and the end of the war in
Cameroon;
German submarine war;
war on the Balkan

1917 America enters the war

1918 Germany and Austria are finished;
the end of the World War

1919 Germany and Austria lose large areas.
New states are formed in which live many Germans too
This year, Rosa Luxemburg and Karl Liebknecht
are also murdered; both were German socialists.
Grand opening of the National Assembly in Weimar.
Establishment of the League of Nations

Hitler appears on the political scene

1920 Kapp Putsch (Cape Putsch)

French occupation of the cities of Frankfurt,

Darmstadt and Hanau

France takes over the management of Germany in

Elsaß and Lothringen, which are now called Alsace

and Lorraine

First election in the Weimar Republic

Establishment of the Free State of Danzig

1921 The Allies determine the amount of reparations

Various meetings of the NSDAP (Hitler's party)

1922 The political conflict reached its climax in

Germany

Renewed change of government in Germany, as

in the previous year

1923 Occupation of the Ruhr by French and Belgian

troops

Revolt of the Ruhr population against the

occupation

Gustav Stresemann forms a new government

Renewed unrest in Germany

End of the revolt in the Ruhr (region)

In Rhineland separatists proclaimed the "Republic

of Rhineland", but it is only a Republic for a few

days

The "Horror inflation"

1924 The Great German National Community and the

Nationalist Bloc came into being.

Charles Dawes and Owen Young in Paris

Germany should pay 2,500,000,000 Deutsch Mark

each year for reparation

Adolf Hitler was sentenced to an imprisonment in

fortress of 5 years

1925 Friedrich Ebert, German President, dies

Field Marshal General Paul von Hindenburg new

President of Germany

1926 Treaty of Berlin by Gustav Stresemann

Raymond Poincaré new French Prime Minister

1927 Hitler, a free man again, gives a speech in
Vilsbiburg and Munich
The Third Reichsparteitag of the Nazis
Inauguration of a war monument in
Tannenberg/East Prussia
Foundation of the German Unemployment
Insurance

1928 Chancellor Müller (SPD)
Extreme right-wing demonstrations

1929 Heinrich Himmler becomes leader of the SS
Opening of an international conference in Paris
Germany has to pay to the Allies 2,050,000,000
Deutsch Mark each year for 37 years,
then 920,000,000 Deutsch Mark till 1988
Gustav Stresemann, German Foreign Minister,
dies
3 million Germans without job

1930 Violent arguments from battle of words between
the organizations of Steel Helmet
Red Front Fighter's Legion, standard of the

Empire and the brutal SA

Heinrich Brüning becomes chancellor of a

minority government

1931 Germany has 65,000,000 inhabitants and

4,900,000 persons without job

Election in Hultschiner Ländchen

The German banks have to pay to foreign

creditors 4,000,000,000 Reichsmark (the

German currency of those years)

The NSDAP becomes largest party in some

German countries

Germany has 5,400,000 persons without job at

the end of this year

1932 Conference of Lausanne/Switzerland, there was

agreed that Germany has to pay

3,000,000,000 Gold Mark as last payment for

reparation

1933 Adolf Hitler, chancellor of the "National Rise"

The first steps of the Nazi government

1934 The first victims of Nazi murders

von Hindenburg, German President, dies and

Hitler takes over his post, but as Führer of the

Reich (Empire)

1935 Saarland becomes a German country again

Hitler has an own standard

"Party Day of Freedom" of the Nazis in

Nuremberg

Mass rally of the ethnic Germans in

Czechoslovakia

The beginning of the persecution of Jews

1936 Wilhelm Gustloff, the leader of the Swiss Nazis, is

murdered by a Jew

Hitler's book "Mein Kampf" bestseller in Germany

Foundation of "Ordensburgen" to breed a new

„Germanic human race"

Intervention in the Spanish Civil War

Hitler's second residence on the mountain

"Obersalzberg"

The "Anti-Comintern Pact"

1937　Hitler's goal, the Habitat War

Foundation of Great-Hamburg

Burckhardt, Commissioner of the League of

Nations for the "Free City of Danzig"

Germany's new car, the People's Car =

Volkswagen (VW)

This year was launched the "Wilhelm Gustloff",

Germany's fate ship

The German zeppelin, the "Hindenburg", went up

in flames

Focke's first helicopter of the world

The minorities' statement between Germany and

Poland

Measures against Jews

1938　Austria, a part of Germany

Sudetenland that belonged to Czechoslovakia

now a part of Germany

Ernst von Rath, an employee of the German

embassy in Paris, is murdered by a Jew

Reichskristallnacht

1939　Hitler's new Reich Chancellery

German troops in the Czech city of Ostrava

Slovakia an independent state

Foundation of the "Protectorate Bohemia-Moravia"

Konstantin Freiherr von Neurath Reich Protector of Bohemia-Moravia

Hitler's nonaggression treaty with Stalin

Dissolution of the last Czech parliament

Memel a part of Germany again

Attack on the radio station of Gleiwitz

Beginning of World War II

Conquest of Poland

First attack of the Royal Air Force

1940 German occupation of Denmark and Norway

Attack on Belgium and France

German troops in Paris

Italy declares war on France

The battle for England

Meeting of Franco and Hitler

Italian attack on Greece

German troops in Africa

Agreement between Italy, Japan and Germany, it

followed Bulgaria and Romania

Operation "Barbarossa"

1941 The Royal Air Force bombs Bremen

General Rommel in Tripoli

Extermination of Jews

Sea battles and the beginning of the air war

German troops in Greece

Beginning of the war against the Soviet Union

Japan attacks the American Pacific navy

1942 Battles in Africa

The "Kreisauer Kreis"

Assassination attempt on Rainhard Heydrich

Germany occupies the remainder of France

1943 The catastrophe of Stalingrad

Goebbels' question: "Wollt ihr den totalen Krieg?"

The resistance group „Weiße Rose"

Introduction of German right in Elsaß-Lothringen

The last battles in Africa

Operation "Zitadelle"

Air raids on Germany

German troops occupy Rome

The largest air battle over Germany

1944 Report from the Russian front lines "South"

Russian recaptures

D-Day

Attempt on Hitler's life

Attacks of the air forces of the Allies

French troops in Paris again

Battles in France and the Netherlands

The "Deutsche Volkssturm"

Russian troops in East Prussia

The beginning of the great escape of Germans

1945 The first Russian soldiers passed the German
frontier
The German Air Force attacks the airfields of the
Allies in northern France, Belgium and the
Netherlands
1,000 aero-planes of the Allies bombard the cities
of Ludwigshafen, Nuremberg and Berlin
Successes of the German army in Hungary
Beginning of the great Soviet offensive on all

fronts in the eastern part of Europe

The greatest escape of the world history

The last days of East Prussia

The sinking of the ship with the name "Wilhelm Gustloff"; this is also the biggest maritime disaster of the world history

The last battle for the city of Breslau

The catastrophe of Dresden

American soldiers in West Germany

Hitler's order: Scorched Earth

For the Russians the Germans are pigs and pigs have to be slaughtered

American troops in the middle of Germany and Bohemia

The death of Mussolini

Russian soldiers in Berlin

The death of Hitler

Dönitz, chancellor of Germany

The end of World War II

Occupation of Germany and division into four zones

Expulsion of the Germans from the eastern areas of Germany and the Sudetenland

The end of the German Empire forever, by it also the end of the Third Reich

Important persons

Ahmed Maher Pasha; 1944 – 45 Prime Minister of Egypt
(1888 – 1945)

Alexander Count of Hoyos; head of the Austro-Hungarian cabinet (1838 – 1922)

Alexej Brussilov; Russian General (1853 – 1926)

Ante Pavelić; Croatian fascist leader (1889 – 1959)

Antonescu, Ion; 1940 - 1944 Romanian dictator
(1882 – 1946)

Arnim, Hans-Jürgen von…; German Colonel General,
1942 commander in Tunisia (1889 – 1962)

Attlee, Clement; 1945 – 1951 British Prime Minister
(1883 – 1967)

Badoglio, Pietro; Italian field marshal in 1926, governor
in Libya in 1928 (1871 – 1956)

Barlach, Ernst; German expressionist sculptor
(1870 – 1938)

Beck, Ludwig; in 1938 German lieutenant general, 1944
plotter against Hitler (1880 – 1944)

Beneš, Edvard; 1935-1938 and 1945—1948 President of
Czechoslovakia (1884—1948)

Benesch, Eduard; German spelling of Beneš, Edvard

Bernadotte, Folke; Count of Wisborg, Swedish diplomat
(1895 – 1948)

Bethmann Hollweg, Theobald von ...; German Chancellor
(1856 – 1921)

Blomberg, Werner von ...; 1933 –1938 German Minister
of War (1878 – 1946)

Bock, Fedor von ...; 1940 –1942 German field marshal
(1880 – 1945)

Bonhoeffer, Dieter; German theologian, opponent of
Hitler (1906 – 1945)

Bonnet, M. Georges; 1938 – 39 French Foreign Minister
(1889 – 1973)

Bormann, Martin; 1933-1941 secretary of Heß, his skele-
ton was found 1972 in Berlin (1900 - ?)

Bose, Herbert von ...; political speaker of Franz von
Papen (1893 – 1934)

Botha, Louis; general of South Africa (1862 – 1919)

Brauchitsch, Walther von ...; Field Marshal, Commander-
in-Chief of the German Army 1938-1941
(1881 – 1948)

Braun, Eva; mistress of Hitler and in 1945 his wife for 40
hours (1912 – 1945)

Brecht, Berthold; German poet (1898 – 1956)

Breitscheid, Rudolf; politician of the SPD (1874 – 1944)

Briand, Aristide; French Prime Minister (1862 – 1932)

Brigade Ehrhardt*; 1919/20, named after the leader of a
Marine Brigade

Brockdorff-Rantzau; Count, first Foreign Minister of the
Weimar Republic (1869 – 1928)

Brüning, Heinrich; German chancellor 1930 – 1932
(1885 –1970)

Burckhardt, Carl Jacob; Swiss professor, 1937-1939 High
Commissioner of Danzig (1891 – 1974)

Burián; Austrian Foreign Minister (1852 – 1922)

Canaris, Wilhelm Franz; German admiral and senior
intelligence officer (1887 – 1945)

Chamberlain, Neville; 1937 – 1940 Prime Minister of
Great Britain (1869 – 1940)

Chernyakhovsky, Ivan Danilovich; Soviet general in
World War II (1906 – 1945)

Churchill, Winston; 1940 – 1945 and 1951 – 1955 British
Prime Minister (1874 – 1965)

Clay, Lucius D. ; American general in World War II
(1897 – 1978)

Clemenceau, Georges; French Prime Minister
1906-1909, 1917-1920 (1841 – 1929)

Cuno, Wilhelm; German Chancellor 1922/23

    (1876 – 1933)

Curtius, Julius; German Foreign Minister 1929 – 1931

    (1877 – 1948)

Daladier, Edouard; 1933, 1934, 1938 – 1940 French

    Prime Minister (1884 – 1970)

David Lloyd George; British politician (1863 – 1945)

Dawes, Charles; American banker and politician

    (1865 – 1951)

de Gaulle, Charles; French general in World War II, later

    French president (1890 – 1970)

Delp, Alfred, Jesuit priest, in 1944 plotter against Hitler

    (1907 – 1945)

Désire Mercier; cardinal and bishop of Brussels

    (1851 – 1926)

Dönitz, Karl; German naval commander, in 1945 chan-

    cellor for few days (1891 – 1980)

Dragiša Cvetković; 1939 – 1941 Yugoslavian Prime Min-

    ister (1893 – 1969)

Dragutin Dimitrijević; also called Apis after the sacred

    cow of Egypt (1876 – 1917)

Dušan Simović; 1938 – 1940 chief Yugoslav General Staff

    then head of government

(1882 – 1962)

Ebert; German President (1871 – 1925)

Edward Grey; English permanent secretary (1862—1933)

Edward VIII; 1936 King of the United Kingdom and
Emperor of India (1894 – 1972)

Ehrenburg, Ilya Grigoryevich; Soviet writer (1891 – 1967)

Ehrhardt*, Hermann; leader of a Marine Brigade
(1881 – 1971)

Einstein; physicist (1879 – 1955)

Eisenhower, Dwight D.; five-star general and 1953 –1961
President of the U.S. (1890 – 1969)

Eleutherios Venizelos; Greek Prime Minister
(1864 – 1936)

Eltz-Rübenach, Freiherr von ...; 1932- 37 Reich Minister
for Mail and Transport (1875 – 1943)

Erzberger; German politician (1875 – 1921)

Falkenhayn, Erich von ...;   German General and War
Minister (1861 – 1922)

Fehrenbach; German Parliament President 1920/21
(1867 – 1945)

Foch; marshal and commander-in-chief of the allies
(1851 – 1929)

Focke, Heinrich; German designer of airplanes and

helicopters (1890 – 1979)

Forster, Albert; 1930 – 45 Nazi Gauleiter in Danzig, since 1939 also governor (1902 – 1952)

Franco, Francisco; 1939 – 1975 dictator of Spain (1892 – 1975)

Frank, Hans; German Governor General in Poland during the World War II (1900 – 1946)

Frankfurter, David; Croatian-Jewish student and murderer of Wilhelm Gustloff (1909 – 1982)

Franz Ferdinand; Archduke of Austria (1863 – 1914)

Franz Joseph I; Austrian Emperor (1830 – 1916)

Frick, Wilhelm; 1933-1943 German Minister of the interior, 1943—1945 Reich Protector for Bohemia and Moravia (1877—1946)

Friedeburg, Hans-Georg von …; in 1945 Germany's last commanding admiral (1895 – 1945)

Friedrich VI; Castle Count of Nuremberg (1371 – 1440)

Friedrich Wilhelm of Prussia; the Great Kurfürst/Elector 1640 – 1688 (1620 – 1688)

Gabčik, Josef; Czech resistance fighter (1916 – 1942)

Gavrilo Princip; Serbian student and rebel (1894 – 1918)

Goebbels, Joseph; 1933 – 1945 German Minister of

Propaganda (1897 – 1945)

Goerdeler, Karl Friedrich; German politician, plotter

against Hitler (1884 – 1945)

Göring, Hermann; founder of the Gestapo; under Hitler

Head of the German Air Forces

(1893 – 1946)

Grese, Irma; warden in the concentration camps of

Ravensbrück, Auschwitz and

Bergen-Belsen (1923 – 1945)

Gürtner, Franz; 1932 – 1941 Reich Minister of Justice

(1881 – 1941)

Gustloff, Wilhelm; founder of the Swiss Nazi Party

(1895 – 1936)

Hacha, Emil; 1918 – 1938 Czech president

(1872 – 1945)

Haeften, Werner Karl von …; 1943 – 1944 Stauffenberg's

orderly officer (1908 – 1944)

Hahn, Otto, German Chemist; 1944 he received the

Nobel Prize for Chemistry

(1879 – 1968)

Hainisch, Michael; President of Austria 1920 – 1928

(1858 – 1940)

Hanke, Karl August; 1941-1945 governor of Lower Silesia

In 1945 final leader of SS

(1903 – 1945)

Harris, Arthur Travers; British Air Officer Commanding-

in-Chief in World War II

(1892 – 1984)

Hassell, Ulrich von ...; 1926 – 1938 German ambassador

in Denmark, Serbia and Italy

1881 – 1944)

Heldt, Max; German labor unionist and politician

(1872 – 1933)

Henlein, Konrad; leader of the Sudeten, 1939 Reichs-

statthalter in Sudetenland

(1898 – 1945)

Heß, Rudolf; German Nazi politician and 1933 – 1941

Deputy Führer to Hitler

(1894 – 1987)

Hesse, Hermann; German poet (1877 – 1962)

Heydrich, Reinhard; 1941/42 Reich Protector of Bohemia

and Moravia (1904 – 1942)

Hilferding, Rudolf; German Minister of Finance from

1923 to 1929 (1871 – 1941)

Himmler, Heinrich; leader of the SS (1900 – 1945)

Hindenburg, Paul von ...; general and last President of

the German Empire

(1847 – 1934)

Hitler, Adolf; German Reich Führer 1933 - 1945

(1889 – 1945)

Höfer, Karl; German General, also called "Teuton

Commander" (1862 – 1939)

Hoffmann, Paul; SS man on the staff of the concentra-

tion camp of Majdanek

(1907 – 1945)

Hoover, Herbert Clark; 31st President of the United

States (1874 – 1964)

Hoßbach-Protokoll; Hoßbach was military adjutant of

Hitler, 1937 writer about a

conference

Hoth, Hermann; German general during World War II

(1885 – 1971)

Hötzendorf, Franz Conrad von ...; head of the Austrian

General Staff (1852 – 1925)

Hugenberg, Alfred; 1933 German Minister for Economy

and Agriculture (1865—1951)

Jagow, Gottlieb von ...; permanent secretary in Berlin

(1863 – 1935)

Jodl, Ferdinand Alfred Friedrich; German general in World War II (1896 – 1956)

Jung, Edgar Julius; lawyer and political philosopher (1894 – 1934)

Junkers; aircraft designer (1859 – 1935)

Kahr, Gustav Ritter von …; 1920/21 Bavarian Minister President, he was also Bavarian General State Commissioner 1923/24 (1862 – 1934)

Kapp, Wolfgang; German coup leader, born in New York (1858 – 1922)

Karl I; Emperor of Austria 1916 – 1918 (1887 – 1922)

Keitel, Wilhelm Bodewin Johann Gustav; German Field-Marshal in World War II (1882-1946)

Kempf, Werner; German Panzer General during World War II (1886 – 1964)

Kollwitz, Käthe; German printmaker and sculptor (1867 – 1945)

Kramer, Josef; commandant of the concentration camp of Bergen-Belsen (1906 – 1945)

Krosigk, Joh. Ludwig von …; 1932 German Minister of Finance, 1945 Chancellor (1887 – 1977)

Kubiš, Jan; Czech resistance fighter (1913 – 1942)

Ladislaus Count of Szögyény-Marich; Austro-Hungarian
ambassador in Berlin (1841 – 1916)

Landsberg; a member of the SPD (1869 – 1957)

Laval, Pierre; French politician and friend of the German
Nazis (1883 – 1945)

Leber, Julius; member of the resistance movement
against Hitler (1891 – 1945)

Leclerc, Philippe; French general in World War II
(1902 – 1947)

Leopold Count Berchtold; Austrian Foreign Minister
(1863 – 1942)

Lettow-Vorbeck; German General in Africa (1870 – 1964)

Leuschner, Wilhelm; member of the resistance movement against Hitler (1890 – 1944)

Ley, Robert; German politician and 1933 – 1945 head of
the Nazi Labor Front (1890 – 1945)

Liebknecht, Karl; German left politician (1871 – 1919)

Lipski, Józef; Polish diplomat, 1934 – 1939 Ambassador
to Nazi Germany (1894 – 1958)

Litowski; archbishop of Posen and Gniezno 1914 – 1915

Löbe; President of the Reichstag 1920 – 1932
(1875 – 1967)

Lord Halifax; 1935–1937 Lord Privy Seal, 1937/38 Lord
President of the Council (1881 – 1959)

Lossow, Otto Hermann von; German General
(1868 – 1938)

Ludendorff, Erich; German general and politician
(1865 – 1937)

Lüttwitz, Walther von; German general (1859 – 1942)

Luxemburg, Rosa;, German left politician (1871 – 1919)

Mackensen; German general (1849 – 1945)

Maercker, Georg Ludwig Rudolf; German general
(1865 – 1924)

Mann, Heinrich; German writer (1871 – 1950)

Manstein, Erich von ...; German General field marshal
during the World War II
(1887 – 1973)

Marinesko, Alexander Ivanovich; Soviet naval officer in
World War II (1913 – 1963)

Marx, Wilhelm; German politician, Zentrumspartei –
Republic Rhineland –
(1863 – 1946)

Max von/of Baden; German chancellor (1867 – 1929)

Mayr, Michael; first chancellor of the Republic Austria
(1864 – 1922)

McKenna, Reginald; British statesman, lord of the
Admiralty (1863 – 1943)

Molotov, Vyacheslav Mikhaylowich; 1939 – 1949 and
1953-1956 Russian Foreign Minister
(1890 – 1986)

Moltke, Helmuth von ...; chief of the German General
Staff (1848 – 1916)

Montgomery, Bernard; British general in World War II
(1887 – 1976)

Müller, Hermann; German Foreign Minister and 1920
Chancellor (1876 – 1931)

Mussolini, Benito; 1925 – 1945 Italian dictator
(1883 – 1945)

Neurath, Constantin von ...; 1932 – 1938 German Foreign Minister and 1939 –1941
Reich Protector of Bohemia
and Moravia (1873 – 1956)

Nicholas II; Russian Tsar (1868 – 1918)

Niehoff, Hermann; German general in World War II
(1897 – 1980)

Nikola Pašić; Serbian Prime Minister (1845 – 1926)

Noske, Gustav; German minister 1919/20 (1868 – 1946)

Olbricht, Friedrich; German general, in 1944 one of the

plotters against Hitler

(1888 – 1944)

Oster, Hans Paul; German general, opponent of Hitler

and Nazism (1887 – 1945)

Papen, Franz von ...; German chancellor 1932 and vice-

chancellor 1933 – 1934

(1879 – 1969)

Patton, George S.; American general and commander in

World War II (1885 – 1945)

Paulus, Friedrich v...; commander in chief of the German

6th Army at Stalingrad

(1880 – 1957)

Petacci, Clara; mistress of Mussolini (1912 – 1945)

Pétain, Philippe; French marshal, 1940-1944 Chief of the

State of Vichy France

(1856 – 1951)

Pieck, Wilhelm; politician and President of the GDR/East

Germany (1876 – 1960)

Pilsudski, Jósef; Polish rebel (1867 – 1935)

Planck, Max; physicist (1858 – 1947)

Poincaré, Raymond; French Prime Minister 1912-1914

and President 1914 – 1918

(1860 – 1934)

Pokorný, Bedřich; in 1945 organizer of the Brno death
march of the Germans
(1904 – 1968)

Porsche, Ferdinand; German car design, founder of the
Porsche Company (1875—1951)

Prince Paul of Yugoslavia; regent 1934 – 1941
(1893 – 1976)

Prince Peter of Yugoslavia; 1941 – 1945 King Peter II of
Yugoslavia (1923 – 1970)

Probst, Christoph; German resistance fighter
(1919 – 1943)

Puttwitz, von …; general and commander-in-chief in
Prussia (about 1914)

Quirnheim, Albrecht Mertz von …; German colonel and
resistance fighter (1905 – 1944)

Quisling, Vidkun; 1942 – 1945 Norwegian Minister President (1887 – 1945)

Raeder, Erich; German Grand Admiral and 1939-1943
leader of the German Navy
(1876 – 1960)

Rath, Ernst von …; 1938 Counsellor at the German Embassy in Paris (1909 – 1938)

Ribbentrop, Joachim von…; Hitler's chief agent, ambassador, foreign minister

(1893 – 1946)

Röhm, Ernst; German politician and head of the SA

(1887 – 1934)

Rommel, Erwin; Hitler's favorite general, 1941-1943

commander of the Africa Corps

(1891 – 1944)

Roosevelt, Franklin Delano; 1933 – 1945 President of the

United States (1882 – 1945)

Rosenberg, Alfred; ideologist of the NSDAP (1893-1946)

Rundstedt, Gerd; German General field marshal during

the Second World War

(1875 – 1953)

Runge, Otto; German soldier (1875 – 1945)

Sahm, Heinrich; Senate President in Danzig 1920-1930,

Lord Mayor in Berlin 1931-1935

(1877 - 1939)

Scheidemann, Philipp; head of the SPD (1865 – 1939)

Schicklgruber, Alois; father of Hitler (1837 – 1903)

Schleicher, Kurt von ...; 1929 head of the Ministerial

Office, in 1932 Chancellor

(1882 – 1934)

Schlieffen; German general (1833 – 1913)

Scholl, Hans; German resistance fighter (1918 – 1943)

Scholl, Sophie; German resistance fighter (1921 – 1943)

Schröder, Kurt von ...; German banker (1889 – 1966)

Schulenburg, Friedrich Werner Graf von ...;1934-1941
Germam ambassador, plotter
(1875-1944)

Schuschnigg, Kurt; 1934 – 1938 Austrian Chancellor
(1897 – 1977)

Seeckt; Major General of the German-Austrian troops
(1866 – 1936)

Seldte, Franz; German Minister for Labor 1933 – 1945
(1882 – 1947)

Seyß-Inqart, Arthur; lawyer and Austrian Nazi
(1892 – 1946)

Skorzeny, Otto; German SS-Main-Storm leader
(1908 – 1975)

Sophie of Hohenberg; wife of Archduke Franz Ferdinand
(1868 – 1914)

Spee, Graf/Count ... von/of; German Admiral
(1861 – 1914)

Speer, Albert; 1942 - 1945 German Minister for Arma-
ments (1905 – 1981)

Stalin, Joseph; 1929 – 1953 dictator of the Soviet Union

(1879 – 1953)

Stauffenberg, Claus Philipp Maria Schenk Graf von ...;
in 1944 plotter against Hitler
(1907 – 1944)

Stefan Count Tisza; Hungarian Prime Minister
(1861 – 1918)

Strasser, Georg;   German politician of the Nazi Party
(1892 – 1934)

Strecker, Karl; German lieutenant general during World
War II (1884 – 1973)

Streicher, Julius; German Nazi and 1928-1940 district
leader of Middle Franconia
(1885 – 1946)

Stresemann, Gustav; German Foreign Minister 1923-
1929 (1878 – 1929)

Stroop, Jürgen; German SS-Brigade leader (1895 – 1952)

Stülpnagel, Carl Heinrich von ...; German general, in 1944
plotter against Hitler (1886--1944)

Stumpff, Hans-Jürgen; German Colonel General in World
War II (1889 – 1968)

Timoshenko, Semyon; Soviet marshal and military commander (1895 – 1970)

Tirpitz, Alfred von; German Admiral (1849 – 1930)

Tiso, Jozef; Catholic prelate, Slovakian President during

World War II (1887—1947)

Todt, Fritz; German engineer and senior Nazi figure

(1891 – 1942)

Tomáš Masaryk; Czech professor of philosophy

(1850 – 1937)

Trimborn, Carl; German politician, Zentrumspartei –

Republic Rhineland – (1854-1921)

Trott zu Solz, Friedrich Adam Freiherr von ...; German

diplomat and plotter

(1909 – 1944)

Truman, Harry S.; 1945 – 1953 President of the United

States (1884 – 1972)

Tschirschky; German ambassador in Vienna

(1858 – 1916)

Vaclic, Josef; Czech resistance fighter (? – 1942)

Verlaine, Paul; French poet (1844 – 1896)

Victor Emanuel III; King of Italy 1900 – 1946

(1869 – 1947)

Vogel, Kurt; lieutenant of the German army (1889-1967)

von-dem-Bach-Zelewski, Erich; German SS leader

(1899 – 1972)

Weidling, Helmuth Otto Ludwig; German general in

World War II (1891 – 1955)

Weigel, Helene; German actress and director of a Berlin
theatre (1900 – 1971)

Wels, Otto; city commander and member of the SPD
(1873 – 1939)

Wilhelm II; German Emperor (1859 – 1941)

Wilson, Thomas Woodrow;   1913 – 1921   American
President (1856 – 1924)

Wirth, Joseph;   German   Chancellor   1921/22
(1879 – 1956)

Witzleben, Erwin von…;   German field marshal general,
1944 plotter against Hitler
(1881 – 1944)

Wojciech Korfanty;   Polish nationalist activist
(1873 – 1939)

Yorck von Wartenburg, Graf/Count …;   German
resistance fighter (1904—1944)

Young, Owen;   American industrialist, businessman,
lawyer and diplomat
(1874 – 1962)

Zawadzki, Alexander;   1945 Polish major general, later
head of state in Poland
(1899 – 1964)

Zeigner, Erich; Minister President of Saxony in 1923

(1886 – 1949)

Zimmermann;   sub-secretary in Berlin (1864 – 1940)

Zuckmayer, Carl;   German author (1896 – 1977)

Zuse, Konrad; German computer pioneer (1910 – 1995)

Bibliography

Deutsche Geschichte, Band 11; Heinrich Pleticha, 1984

Die Große Bertelsmann Lexikothek, Band 1 – 15, 1988

Bildatlas der deutschen Geschichte, Wilhelm J. Wagner,

1999

Daten der Weltgeschichte, Gerhard Hellwig,

Dr. Gerhard Linne, 1975

Der Zweite Weltkrieg, Christian Zentner, 1995

Die große Flucht, Guido Knopp, 2001

Chronik 1943, Ausgabe des Chronik Verlags, 1999

Die Deutschen und der Osten, Hermann Schreiber, 1984

Die Chronik, Geschichte des 20. Jahrhunderts bis heute,

2006

Freud und Leid einer Familia; novel by E. Harings, 2013

Flucht aus Königsberg; novel by E.Harings, 2017 --

(publisher: tredition)

Wikipedia

Note

Due to lack of imaging permissions, no strange photos were taken that are less than 70 years old. But there are also some copies of private photos in this book. The drawings were made by myself.

References to specialist literature on each page were deliberately omitted because it is no scientist work.

Nevertheless, this book, like all books of the series German history, should be suitable for schools and universities.

The author

Books about German history by Egon Harings

German(ic) History Volume 1 *The great time of the* *Germanic tribes*	published by August von Goethe Literatur- verlag/Frankfurt in 2010 and Fouqué Publishers/ New York in 2012
German History Volume 2 *Germany in the* *Middle Ages*	published by August von Goethe Literatur- verlag/Frankfurt in 2011
Germany before and after the Thirty-Years' War *From Martin Luther to the* *French Revolution*	not published yet
Germany before World War I *Fron Napoleon to the signs* *of World War I*	not published yet

Germany and two World Wars
From the German Reich to the
end of the Nazi regime

Germany after World War II	published by
Two German states and the	tredition in March
reunification	2018
The Great Age of Angela Merkel	published by
	tredition in 2017
The last years of the reign of	publication
Angela Merkel	planned